Show Biz

FROM VAUDE TO VIDEO

SHOW

by ABEL GREEN &

KENNIKAT PRESS
Port Washington, N.Y. // London

BIZ

from

VAUDE

to

VIDEO

JOE LAURIE, Jr.

Volume Two

SHOW BIZ

Manufactured by Taylor Publishing Company   Dallas, Texas

PART FOUR

BIG BUST

1930 - 1932

38

'Stay Out of Hollywood!'

★

    Film business slumped so badly in 1930 that one theatre offered 2-for-1 tickets and coupons entitling patrons to free marcel waves. Fox Theatres were in double trouble, indicated by the numerous suits filed by the divers Fox companies against William Fox, alleging malfeasance in office, manipulations of assets and misappropriation of funds.

    Fox was ousted from the company he had built, although managing to retain the title of "consultant" at a $500,000 annual salary. The reorganization took 22 lawyers, at a cost of millions, with

Samuel Untermyer's bill alone coming to $1,000,000. Harley L. Clarke was made president of the new Fox company, now called the Fox Film Corp. The name of William Fox was ordered off all billing, film credits and ads.

Hearst Metrotone News scored a scoop in 1930 by getting John D. Rockefeller before their cameras, at the age of 93. The excuse was the 60th anniversary of Standard Oil. The following year, newsreel favorites were President Herbert Hoover, Benito Mussolini, Prime Minister Ramsay MacDonald, Mayor Jimmy Walker and Governor Franklin D. Roosevelt.

Theatres ran contests to discover patrons who looked most like Greta Garbo. The Hays Office ordered the use of Mexicans as movie heavies stopped, because of the sizable market below the Rio Grande. To compensate, Hays gave the nod for Russian villains because Soviet restrictions were keeping out American films.

And from far-off Jerusalem Variety reported that the talkies were being called "hearies" there . . . a term derived from the Hebrew word, *hashmonua* (meaning "hearies").

If 1930 was bad for Hollywood, 1931 was terrible. The boxoffice, crippled by the depression, was hit equally hard by public charges that the films being made were lemons, and the stars grossly overpaid. Film attendance dropped 40 per cent, forcing cuts in studio and theatre overhead. Bankers, previously lenient with the industry, began to demand more concrete collateral for loans—and the only collateral producers could offer was the diminishing interest of the public in films.

Some theatres, desperate for business, experimented with vaudeville. Most hit upon the double-feature bill, plus dishes, bank nights and other come-ons. One Broadway theatre tried television, and quickly scrapped it. Variety ironically noted February 17 as the 18th anniversary of the first showing of talking films—Thomas A. Edison's screening of a scene from *Julius Caesar* at the Colonial Theatre, New York.

k.o. to the silents   Depression or not, the talkers definitely signed the death warrant of the old silents. By 1931 only 1,500 out of 22,000 film theatres were without sound—the 1,500 being mostly of barn and store proportions. Warner Bros., who had brought all this about, went deeply into the red with about $30,000,000 in operating losses between 1930 and 1934. But so well had the organization been built that Warners survived the depression without "going through the wringer" of bankruptcy or reorganization, as others did.

There was little doubt but that the film industry still led all wings of show business in popularity even in the business debacle. A Chicago poll taken in 1931 showed the greatest familiarity with names in the following fields: (1) film actors, (2) gangsters, (3) athletes, (4) politicians, (5) musicians, (6) big business executives, (7) legitimate actors, (8) radio talent, (9) journalists and (10) film directors.

The talkers hit heavily at the ranks of the old silent stars. By 1931 there were only three stars remaining from the old silent days of 1921, and 26 new talkie stars. Among the fallen were John Gilbert, William Haines and Ramon Navarro, who retired to a monastery for a time. Even Douglas Fairbanks and Mary Pickford were slipping, whereupon she announced her imminent retirement. Billie Dove, Norma Talmadge and Marion Davies already had slid in public favor, despite the heavy Hearst publicity behind the latter.

Bert Wheeler and Robert Woolsey, Lew Ayres, Conrad Nagel, Buster Keaton, Bebe Daniels, Charles Farrell and Edmund Lowe continued to get top billing—but dwindling fan mail. Charles Bickford and Adolphe Menjou, starting the year as major stars, finished up working for independent companies. Even the great John Barrymore was let out by Warner Bros. Jack Oakie and Buddy Rogers slipped down the ladder from "starring" to "featuring." Clara Bow, after some bad publicity, faded and was counted out—only to surprise her detractors by a 1932 comeback with *Call Her Savage*.

Lionel Barrymore, who held a director-actor contract with Metro, was confined to acting only because he was considered too slow and too long on shooting schedules. The top film names of 1931 were almost exclusively those with strong voice personalities—Constance Bennett, Joan Crawford, Marlene Dietrich, Greta Garbo, Marie Dressler, Janet Gaynor, Norma Shearer, George Arliss, Ronald Colman, Wallace Beery, Maurice Chevalier, Clark Gable, Edward G. Robinson and Will Rogers. Tallulah Bankhead also made her first talkie—a film called *Tarnished*. Mickey Mouse in sound made the grade, although one of the cows in a Disney film had its udder removed by the finicky Hays Office.

Gangster films, which enjoyed a strong vogue in 1930 and 1931, began to taper off with Paul Muni in *Scarface* in 1932. Travelogs, representing colorful escapist fare, were highly popular. Not so popular was the habit of many small theatres to show commercial films —because they received these without cost, or were even paid to screen them—as supporting shorts for features. Protests forced many of the theatres to discontinue the practice.

A growing chiseling practice was the theatre owner who rented a film for one house, then "bicycled" it to his other houses in town, or perhaps to the next town. This is a violation of the Copyright Act and the industry soon took drastic means to curb the practice.

Variety noted in 1931, with something like awe, that pioneer theatre showman A. J. Balaban—formerly of Balaban & Katz— threw up his $75,000-a-year career to enter the Christian Science Church. He later returned as managing director of the Roxy.

The price of film tickets was widely considered too high for a depression year. Theatres which lowered prices did the best business of 1931. Many more followed suit in early 1932, when a 10 per cent Government tax was imposed on all tickets over 40¢. Those which refused to shave prices were forced to pass the 10 per cent levy on to patrons, hurting their b.o. still further.

cuts As bad as 1931 was for Hollywood—with West Coast sages predicting that things could not possibly get worse—1932 set an all-time low for the film industry. United Artists cut the salaries of their executives 40 per cent, while Metro-Loew salaries went under the meat-chopper for a 35 per cent trimming.

Studios paid settlements to get out of crippling contracts with actors and directors, engaging stars on a day-to-day shooting basis. Publix Theatres warned its personnel against overuse of postage stamps, phones and telegrams. Paramount issued a salary cut—its third—of 5 per cent of all salaries up to $150, while Fox put through a second slice of 5 to 35 per cent, and Warners did likewise with a flat downbeat of 10.

Story prices slumped to an all-time low, and film operators as well as stagehands throughout the country were handed trimmed paychecks. Will Hays took a 60 per cent salary slice, and reduced his budget from $600,000 a year to $240,000. All with the same groaning and head-shaking that accompanied exactly the same financial shakeup that hit Hollywood after World War II.

National theatre advertising for and by film chains fell off 50 per cent. Practically all theatre-building ceased, and the Roxy—harried by terrible business and a staggering overhead—closed for several weeks. With labor being promised a New Deal from the White House, film theatre unions began to war against each other with jurisdictional strikes . . . the clashes driving away patrons in some cities to the extent of a 40 per cent boxoffice dip.

Alarmed at the ugly temper of unemployed America, film stars began to take out kidnap insurance policies from Lloyds of London, agreeing to Lloyds' provision that the policies would become void if the stars let the fact be known for publicity. The stars reasoned that if Lindbergh's baby wasn't safe, neither were they.

The economy move that pared Hollywood's expenses by $18,000,000 a year brought a new idea into film production—loanouts of stars, supporting players and directors. Film companies agreed the plan would work to everyone's benefit—helping the company which had highly-paid personnel under contract and idle, and also the company which needed them for special productions. This led to a growing realization by stars that they might serve their own interests better as independents, rather than under contract to a single studio.

The loanout system, essentially a sound idea, ran into difficulties later when stars began to balk at being "sold on the block" to other studios for film roles which they did not want to play. They also objected to producers renting them out to other producers for huge sums, cleaning up on the loanout deal, while the stars themselves were being paid relatively modest salaries. Some stars refused to accept loanout assignments, resulting in studio suspensions and lawsuits.

A few feeble attempts were made to bolster film business during the depression. Some film companies tried exclusive one-theatre release of first-run films. Some theatres tried not double, but triple features. Film companies refused to rent product to any theatre which did not keep admissions above a dime. The theatres promised. . . . then flooded their neighborhoods with half-price admission coupons.

Paramount tried to woo the critics by inviting them from all cities to New York previews. Warners inaugurated "trade showings" in key areas for exhibitors. But nothing could help the b.o. except the man who bought the tickets—and he just didn't have the cash in his pockets.

jolson's $5,000,000 gross   The top money-maker in soundpix up to the end of 1932 was Al Jolson's *The Singing Fool,* which had grossed $5,000,000. Runnerup was Charles Chaplin's *City Lights,* for the most part silent save for a synchronized score and other sound effects, with over $4,000,000. (It was revived in 1950 and, in face of exhibitor fear in some quarters that Chaplin's political ideologies might militate against his b.o., it did smash biz.) The third top grosser of the period was Warner Bros.' *Golddiggers of Broadway,* also in the $4,000,000 bracket. Hollywood eyed those figures, thought of the $10,000,000 grosses each earned by *The Big Parade, Ben Hur* and *Birth of a Nation,* and sighed. (It has since been estimated that *Birth of a Nation* probably grossed nearer $40,000,000 for its sundry states rights' owners.)

"One more 'improvement' in films," said one diehard silent film producer, "and we're sunk." Sound, of course, was to prove the salvation of Hollywood.

After the beating it took in the 1920s, vaudeville was in no condition to weather a brutal depression. Variety described its plight succinctly by reporting, "Vaudeville in 1930 stood motionless on a treadmill that moved backward." The Loew Circuit dropped vaudeville as a useless expense which would drag Loew operations into the red. Independent circuits practically disappeared.

What was left of vaudeville "time" was patched together under the tattered banner of RKO, which reduced all bills to four acts, sliced the package price of each bill from $5,000 to $3,000, and shipped them out as units on a 50-week route. This reorganization meant a reasonable break for good acts, but the death knell for fair or poor acts, which were crowded out of show business. Some 1,500 acts fled vaudeville in 1930. Another 3,500 "flash" acts found their expenses too heavy for vaudeville's rewards.

The Palace, once the proud pillar of vaudeville, was now cracking at the seams. During 1930 it was losing $4,000 a week. The great showplace found itself caught in a web of its own contradictions. It had helped wreck vaudeville by raising salaries to astronomical heights. Now it sought headliners in vain. The headliners had largely deserted to other fields, since the rest of vaudeville had crumpled. The headliner shortage compelled the Palace to hold acts for two and four weeks, and to repeat them frequently . . . but that didn't add up to a year's salary.

In desperation the Palace began to entice headliners from other fields—radio, Hollywood, musicals and night clubs. It hopefully featured top-name masters of ceremonies, and encouraged ad-libbing. It even copied a page out of the old Winter Garden Sunday night shows, and had the emcees call on celebrities in the audience to stand up for bows, or to go onstage for guest shots. It tried to send audiences away tingling by using headliners to close the show.

To little avail. Bills that cost between $10,000 to $13,000 a week did well if they grossed $20,000 or $25,000. In the old days, Palace bills had cost about $8,000 a week, and had paid off an average $800,000 a year net profit. To make the 1930 picture blacker, Keith's was paying off $120,000 to acts they couldn't use—mostly "production" turns and adagio acts, which audiences were walking out on.

It was during the emcee era of the Palace that Al Jolson made his first, and last, "appearance" there because, actually, neither he nor George M. Cohan, of all the contemporary greats, ever played the Palace officially. Jolson obliged from the audience when Dave Apollon, as conferencier, called on him, and he got up and sang one number ad lib.

In later years, more of the desperation "policy" was essayed with super-vaude shows emceed by Lou Holtz, the Eddie Cantor-George Jessel bill, another sparked by Frank Fay, wherein headliners worked in and out of the supporting bill. This was not vaudeville in the real sense; it was more like a makeshift revue with neo-nite club overtones.

The Palace tried to snare Amos 'n' Andy, but the radio team refused. Their reason was that their act didn't register with actors, and the Palace catered to the footlight trade. They accepted an RKO circuit booking for all theatres except the greatest vaudeville showhouse of them all. And when they did, Variety ran an ad by McIntyre & Heath, oldest and most famous minstrel team, which claimed that Amos 'n' Andy were a "pale copy" of McIntyre & Heath, so "book the original!"

the end of the palace   In April 1930, all of Broadway was shocked and saddened by the news that their beloved Palace had undergone the final ignominy. It had been wired for sound.

There were other tokens of the evil days vaudeville had fallen upon. Loew's declared it was through booking top names because of the expense. The Vaudeville Managers Protective Association, once-powerful combine formed by E. F. Albee, folded up with no money in its treasury and no interest among managers. NVA dropped its payments of insurance and weekly gratuities to ailing vaudevillians. The White Rats officially admitted their finish, explaining there just weren't enough vaudeville actors to pay dues, and handed over their A.F. of L. charter to the new "Four A's"—the Associated Actors & Artistes of America.

By an ironic quirk, even the official name of vaudeville was changed in 1930 to "RKO Varieties"—which was the original name of vaudeville when Keith first tucked the ball under his arm and ran down the field of show business.

Eva Tanguay was typical of one-time great vaudeville stars who felt the pinch that first year of depression. Once the highest-priced single act in vaudeville—$3,500 a week—she was asked in 1930 to "show" her act. At first she indignantly refused, then thought better of her refusal. RKO gave her a "showing" date of three days at the Bushwick Theatre in Brooklyn, for $150.

RKO, trying to get away from the routine vaudeville act which made audiences yawn, booked stunt acts like Francille, who milked cows via radio, and operated miniature battleships and autos by remote control. Mae West was rejected (also by Loew's) because, as RKO's new president Hiram S. Brown explained, "Spice is all right, but dirt is out." Mae shrugged and signed with Fox, who let her do anything she wanted except cooch.

RKO went so far as to appoint a Mrs. Beatrice Mindlin as "fashion counselor" for the circuit. Her job was to tell actresses what they could and could not wear, and to impress upon male thespians the wisdom of keeping their pants pressed. She also kept a watchful eye open for any violations of the newly-restored RKO ruling—no bare legs.

Sentiment among theatre managers helped vaudeville in 1930, but sentiment died in 1931 along with most of business. RKO baldly announced that it wouldn't "bother" with vaudeville at all, if it could get enough decent films. The films were so bad that year, RKO found, that they made the four-act vaudeville bills look good by comparison. This acid view of vaude from the circuit that booked 70 per cent of the 102 weeks of vaudeville "time."

The second largest user of vaudeville acts in 1931 was the Publix Theatres 14 weeks. Warners offered 14 weeks as well, and Loew's dropped to about only 6 weeks of "time." All in all, only some 675 vaudeville acts were working a full week at any time during 1931.

The N.V.A. Club was abandoned, although it announced it would continue to maintain its sanitarium. The New York *Star,* merged with *Vaudeville News,* which was begun by Albee "to put Variety out of business," passed quietly out of the picture after 20 years. Variety discontinued its 25-year-old Correspondence Department from all towns, which were now mostly "film" towns, and in its place just reported the live stuff in key cities.

Already the name "Albee" was becoming unfamiliar to American theatregoers, who went to "RKO" theatres instead. RKO whetted the axe once again and sliced headliners' salaries, frequently more than half, and shrank its 23-week route to include cut salaries for six weeks. Now contemptuous of tradition, RKO cut actors' first names off their billing, explaining they could get the last names in bigger type by this device.

Many standard acts quit show business in despair. Even those who clung to the sinking ship felt hopeless about their future. The four- or five-a-day grind most were forced to work killed what spark their performances originally may have had. And most were working with old, hackneyed material. Vaudeville writers had fled to the Hollywood hills. To make matters worse, old vaude routines were turning up in talking film shorts, as well as on radio, hurting the original live acts in vaudeville.

The Palace continued to sink deeper into the red, and found it increasingly tougher to get headliners. To foster the illusion that vaudeville was still Broadway's favorite entertainment, the manager put a blackboard in the lobby, listing the names of celebrities attending each performance

RKO still pretended to offer "clean" shows, ruling off "pansy" bits and actors who indulged in Bronx cheers for humor. Small acts didn't dare talk or sing off-hue—bookings were too tough—but the headliners were allowed to get as blue as they preferred.

The Midwest raised some wry smiles in show business by featuring acts as "Gloryfied Vaudeville."

There was a faint glimmer of hope for vaude as 1931 slipped into 1932. David Sarnoff, speaking for RKO, declared that the circuit's four-act bills had kept RKO theatres from diving heavily into the red. They had served as insurance against the extremely bad RKO films of that year.

Bad films generally forced bigtime film theatres like the Paramount and the Capitol to strengthen their bills with name acts on the stage. They went into competition with the Palace for headliners, and star salaries enjoyed a brief spurt upward. The Palace offered a $16,500 bill. The Paramount countered with a $17,000 stage attraction, and the Capitol upped the ante to $20,000.

radio's hypo to talent   Good acts—in the midst of depression—were bewildered to find themselves being offered up to 50 per cent over their accustomed salaries. Radio acts, which had not yet even proved themselves on the air, were startled to find themselves in front of microphones on theatre stages. The most important drawing cards were rated as film personalities, musical comedy stars, radio stars and vaudeville headliners, in that order.

Jolson was paid his highest price—$15,000 straight salary, plus a percentage of the gross. Jack Pearl and Burns & Allen, from radio, were sought after. Warners gambled with Lou Holtz, on a straight vaudeville policy, and lost. The boom died as quickly as it had risen, with warring theatre interests getting together to control salaries. The issue quickly lost importance as Hollywood, having found its way through the maze of vocal problems, began to turn out better films. Before 1933 was over, vaudeville, which had drawn business for bad pictures, was considered to be keeping business away from good pictures.

RKO gave up the New York Hippodrome to Cooper & Carroll, 10¢ film operators, who made a pitch for the depression trade by offering vaudfilm shows at 15¢-25¢. The stage bills cost $150 a day, and films were scraped from the bottom of the barrel. The price lure won business at first, but the bad shows eventually K.O.'d Cooper & Carroll.

By the end of the year vaudeville found itself in a deeper hole than ever. Loew's, which had produced some of its own unit shows, closed its production department. Warners, which had 11 theatres offering stage presentations, dropped them gradually until their theatres offered films only. The Publix bookings disappeared. Vaudeville time dwindled from 102 weeks at the beginning of the year to only 25 weeks at its close. The 800 acts working a full week at first fell off to only 200 at the finish.

Only 200 in the entire United States! Vaudeville, which had ample room for 20,000 full-week acts in 1916!

One of the showmen who hearkened mournfully back to the good old days was Lee Lash, who originated and controlled the sale of advertising space on theatre backdrops. In his heyday, Lash had earned over a quarter of a million dollars a year with his idea, holding contracts with 1,700 theatres. 1932 found him with a bare handful of theatres left. And these took one-third of the $80 revenue from each 10-ad curtain.

The career of the Palace plunged further downhill—if that was possible. From its haughty two-a-day policy it had gone into straight grind vaudeville. Then it threw in films with its vaudeville, in the fall of 1932. Nothing helped. Losing $2,000 and $3,000 a week, the Palace finally announced in November 1932 it was turning into a straight picture house, booking as its first film under that policy Eddie Cantor in *The Kid From Spain*.

That was the official kiss of death. The desertion of the Palace left only one week of RKO vaudeville in the nation—the last hold-out, the Chicago Palace. Broadway, and most of the nation, were stunned by the news that live acts would no longer tread the famous boards of the Palace. As nothing else, the news sharply pointed up the passing of an era.

"Vaude never knew what the Palace meant to it," observed Variety soberly, "until the Palace passed and the newspapers all over the country wrote farewell tributes." Seventeen years later, in the spring of 1949, a form of vaudfilm was to come back to the Palace. The nation's press again sentimentally, almost lachrymosely, heralded "the return of vaudeville" to the famed flagship of the bigtime. This was fallacious enthusiasm because eight acts, at $3,000-$4,000 gross cost for the entire bill, doing four shows a day, plus a first-run film, at 95¢ top, was but a lukewarm, considerably watered-down variation of the theme.

39

The Shuberts Go Boom

★

Broadway applauded Robert Benchley when he wrote, toward the end of 1930, "I am now definitely ready to announce that Sex, as a theatrical property, is as tiresome as the Old Mortgage, and that I don't want to hear it mentioned ever again." He added, "I am sick of rebellious youth and I am sick of Victorian parents and I don't care if all the little girls in all sections of the United States get ruined or want to get ruined or keep from getting ruined. All I ask is: don't write plays about it and ask me to sit through them."

Although legit produced few notable attractions during the depression years, it did, by and large, heed Benchley. Not only was the public sick and tired of the trite themes of the Twenties, but it had no pennies to spend on them even if it had continued to like them.

The depression, which checked the sudden expansion of the new talkies, caught a lot of stage people in Hollywood short. All through 1930 they came trickling back to Broadway—to find that there was a depression on the Main Stem, too.

Some producers tried to shake some life into the legitimate by arranging to have their shows raided. Earl Carroll and 10 of his *Vanities* girls were given a ride in a police sedan, but the grand jury failed to indict. Another jury disagreed on the salacious qualities of Mae West's *Pleasure Man,* and the case was finally tossed out by the prosecutor himself.

The Shuberts made the legitimate's most depressing depression headlines. During 1930, with actors growing daily more desperate for work, the Shuberts announced they were bringing in 20 plays from abroad—complete with casts. It was small consolation to embittered American actors that most of the Shubert importations flopped.

Although Broadway hadn't fully realized it, the stock market crash had shaken the Shubert corporation severely. Lee Shubert suddenly made his corporation investors quake for their $8,000,000 by applying in 1931 for equity receivership. The Irving Trust Co. and Lee Shubert were appointed co-receivers by the court, under the peculiar arrangement that permitted the Shuberts to continue in business "for the expected benefit of the creditors." The court twice extended the period of receivership. In the spring of 1932, had Shubert theatres been sold at the prevailing low price of real estate, creditors would have received 4¢ on the dollar. The only chance the corporation had to pay off was by producing successful shows. This it failed to do. By the end of 1932, Variety reported that it was doubtful if Shubert creditors could hope to realize even 1¢ on the dollar.

Legit found 1931 its most dismal year in almost two decades. Through most of the year, Broadway was about 45 per cent dark. During the summer there were only 12 plays on the boards. Musicals lost $2,000,000 on the season. Productions closed faster than new ones could take their place.

An idea of the mortality rate is that Jessie Royce Landis in Booth Tarkington's *Colonel Satan* only lasted 17 performances; Lynn Riggs' *Green Grow the Lilacs,* which was to bloom into *Oklahoma!,* when musicalized by Rodgers & Hammerstein in later years, only flourished for 64 performances despite the cast presence of Franchot Tone, Helen Westley and June Walker. *Rock Me, Julie,* with Paul Muni, Jean Adair and Helen Menken, only kept rocking for seven performances; and Paul Kelly in *Hobo* only lasted five shows.

Even Jolson's *Wonder Bar* could only last 76 performances but on the more definite hit side there were Earl Carroll's *Vanities* (with Jack Benny), *Fine and Dandy* (Joe Cook), Moss Hart and George S. Kaufman's *Once In a Lifetime, The Greeks Had a Word for It, You Said It* (Lou Holtz and Lyda Roberti), and Katharine Cornell in *The Barretts of Wimpole Street.* Ziegfeld's *Hot-Cha!,* with Bert Lahr, Buddy Rogers, Lupe Velez, Marjorie White, June Knight and Lynne Overman heading the cast finished in the red.

In addition to the Shuberts, A. H. Woods went into bankruptcy. So did Arthur Hammerstein, who had made over $2,500,000 on *Rose Marie,* but sunk it into building a theatre to perpetuate his father's name (it's now a CBS Radio Playhouse at 53d and Broadway, New York). Other managers, caught with their plans down by the market crash, crowded the 77-B corner along with them.

For the first year in a long while, no *Uncle Tom's Cabin* troupe took to the road. Equity, with almost half its members unemployed, barred new members by raising initiation fees. Employed actors accepted salary cuts, glad to be working. Equity, which frowned on Sunday shows, waived the rules to allow three Sunday legitimate shows to play benefits for the unemployed.

Incongruously, 1931 was the year chosen by Earl Carroll to open the new Earl Carroll Theatre, which cost—including the show—$4,500,000. And Flo Ziegfeld put on his first *Follies* (with Helen Morgan, Harry Richman and Jack Pearl) since 1927. Somebody forgot to tell them what year it was.

1932 found 152 plays offered by producers, considerably less than the number introduced in previous seasons. The number of flops was high—fully 121. Only 16 shows were rated as hits, and another 15 as moderate successes. During late August, there were only six plays open on Broadway.

more banks than managers   The banks moved in as theatre operators. Shubert had tossed many theatres into their hands by defaulting on mortgages. A. L. Erlanger did the same. The banks foreclosed on Charles Dillingham and took over the Globe Theatre on Broadway. By the end of 1932, there were more banks in show business than there were Shubert and Erlanger theatres combined.

Taxes had a sobering effect on ticket prices. Most musicals were limited to a $4.40 top, with no show exceeding a $5.50 top. Some straight dramas charged $3 top, and out of this paid the 27¢ tax themselves.

There was no depression for one playwright—George S. Kaufman, who was earning about $7,000 a week. He owned 25 per cent of *Dinner At Eight,* besides his royalties as co-author and 35 per cent of the hit musical satire, *Of Thee I Sing,* which he also co-authored and which had two companies on the road.

In 1930 Al Jolson appeared at the Capitol for $15,000 a week, plus 50 per cent of the take above $100,000. Most of Broadway bet the gross would go over the top, but Jolie actually hit only $80,000, despite his five and six appearances a day. The reason was not the failure of Jolson to draw—but his refusal to sing the same songs at

every show. People stayed to hear his new songs . . . and the turn-
over suffered.

Later that year Jolson gave a concert at the New Orleans Auditorium, joking and singing for two hours before a packed house of
12,000. In 1931 he went into the musical, *Wonder Bar,* for the Shuberts. And in 1932 he was topping all salaries with $17,500 a week,
plus a percentage of the gross.

Eddie Cantor, playing the Palace in 1930, received $7,700 a week.
Booked again at the Palace the following year with George Jessel,
his salary went to $8,000, with another $8,000 going to Jessel and the
rest of the bill. The show, breaking all Palace records, was the first
in Palace history to run for eight weeks.

winchell reverts to greasepaint   Walter Winchell
put on greasepaint in 1930 by making a Vitaphone short called "The
Bard Of Broadway," with Madge Evans. Winchell's take was $1,750.
That year, with his New York *Mirror* contract at $500 a week still
good for three more years, it was torn up and replaced with another
at $1,000 a week . . . plus syndicate money. But the ubiquitous
Winchell could not be confined to print, even at $1,000 a week. He
was signed for a radio show by WABC, offering a guest star with
each broadcast.

In 1931 he accepted his first professional stage booking in 10 years
—a $3,500-a-week engagement at the Palace, following vaudeville ap-
pearances by fellow journalists Heywood Broun, Floyd Gibbons,
Mark Hellinger and Harry Hershfield.

Winchell turned in his own review of his act to Variety. "Another
freak attraction on the current Palace bill," he wrote, "is Walter
Winchell. . . . This sort of headliner is too anemic for the best-
known music hall. His appearance is oke—he has a natty tone about
him. He can be heard in the last rows, too. But he is hardly bigtime
material. He simply won't do. . . . Winchell should have known
better and should stick to columning."

But Winchell didn't take his own advice. That year he signed
with not one, but two radio sponsors—Lucky Strike on NBC, and
Geraldine Hair Tonic via CBS. He also branched out into Tin Pan
Alley, doing the lyrics for a song published by Bibo-Lang called
"Things I Never Knew Till Now," with music by Al Van.

Since 1927 Lee Shubert and Walter Winchell had rarely seen eye to eye. Winchell as a dramatic critic was barred from all Shubert theatres. The columnist's favorite comment on the feud was, "I can't go to Shubert openings. So I wait three nights and go to their closings." When he wrote in his column, "The Shuberts lousy? Why, they are the best producers in show business," Lee Shubert sued him for libel—and lost.

In 1931 the dam broke, and Shubert invited Winchell to the opening of Al Jolson in *Wonder Bar*. The producer had decided to end the four-year ban, not out of any love for Winchell, but because Winchell's "opposition" had proved too costly. He covered the Jolson show. The Shuberts were to enjoy even greater boxoffice benevolence from the columnist in later years when, almost single-handedly, in face of a set of mediocre to downright bad notices, Winchell's plugging did a lot to put over Olsen & Johnson's *Hellzapoppin*. The Winchellian "orchids" for pix, plays, books, et cetera became a one-man boxoffice Oscar of no small potency. As far back as 1931 songsmiths Abner Silver and L. Wolfe Gilbert paid tribute to the grip he held on the popular imagination with a ditty titled "Mrs. Winchell's Boy." It was a very confidential hit.

guinan, vallee & benny   Variety glimpsed other stars cutting their way through the depression years. In 1930, Texas Guinan was writing a brief daily column in the ill-fated New York *Graphic;* Weber & Fields were on WOR every Monday night touting Webster Cigars; Will Osborne was crooning at the Brooklyn Fox, billed as originator of the style, while the "copy," Vallee, was soothing feminine hearts at the Paramount on Broadway. Copy or no copy act, Vallee had jumped in two and a half years from $3,000 to $4,500 weekly salary. And in late 1931 Variety revealed that the only new actor millionaires created since the market crash were Vallee, Maurice Chevalier and Amos 'n' Andy. Chevalier received $12,000 a week from the Chicago Theatre, which lost $15,000 on the deal, as Chevalier explained he had been the victim of sharing the bill with a bad film.

Jack Benny spent 1930 in Earl Carroll's *Vanities*. That year Fanny Brice went on tour with a big electric sign spelling out her name, for use at all theatres where she appeared. Primo Carnera entered vaudeville. Bob Burns was glimpsed coming up the ladder, as half of the team of Burns & (John) Swor, whom Fox was trying—unsuccessfully—to build up as another Moran & Mack. Mary Margaret McBride, housewife's companion of the 1940s, was noted as a cub reporter on the Cleveland *Press,* doing occasional lecture turns at women's clubs.

Harry Lauder, before returning to Europe after an American tour, broke Scottish precedent by throwing a party for 28 guests at a New York hotel. He amazed William Morris with the gift of a traveling clock, and a diamond wristwatch for Mrs. Morris. Lauder warned the guests they could only stay two hours until the maitre d'hotel assured him there would be no extra charge if the guests stayed later, whereupon Sir Harry magnanimously invited them to stay as long as they liked. "I'd also invite you all to the theatre," he added, "but I'm not playing this week, and I've spent so damn much money on this food that I haven't any left for theatre tickets."

From France came the belated report that Gaby Deslys, once the toast of Broadway and the *grands boulevards,* had been a distinguished World War I spy for the French Government. She had impersonated an Hungarian woman named Hedwige Navratil, whom she resembled, and had taken the Germans for all the secrets in their pants pockets.

Kate Smith's first radio commercial in 1931, when she hoisted her moon over the mountain for La Palina Cigars, scored a big hit. She played 11 consecutive weeks at the Palace, just missing the previous marks set by dancers Adelaide & Hughes, for 12 weeks, and songstress-comedienne Ruth Roye whose three months' stock run holds the record.

Bing Crosby hit stardom in 1931 when Paramount billed his name above the film. CBS, however, stopped him from whistling with his songs over the air because another CBS chirper, Morton Downey, had been first with the technique. Downey was broadcasting from the Club Delmonico, New York, on Friday and Saturday afternoons.

Will Rogers was on a three-week tour for the Red Cross, along with Frank Hawks, the flier, and The Revelers. Not only did Rogers work on the cuff, but paid his own expenses as well. His generosity netted the Red Cross as high as $8,900 a night, with Texas alone kicking in $50,000.

schnoz goes single The famed Clayton, Jackson & Durante combo broke up in 1931, after consulting with *Sime.* The boys had started together at the Durante Club in 1923. The cold facts were that Lou Clayton and Eddie Jackson would anchor the talented Schnozzola, who would undoubtedly soar much higher solo. So did Variety's editor-founder counsel them. The boys were all for the change; Lou Clayton became Durante's manager, and Jimmy took good care of Eddie Jackson as well, as he did drummer Jack Roth and piano accompanist Harry Donnelly.

Eva Tanguay was still going in 1931, but at a limping pace. She opened in Brooklyn's Rockwell Terrace, a small cabaret, and later joined a Fancho & Marco unit, doing four and five a day. Babe Ruth opened a Broadway haberdashery, and closed it after five months. Ethel Barrymore, whose dressing room at the Barrymore Theatre was never used by anyone save herself, showed how she felt about Billie Burke by giving her the key, when Miss Burke appeared there in *The Truth Game.*

Lou Holtz headed an eight-week vaude show at Warners' Hollywood Theatre, New York, at $2 top, but the policy flopped. Ed Wynn, knocking them dead in *The Laugh Parade,* closed that legit musical every Tuesday to broadcast his Texaco "Fire Chief" program. Later in the year he decided to broadcast from the stage, charging admission, the proceeds to charity. He was the first to do this, and the practice became standard with many radio shows Vaudeville's highest-priced act of 1932 was the Four Marx Bros. at $10,000 a week.

Show business was further depressed during the depression by the passing of many of its favorite figures. One of the first to go was James Churchill, at 66, whose restaurant had been one of Broadway's favorite haunts before it succumbed to the Chinese restaurant invasion. Less mourned was E. F. Albee, who left only $250,000 out of his $25,000,000 to actors' charities. Bulk of that went to the Actors' Fund of America and not to the pet National Vaudeville Artists, the NVA Club which he had subsidized. Albee died a broken-hearted man; his own vaudevillians had turned on him.

A. L. Erlanger, who also died in 1930, did much worse—not one cent of his $12,000,000 going to any charity. The estate was thrown into protracted, expensive litigation on a "common law wife" suit. Although the estate had claims against it of some $7,000,000 with only $124 available as cash on hand, the Erlanger firm continued in business under the aegis of Judge Mitchell Erlanger, Abe Erlanger's brother.

Broadway grief was more readily expressed in 1931 for two of its great and respected showmen—David Belasco, who died at 78, and Joe Leblang, the cut-rate ticket broker, at 57. The same year also saw the passing of Lon Chaney, author Frank Harris, and Charles E. Manchez, inventor of the ice cream cone which symbolized Coney Island.

Flo Ziegfeld died in July 1932. His career, full of spectacular ups and downs, ended on a depressing note. He had lost two fortunes made in show business and Wall Street, the market collapse taking him for over $2,000,000. His last production, *Hot-Cha!* finished in the red, and only his final show, a revival of *Show Boat,* saved him from bankruptcy before his death.

Even more deeply mourned by all of show business was William Morris, who died at the age of 59, two years after the death of his lifelong enemy, E. F. Albee. Variety, which had so often cheered Morris in his courageous battles against the monopolies of show business, termed him "one of the greatest, if not the greatest, of agents and managers in show business."

Other deaths of 1932 included those of Mrs. (Minnie Maddern) Fiske, at 67; Chauncey Olcott at 71; Billy Minsky at 41; John Philip Sousa at 77; George Eastman, founder of Eastman Kodak, at 77; and novelist Edgar Wallace, who had turned out 200 novels and 23 plays during his lifetime, at 56.

Albee, Erlanger, Belasco, Ziegfeld and Morris—the greats were passing, and with them the chapters of theatrical history that had made the first three decades of the 20th century a fabulous tale of Scheherazade to intrigue students of the growth of American show business.

PART FIVE

NEW DEAL

1933 - 1940

The FDR Years

★

The era began, sternly and grimly, with the three harsh years of the depression, then sank to an all-time low in 1933.

In 1934 the nation was so sobered that even Hollywood reported only 60 divorces. Ironically, the depresh proved a boon to family life, drawn closer together in the common fight against the economic wolf. A 1933 survey of favorite American recreations gave first place to reading, radio second. Films, the ranking mass entertainment of the 1920s, placed third.

America's serious mood proved a boon to the apostles of view-

point and opinion. The lecture circuit of show biz climbed out of
the depths for richer dividends. Usual rates for the platform pun-
dits were $100 a night, with $250 for outstanding personalities and
$500 for the real big names. Above that level, only Eleanor Roose-
velt and Admiral Byrd commanded between $700-$1,000 a night.

The national hunger for enlightenment also boomed the stocks of
columnists, who were respected as repositories of encyclopedic wisdom. Top salaries and top syndication went to Walter Winchell,
Walter Lippmann, Westbrook Pegler, Heywood Broun, Mark Sullivan, F.P.A., Arthur Krock and Mrs. Roosevelt among others. The
same thing, of course, was to see itself repeated with World War II,
and with the Korean crisis the political commentators and columnists
once again got the spotlight.

Federal relief began in May of 1933, and ended at the close of
1935. During that period the economic tide began to change rapidly.
"Prosperity's return to Broadway" was keynoted by the Parmalee
(Yellow Cab) Co. report that its 2,000 hackies on the streets of New
York showed an average uppage in tips of 25¢ per fare.

In 1933, Broadway legit sold an average of $228,000 worth of
tickets per week. By the end of 1934, the weekly average had tilted to
$381,000.

Niteries and hotels were equally enthusiastic about recovery under
the New Deal, if not about New Deal taxes. Average checks rose
from $2.80 to $3.40. Leon & Eddie's, a standard tourist spot, reported
once-a-week 1933 patrons were dropping in three times a week during 1934. Broadway was an accurate barometer of what was going
on in general business throughout the country.

Curves on office charts rose steadily upward. In 1936, show business divided $24,000,000 in bonuses and dividends among its em-
ployees. The number of dice, card and wheel games rose to its greatest height since the 1920s. The following year football pools were
reported to be grossing more than $1,500,000 weekly, with an equal
bonanza for numbers racketeers. Steamship companies reported 1,-
000,000 passengers booked annually for ocean cruises, and theatres
began to raise their prices.

jukeboxes and repeal   Jukeboxes reflected the rising
tide of national joy, sweeping into every crossroads town by 1939.
Adolescents jitterbugged to the hot licks of the nation's top bands—

for a nickel a dance. In 1940 there were 400,000 jukeboxes flashing colored lights and making music to celebrate a $65,000,000 new industry. Bars began to install "Talk-A-Vision" machines which offered musical movies at the insertion of a coin.

In the first months of 1933, when repeal seemed likely, if not an absolute certainty, radio jumped the gun by inviting liquor advertising. CBS' St. Louis outlet, KMOX, had one announcer telling the radio audience, "Put in your orders now for Blank's Whiskey. If the repeal of the Volstead Act does not materialize as expected, your money will be cheerfully refunded."

Legalization of 3.2 beer in March evoked a wave of repeal celebrations all over the country. In New York, film theatres found that business perked as film fans went for 3.2 and a film. The more sophisticated legit trade, however, turned up its nose at the plebeian offering and sought its usual refreshment in its usual speakeasies.

When full repeal was established, New York speakeasies quickly realized that their main attraction had vanished—the little peephole in the door through which patrons whispered, "Benny sent me." With liquor flowing copiously anywhere, there was no need of Benny to send anybody any place. The speaks rapidly converted into night clubs, and there was a huge demand for talent to lure trade. Some clubs tried to make patrons as anxious to get in as they had been in Prohibition days by deliberately making it tough—"reservations," a mythical "membership," and the rest of the "exclusive" paraphernalia. There are still remnants of that to this day.

The outstanding event of 1934, outside of the world-shaking events abroad, was the arrest of Bruno Richard Hauptmann for the kidnaping and murder of the Lindbergh baby in May 1932. Tried in Flemington, New Jersey, Hauptmann brought a $50,000 weekly boom to that obscure town as curiosity-seekers flocked in by car, bus and train. The trial was given the biggest newspaper and radio coverage of any trial in American history.

murder, inc.   There were further thrills in 1934 for readers and dialers in the capture and slaying of John Dillinger. The following year headline writers had a holiday with the long delayed extermination of Dutch Schultz. The era in crime closed with the sensational expose of Murder, Incorporated, a phrase coined by the New York *World-Telegram*.

England dominated the world's news in 1936, with the death of King George V; the ascension of Edward VIII to the throne; and the historic romantic abdication before the end of the year to marry "the woman I love." Edward and his American-born wife continued to win headlines all through the decade, despite the crowning of George VI and Elizabeth in 1937. The coronation was overshadowed that year by the marriage of the newly-styled Duke of Windsor to Mrs. Simpson in France. To mend England's fences in the United States, King George and Queen Elizabeth paid a 1939 visit to the Roosevelts in Washington and Hyde Park. The following year they exiled the embarrassing ex-King to the Bahamas as "Governor and Commander-in-Chief." United States show business, showing rare consideration for our English cousins, banned all Wally Simpson gags on radio, and passed up thinly-disguised "royal romance" themes for pictures as "too hot to handle."

Apart from floods and strikes, newsreels enjoyed a boom in disaster during 1937 with the explosion of the *Hindenburg* at Lakehurst, New Jersey, fortuitously filmed at the exact moment it happened by a surprised cameraman; and the disappearance into thin air of round-the-world flier Amelia Earhart. England's Coronation ceremony also won heavy newsreel footage.

The following year more air news was made by Douglas ("Wrong Way") Corrigan, who flew from Brooklyn to Dublin with neither permit nor permission. Corrigan received offers totaling $200,000 from show business, but refused them all. The rest of 1938 was taken up by war news from abroad; the arrest of ex-President Whitney of the New York Stock Exchange; the tearing down of New York's 6th Avenue Elevated after 60 years of operation; and Mexico's appropriation of foreign-held land, including 17,980 acres belonging to William Randolph Hearst—who didn't like the idea.

The news event of 1939 was, of course, the outbreak of World War II in September of that year. Slightly more than one year later America had a new Selective Service Act—the first "peacetime" compulsory military service in its history.

fdr—no. 1 showman   Unquestionably the biggest figure in all show business of 1940 was Franklin Delano Roosevelt, whose radio rating hit a new high, with a Crossley grade of 38.7. His election for a third time demonstrated, as nothing else could, the power of

American radio. More than a political contest, the 1940 election was a battle between newspapers and radio to test which medium exercised the greatest influence on the American public. When the newspapers lined up about 90 per cent solidly against a third term, Roosevelt took his case to the people via the airwaves. Newspapers denied that the victory had been a clear-cut one, claiming that the Roosevelt voice and personality were as much of a factor in the victory as the medium of radio.

On the lighter side of the ledger for the 1930s were the usual fads and foibles that always fascinated the American public come war, peace or atom bombs. A new era in publishing history began in 1933 with the appearance of *Esquire,* a magazine frankly aimed at being lusty in a slick way, offering juicy Petty and Varga pin-up girls for bachelor quarters. With the perversity of the sex—as though the publishers didn't know—women also flocked to buy it.

The Chicago *Tribune* made all of the Windy City fragrant in 1929 by running a rose-scented ad for the Allied Florists Association of Illinois. Sixty pounds of perfume were mixed with the regular ink for this aromatic scoop. The last footnote on the history of journalism of the 1930s was the appearance of New York's liberal newspaper, *P.M.,* the first big-city journal to line up openly on labor's side. Chicago millionaire Marshall Field III bankrolled it—but even he ran out of money some 10 years later.

The first of the 1930s fads was long fingernails, introduced in 1933 by Marlene Dietrich. It was also the year of the jigsaw puzzle craze, which enjoyed a long—depression-nurtured—vogue until 1936, when "knock-knock-who's-there?" games and gags, along with a candid camera craze, occupied the idle time and minds of the nation. Bars increased their take that year by installing skee-ball alleys. In 1939 and 1940, the top divertissements were gambling—pinball machines, which graduated out of the penny arcade class; and the newly-improved game of gin rummy, a Hollywood favorite.

The pace of the 1930s saw many changes, besides those in economic and political spheres. Show business rejoiced in 1933 when increasing bus competition forced the railroads to restore old party rates. Niagara Falls hotel men claimed that no honeymooners were arriving —by train, bus or car—because show business comics had ruined the town's reputation with corny gags about it.

Variety noted in 1936 that the old aspiration of youngsters to see their names in lights on Broadway had practically vanished, replaced by a determined migration to Hollywood, the new mecca. Broadway was further depressed that year by the disappearance of the old Criterion Theatre, replaced by a large and gaudy Woolworth's.

The same year, Max Schmeling made Teutonic hearts rejoice by knocking out Joe Louis. Two years later Louis made American hearts rejoice by knocking out Max Schmeling.

a couple of exes   A further token of change was noted in 1936 when Churchill met Paderewski at England's Denham Film Studios, where Paderewski was making a picture. "The last time I met you," the great Pole said sadly, "you were at the War Office." Churchill replied, "The last time I met you, you were a president."

Perhaps the most startling change of all took place in 1939, when sedate Philadelphia agreed to permit Sunday dancing but stood firm on no Sunday drinking.

When the era drew to a close, Variety revealed its usual list of the year's top salaries—implying, thereby, Americans considered most indispensable. Top of the list was Claudette Colbert, with $301,944. Next, surprisingly, came Warner Baxter, with $279,907. In the third slot was Bing Crosby's take of $260,000. Runners-up were Jack Benny ($250,000), Joseph Pulitzer ($180,000), William S. Paley ($171,849), Bob Burns ($155,900), Robert L. Ripley ($145,000), and W. R. Hearst ($100,000).

The curtain rose on 1933 to Wagnerian music offstage. On January 30, Adolf Hitler was named Chancellor of Germany—32 days before Franklin Delano Roosevelt was named President of the United States, and 27 days before the famous hoax of the Reichstag fire which Hitler used as a pretext for liquidating his opposition.

While Hitler was busy paving the way for mastery of the world, Roosevelt was busy pumping new life into our end of it. Two days after he took the oath of office, F.D.R. shut the nation's banks, stock and commodity exchanges. Six days after this moratorium he delivered his first fireside chat, to tell the nation what he was going to do.

Show business, along with the rest of the nation, hung onto every word. Something was radically wrong when stagehands were being paid more than actors, and janitors earned more money than the managers of film theatres.

nra theme song   On June 13 the New Deal became law, with the passing of the N.R.A. Act by Congress. Tin Pan Alley immediately celebrated with a song called "Nira"—after National Industrial Recovery Act; and N.R.A. quickly became the three most-frequently used initials in the alphabet of all show business comics.

Under the N.R.A.'s vaudeville code, the legal minimum wage for actors became $7.50 a day—$40 for the full week. Many independent theatre managers wailed that they couldn't afford to pay those salaries. Actors retorted that any theatres which couldn't, shouldn't be allowed to employ actors.

In November big things were rumored to be under way for show business. The Blue Eagle was reported to be hatching a blueprint to save the legitimate theatre. A theatre "recovery" movement was sparked by Gustav Blum, an indie producer, with the enthusiastic endorsement of Frank Gillmore, president of Actors Equity.

Blum's plan was for a Federal-subsidized stock theatre, with everyone connected working for nominal wages, to produce "the best plays" for 25¢ and 50¢. Meanwhile, Eva LeGallienne won the ear of Mrs. Roosevelt for her own scheme—a national theatre patterned after her Civic Repertory, with a 25¢-$1 admission.

The Blum plan won out early in 1944. On January 15, several thousand actors stormed Equity's offices for jobs in the free shows which had begun playing in school auditoriums and institutions under the Civil Works Administration. The Government's first grant was $28,000, budgeted to give 150 unemployed actors work for 32 days, each player getting $25 to $30 a week.

Angry that there weren't enough jobs to go around, 100 vaude actors marched with picket signs to New York's City Hall to demand that Mayor Fiorello H. LaGuardia shake more jobs out of Washington's pockets. Their signs read, WE DON'T WANT A DOLE—WE WANT WORK! and WE ALWAYS GIVE WHEN ASKED FOR ANY BENEFITS, FOR ANY EMERGENCY—WHAT ABOUT GIVING US A NEW DEAL?

Appropriations were increased, and the movement extended month after month, until it was taken over by New York's Public Works Division of the Emergency Relief Administration.

Early in the fall of 1934, the Government appropriated another $300,000 for W.P.A. shows to be sent into the C.C.C. camps—another New Deal innovation. These burgeoned into 20 units—four vaudeville, employing a total of 300, and the rest New York City units. These actors received $24 weekly, plus bed and board.

The W.P.A. also set up stages in the city's parks during the summer, using trucks for transportation and amplifying equipment for acoustics. At one Staten Island park performance, the audience tallied 20,000, which led some neighborhood theatres to complain that this was too much "opposition."

1935 brought a $4,880,000,000 Works Relief Bill in April. New York State revealed that it was helping to keep 2,000 actors alive. Elmer Rice was appointed regional director of a new theatre scheme for New York, which planned to try out new plays in the Bronx, Queens and Brooklyn—omitting Manhattan because of the obvious high rental cost of theatres. The question of the Government running in direct opposition with the commercial theatres soon arose.

Out of the giant fund for relief, the W.P.A. came into existence with an allotment of $27,315,000. Of this sum $10,000,000 was earmarked for the wages of actors, writers, and other unemployed but willing digits of show business.

rise and fall of the ftp   In 1936 Washington appropriated $7,000,000 for W.P.A. shows. Over 9,000 show people worked in the Federal Theatre Project in 20 states, entertaining a national audience of 350,000 nightly. In New York alone, 4,700, or over half the Federal Theatre's personnel, were employed.

The Federal Theatre saw itself maligned in some newspaper headlines and by the same papers' dramatic critics. It was not, certain writers stressed, a boondoggling project, but "one of the greatest stimulants of the American theatre had ever known." It produced great things; introduced millions of Americans who had never seen a stage performance to the legitimate theatre; and gave hundreds of talented actors, writers, composers and directors a chance to show what they had. Orson Welles, for example, was a simonpure W.P.A. product.

A memorable division of the Federal Theatre was the *Living Newspaper* troupe, which introduced a new note to Broadway—documentary plays. Among the themes tackled by the *Living Newspaper* were the power trusts, the problem of erosion, and monopolies. The staging, writing, direction and lighting were sometimes brilliant.

No troupe of the Federal Theatre Project aroused the bitter enmity of the Roosevelt-haters as did the *Living Newspaper,* which was effective propaganda for the New Deal and against the Old Guard. It was the basis for the charge that the Federal Theatre "was shot through with Communism"—because the *Living Newspaper* was pro-New Deal—and wasn't the New Deal communistic?

In 1937 all of show business, including theatre managers and show business executives, helped the agitation for a five-day week for all industry. A five-day week meant two full days of leisure—an obvious boom for the nation's boxoffices.

social security theme song Social legislation was still pouring out of the Washington mills. To celebrate Social Security and job insurance, songsmiths Hillie Bell and Willard Egloff wrote, "I'm In Love With 234-0-567"—a number which was never assigned to anyone because the song beat Washington to it.

Show biz unionization gathered momentum. SAG (Screen Actors Guild) invaded the East, signing up all New York local studios except March of Time. In Hollywood, the Screen Publicists Guild was born. In Philadelphia, 28 Jewish cantors (not to be confused with rabbis) applied for an AFL charter—and it wasn't a gag.

Negro Actors Guild came into being. The Dramatists Guild won their first deal—a contract involving film rights to the hit legiter, *The Women*. The IATSE (International Alliance of Theatrical Stage Employees), which embraces stagehands and film theatre projectionists, announced plans "to organize the entire amusement industry 100 per cent." This proved a spurious pitch for the racketeering Browne & Bioff regime, of which more anon.

AFRA (American Federation of Radio Artists) also was formed. As late as 1936 there were cases of factory scripting methods on certain radio soap operas, grinding out several scripts a week for $25, while some radio sponsors were accused of paying off their lesser show talent with merchandise. AFRA did not win its decisive victory, however, until 1939.

The American Theatre Council, representing all theatre groups and unions, held its first convention in May of 1937. Speakers stressed the point that the biggest trouble with show business was Hollywood, which had withdrawn financial backing from Broadway shows because of differences with the Dramatists Guild over contract terms.

1938 shifted the emphasis in show business unionization. The fever suddenly infected "the front of the house." There were managers' unions, agents' unions, treasurers' unions, and press agents' unions. The Ringling Bros. Circus was also hit by a strike of laborers, which lasted two days before Ringling-Barnum & Bailey capitulated.

In 1939, Equity flexed its muscles again and proposed raising its minimum pay for actors from $40 to $50. There was an outcry from the membership, who feared they would be pricing themselves out of the market, and the matter had to be shelved until the following season.

in the red, both ways   The Federal Theatre Project collapsed early in the summer of 1939. Angry solons in Washington denied it funds, charging waste and extravagance. The real complaint, whispered in the cloakrooms, was radicalism. The House voted the Project out of existence. The Senate, more faithful to the New Deal, attempted to save it, but the House refused to compromise. President Roosevelt was forced to sign its death warrant on pain of being forced to reject the entire relief appropriations bill. Unwittingly, show business comics had played into the hands of the reactionary House by popularizing W.P.A. gags like "termites ate through his shovel handle," giving the lower body of Congress apparent justification for slashing W.P.A. funds.

Sticks Nix Hick Pix

★

Morale in Hollywood sank to an all-time low in 1933 because of salary cuts, dropped options, firings and the Damocles' sword that hung over the entire industry as it waited to see what the New Deal could do to put spending money in the nation's pockets. Actors wrote letters of protest to Washington over the influx of some 12,000 European actors into the United States during the depression. Broadway actors blamed Hollywood producers for encouraging the immigration. William Fox privately explained that his reason for enticing foreign stars was the hope of increasing the foreign b.o. of Fox pix.

Producers felt uneasy about the first British films coming into the country. They were good—too good. Critics had a field day, lambasting Hollywood for turning out "puerile tripe" compared to England's masterpiece, *The Private Life of Henry VIII* (Charles Laughton). *Rome Express,* with Esther Ralston, Conrad Veidt and Frank Vosper, who also did part of the dialoging job on this one, was called by Variety "probably the best British film shown over here to date and will get easy booking in the United States."

Theatre grosses declined all through the spring and summer of 1933, showing little improvement over the practically zero business of the bank holidays. Bankruptcy and receiverships were the order of the day for Paramount-Publix, RKO, and the West Coast division of Fox. Only Warner Bros. and Loew's, Inc. weathered the financial storms.

Financial fireworks on the West Coast, four years after Wall Street laid its famous egg, resulted in a general reorganization for greater efficiency. Bankers still clung to their mortgages, but were shrewd enough to turn over production, distribution and theatre management to the men who knew how. Many theatres were allowed to return to their original owners. The end of the depression found showmen once more in the saddle.

The pix biz rode into the black during 1934. Bankruptcies and receiverships were cleared up, and studios began turning out better films. It was the first year of Volsteadian repeal, and Americans were coming out of their homes again—to the benefit of film theatre boxoffices.

The year was not without its setbacks for Hollywood. The summer crop of films was extremely lightweight, and some of these began to provoke agitation from church circles for extreme film censorship. A drought in the Midwest crippled theatre attendance, resulting in film houses offering giveaways—everything except the managers' children—to lure patronage.

Exhibitors yielded to ASCAP's demands for a new music tax schedule—10¢ a seat for theatres seating up to 800; 15¢ a seat for those with a 1,600 capacity, and 20¢ for larger houses. Exhibitors were also battered by union troubles and the usual tiffs with distributors over block-booking which allegedly forced lemons onto theatre bills.

Hollywood came to their rescue—and headed off the church crusade—by releasing its top films, usually held for the favorable box-office weather of the fall, in the middle of August. This strategy succeeded in all aspects, and helped speed the return of patronage to film theatres.

1935 found the film industry the second most important in California, ranking after oil production. Government census figures showed 39 studios in operation, employing 9,022, and valued at the new all-time high for Hollywood of $97,748,377. At its World War II peak, the pix biz was estimated to be a $2,000,000,000 industry.

The optimism engendered by the New Deal, spreading into all the formerly gloomy cracks on the map of America, found a shining mirror that year in Hollywood. Industry was recovering, employment was up, and both unions and relief spending were putting more money in the pockets of more people. Film receipts climbed.

Even conservative producers began to dig deep for expensive advertising campaigns. Warner Bros., which was courageous enough to believe it could sell Shakespeare to Americans of the 1930s, splurged heavily to promote *Midsummer Night's Dream* with James Cagney. They were wrong, but only because they were premature. Not until 1948, with J. Arthur Rank's Oscar-winning production of *Hamlet,* starring Sir Laurence Olivier, did Americans really flock to see Shakespeare on the screen. "The Bard boff at the b.o.," as Variety put it.

The upbeat of 1935 could be detected by a new surge of theatre building activity; higher prices paid to Broadway for screen rights to legitimate hits; and an increasing number of film companies and stars becoming angels for Broadway plays.

The reason for a new interest in Broadway was the realization by Hollywood that the movie tripe of the 1920s was obsolete in the realistic 1930s. With the New Deal "fireside chats," social legislation and other far-reaching stimuli, the "silo belt" was rapidly becoming too sophisticated to be entertained by corn as green as their summer crops. Variety summed up the situation in its famous headline:

STICKS NIX HICK PIX. So it was to Broadway that Hollywood turned for mature story material.

That Hollywood couldn't get it fast enough—and in large enough quantities—was evident by the rapid growth of the give-away fever in movie houses. Since most films were too inconsequential to draw heavy trade, managers vied with each other by turning performances into lotteries. In Denver, theatres were even giving automobiles away.

Urged by the film industry, the N.R.A. stepped in and forbade the practice of movie house giveaways. But—as happened when radio interests tried to stop giveaways on 1948's "Stop the Music" program —the public wouldn't permit it. It *liked* giveaways—even with the individual odds heavily stacked against the ticket-buyer. He still had a chance, didn't he? *Somebody* had to win! So managers were forced to continue with extra-legal forms of giveaways, like "bank night." Even Loew's was compelled to join the indies with screeno. Washington and Hollywood sighed and gave up.

43.945 cinemas wired for sound

A roundup of 1936 showed 18,508 theatres in the United States. Of these, 15,089 were wired for sound. Some 13,130 theatres, which the depression had shut down, still had cobwebs on the cashier's glass. The tally also showed that there were 27,956 theatres wired for sound in all of Europe, including Russia.

Business began to boom for Hollywood in 1936, when it helped the New Deal out to the extent of $100,000,000 in taxes—which it could well afford. The good films made were so good that they made the bad ones on the double feature programs look terrible by contrast— and a demand grew up for abolition of double features. Public polls were held but, like Prohibition, when they voted dry and everybody drank, so did the public actually favor two-for-one film programs.

That films were becoming better was attested to by the recognition they won in Washington, where the National Archives announced that 1936 films would be preserved for exhibition to our descendants in the year 2,436. Even that news, however, was not sufficient to impress exhibitors into killing banko and screeno, which continued even when threatened on grounds of violating lottery laws.

Fords and big jackpot cash prizes were among the inducements offered filmgoers. One exhibitor tried offering films accompanied by basketball and badminton games on the stage. Others went along with the policy of Hollywood, and spent their surplus funds in the orthodox channels of advertising.

During 1936 and 1937 there was so much foreign talent—actors, directors and writers—streaming into the United States that actors again pressured Washington for action. Bills were prepared in Congress to protect home talent, but they died in pigeonholes. Across the Atlantic, English actors began to protest to Parliament that too many Americans were invading the British Isles and keeping English talent unemployed.

Theatres began tilting admission prices about a nickel, estimating that the traffic would bear the increase—and it did. Film-going was once again getting to be a regular habit of Americans, who came and came again, despite their squawks against double features, and the dull similarity of many films. The demand for a constantly better product even inspired a sudden craze for some of the finer old silents, but distributors were reluctant to release them, fearful of a drop in their regular meal-tickets.

Hollywood decided to pull the cork out in 1938, and announced 35 films budgeted at $1,000,000, or more, apiece. This was decided upon, along with a hoopla campaign to plug the slogan, "Movies Are Your Best Entertainment," at an industry-wide conference. Producers hoped by this concerted action to sweep aside criticism of their less admirable efforts, and to buck the trend in giveaways. The Hollywood ballyhooists had a field day with the idea, even playing it for laughs by billposting a maternity ward with the slogan, "Movies Are Your Best Entertainment." The catchphrase, however, suffered a costly deflationary reflex when some captious critic discovered that the key letters of the campaign slogan spelled out MAYBE.

Giveaways were too firmly entrenched by 1938. Borrowing from radio, house managers staged quiz shows and spelling bees for prizes. Cutrate exchange tickets and "twofers" (two-for-one) weren't enough. In the Midwest some exhibitors installed "magic eyes" which snapshotted patrons entering the theatre. The quizzes, spelling contests and other stunts were palpably designed to circumvent the lottery (game of chance) angle by putting the accent on "skill." But with a frankness that hurt, one Fox theatre manager, Roy Hanson by name, heralded on the marquee: WIN $80 AND SEE A LOUSY

SHOW. Some years later, with the boom of double features, another Southern manager, with equal frankness, put up on his marquee, ONE PRETTY GOOD PICTURE AND ONE STINKER.

beginning of gov't suits   Hollywood's biggest headache of the year was the sudden attack by New Deal trust-busters on the close interlocking controls in the movie industry of production, distribution and theatre ownership. The five major studios affected were Paramount, 20th Century-Fox, Loew's, RKO and Warners. All, the Government charged, were guilty of violating the Sherman Anti-Trust Act. It filed suits against the companies, insisting upon a complete divorce between the production and distribution ends, and the theatres. Alarmed, the five companies pooled to fight the suit but the Government won out eventually, although it took them 10 years to do so.

This was the latest and most aggravating of the moves by Washington against Hollywood that had begun in 1933, when the Government had deflated the movie colony's boast to be the fifth largest American industry. It was not, chided Washington, which then revealed that Hollywood ranked somewhere between 20th and 30th.

Hollywood was one of the targets in Washington's heavy tax legislation, levied on top-bracket incomes. In 1938, Hollywood lobbied for a reduction in these taxes, but was ignored. Two years later Hollywood was suddenly hit over the head by Martin Dies, who yelled to the country in black headlines that Communists "dominated" the movie colony. Hollywood's frantic demand for a fair hearing was again ignored. History was to repeat itself a decade later when Congressman J. Parnell Thomas—who himself was found guilty of malfeasance in office—probed Hollywood for Communism and fellow-travelers. The "Unfriendly 10" were eventually found guilty and given fines and jail sentences, including among them notable scripters and directors.

1940 also brought another first-class headache in the shape of New York's Mayor LaGuardia, who had been lighting fires under Hollywood producers to move some of their studios to New York City, in recognition of the enormous income Hollywood derived from Gotham.

"You can tell the film executives for me," the Little Flower exploded in Variety's ear, "that they don't fool me one bit with their

empty gestures of 'we will co-operate,' then giving us the go-by. . . .
If necessary we'll make them recognize our claim. As a matter
of fact, that smug half-dozen or so movie producers already have
stirred up plenty for themselves with the Government because
of their habits. Maybe that will be the medium through which the
City of New York can achieve its just claims. They can't kid me
with their phony sympathies, and as a matter of fact even if we
could blast them out of their self-satisfied strongholds in California,
I'm not so sure that we want them!"

The Little Flower never lived to see Hollywood in New York.
If the studios didn't actually move East, they did come to the
conclusion, in the late 1940s, that it would be a lot less expensive
to shoot films in the actual New York locales. Their look of authen-
ticity, at least, was a plus production value.

During the 1930s, Hollywood's profit was derived—as it was
through most of the 1940s—from the foreign market. Films were
expected to earn their expenses in the United States, then bring
in the gravy from abroad. In 1933 American films were still supreme, despite the fact that Japan led the world in film footage
produced, and Germany was creeping up to the United States as
a competitor.

The tables were suddenly turned in 1934, when Charles Laugh-
ton's *Henry VIII* suddenly made not only the foreign market, but
American as well, aware that England could make remarkably
fine films. Abroad that year, the outstanding foreign boxoffice
records were made by—in the order named—Eddie Cantor, Greta
Garbo, Marlene Dietrich, Norma Shearer, Janet Gaynor, George
Arliss, Paul Muni, Clark Gable, Claudette Colbert and Ronald
Colman.

Two years later the lineup of foreign nation favorites had altered
drastically—with only three of the old 10 holding on. First was
Shirley Temple, followed by Gary Cooper, Clark Gable, the Fred
Astaire-Ginger Rogers team, Charlie Chaplin, Greta Garbo, Marlene Dietrich, Grace Moore, Laurel & Hardy, and Robert Taylor.

One foreign film made the headlines in 1936—*Ecstasy* with Hedy
Lamarr *au naturel*. The outcry against admitting it led to a Supreme
Court decision that, even though the United States Customs Office
admitted a film, any state had the right to ban it if its Board of
Censors saw fit. And most did.

broadway's hollywood invasion   Still in the swaddling clothes of the talkie stage in 1933, Hollywood felt a desperate need for romantic leading men who could both mug and talk expertly. By September of that year it had signed 315 actors from legit. The only new film names of any consequence that year, however, were Mae West and Katharine Hepburn, who scored in *Bill of Divorcement* with John Barrymore. Mae West clicked heavily in her first starring film, *She Done Him Wrong*, which was barred from Australia, where censors considered her "vulgar." It was pointed out that Aussie's headquarters, England, loved Mae West to the extent of smashing boxoffice records to watch her do him wrong.

Kate Smith's first film, *Hello Everybody,* proved so embarrassing to the New York Paramount that the theatre pulled it after six days, a fact which puzzled show business because Kate Smith in person was a powerful drawing card.

In the same year a bit player got her start on the Fox lot when George White, during a film version of his *Scandals,* had a row with the star, Lilian Harvey, who walked out. White promptly summoned a girl who had one song with Rudy Vallee's band, and made her the lead. For her work in the film, Alice Faye won a contract and later stardom.

Top movie personality of 1933, however, was conceded to be Franklin D. Roosevelt in the newsreels . . . termed by a Hollywood wit, "the Barrymore of the White House." Lionel Barrymore, an enemy of the New Deal from the start, did not appreciate the comparison. Of course they meant his "Great Profile" brother, John.

The prevailing trend on the lots that year was the filmusical, in an attempt to jump on the bandwagon of Warner Bros.' *42d Street.* One outstanding short was produced which was constantly repeated by request throughout the era—Walt Disney's *Three Little Pigs,* whose big bad wolf became a symbol for the depression that nobody was afraid of any longer.

1933 was also the year in which Hollywood first took official cognizance of Hitler in a film called *Rafter Romance.* One scene showed actor George Sidney apprehending his son in the act of drawing swastikas on doors and walls. In the words of one entranced Jewish lady who enjoyed the film, "And does he give it to the kid—*mm mm!*"

A survey of 1934 showed that the year had produced a crop of 35 new stars—22 of them in films. Some were European importations, while others were Broadway personalities who scored in their first talkies. Katharine Hepburn won the Academy Award as the year's best actress for her work in *Morning Glory* for RKO. Charles Laughton won the male Oscar for *Henry VIII*, and Frank Lloyd's *Cavalcade*, a film version of the Noel Coward stage success, took best director and film awards for Fox. Incidentally, writing later on *Cavalcade, Goodbye, Mr. Chips, Mrs. Miniver, et al.*, Variety observed, "the best British pix are still the ones made in Hollywood."

1935 was a relatively undistinguished year, offering a cycle of gangster films of which Cagney's *Public Enemy*, based on Dillinger's career, was outstanding. Cagney demonstrated a new "treat-'em-rough" technique, somewhat similar to the caveman style of the old silents' Valentino, by pushing a grapefruit into his screen girl-friend's (Mae Clarke) face. His stock soared 100 per cent as a heart palpitator among femme fans, much as James Mason's did years later with an English brand of sexual sadism. The other notable film event of 1936 was the debut of the March of Time, first documentary-type newsreel.

more new faces New stars continued to pop up during 1935 and 1936—no less than 27 in films—as studio talent scouts scoured Broadway and college campuses for fresh faces. Among the new stars recruited from vaudeville, radio and night clubs by Darryl Zanuck at 20th Century-Fox were the Ritz Bros., Tony Martin, Don Ameche, Dixie Dunbar and Jack Haley. Musicals were still in top favor because, as Joe Schenck reported, they lent themselves easily to plugging and promotion via radio, which had proved that it could publicize any musical into top boxoffice. The craze for musicals accounted for the presence of no less than 63 of the nation's top tunesmiths on Hollywood payrolls.

The five directors of 1936 who were found turning out the most consistent b.o. successes were W. S. Van Dyke, Clarence Brown, David Butler, William Wyler and Norman Taurog. The Academy recognized *Mutiny On the Bounty* (Laughton again) as the year's best film; and gave its acting laurels to Victor McLaglen for a magnificent performance in *The Informer* and Bette Davis for her fine work with Leslie Howard in *Of Human Bondage*.

With *The Informer*, Hollywood proved to its scoffing critics that it was capable of genuine film artistry as fine as any emanating from a foreign source. So enthusiastic was the response of American intellectuals to the film—despite the unfortunate maudlin ending to the O'Flaherty classic tacked on in an effort to meet Havs code requirements—that it is still being revived as an outstanding film.

Much praise—as well as wonder—was poured out at the scene during which McLaglen, as the Informer, appears before the Irish underground court for judgment. His bewilderment and confusion were considered a classic in screen acting. Inside Hollywood gossip awarded the laurels to director John Ford, who, it claimed, had encouraged McLaglen to imbibe freely at a party, under the illusion that there would be no shooting the following day. Then, the story went, Ford had ordered McLaglen awakened roughly after only one hour of sleep, and thrust suddenly in front of the cameras, which had started grinding.

From the b.o. viewpoint, the best pix in 1936 were Chaplin's *Modern Times, San Francisco* (Gable-Spencer Tracy-Jeanette MacDonald), *Swing Time* (Astaire-Rogers). *The Great Ziegfeld* (William Powell-Myrna Loy-Frank Morgan-Luise Rainer, the latter also an Academy winner with *Good Earth* but destined not to continue Hollywood prominence despite a double-win of the coveted Oscar), *The Littlest Rebel* (Shirley Temple), *Rose Marie* (MacDonald-Nelson Eddy), *A Tale of Two Cities* (Ronald Colman) and *The Story of Louis Pasteur* (Paul Muni).

The New York film critics, taking exception to the usual pattern of Academy awards, formed their own Film Critics Circle, à la the legit Critics Circle, and now annually select their own "best" films and performances of the year.

That year was fertile indeed with solid film entertainment, because in addition to the above it produced *Mutiny On the Bounty* (Laughton-Gable-Tone), *Mr. Deeds Goes To Town* (Gary Cooper), *Dodsworth* (Walter Huston-Ruth Chatterton-Mary Astor-Paul Lukas-David Niven) and *Anthony Adverse* (Fredric March).

Sam Goldwyn made Broadway rejoice by paying the top price of 1936 for a stage hit. Sidney Kingsley's *Dead End*—$165,000. David O. Selznick acquired screen rights to the best-selling novel *Gone With the Wind* for $52,000, and turned down another producer's offer of $150,000 for a re-sale.

As a postscript to 1936, Variety revealed that the Louis-Schmeling fight films were "tops in gross for all time," and that a joint attack by the Hearst and Paul Block papers on Mae West's film, *Klondike Annie,* had resulted in a remarkably satisfying burst of business for La West at the b.o.

Hollywood still strove to freshen audience interest in 1937 with new and—it hoped—beguiling faces. Among the "starlets" it unveiled that year were Rochelle Hudson and Judith Barrett, for whom it predicted big things. Ten years later Louis Sobol got around to asking, "Whatever became of their careers?"

A new and startling trend developed in the production of Westerns. Gene Autry had the crackpot idea that Western fans would like their cowboy stars to warble as they rode—and he did. Instead of walking out, audiences lapped it up—even the small fry trade. Overnight every studio began to test its horse opera aspirants for vocal qualifications. Meantime the studios were splurging more and more with Technicolor. Sam Goldwyn announced he would toss the screen's new paintpot over every new film he made—a pronunciamento more enthusiastic than accurate.

The lush market for musicals continued. Many studios showed a sudden interest in opera divas (such as Grace Moore, Gladys Swarthout, Lily Pons and Marta Eggerth), to the consternation of the Met. The death of Jean Harlow, and its attendant publicity, was cashed in on by reissues of her films. Audiences watched the glamorous Harlow move, speak and exude s.a., with something like mingled fascination and horror.

RKO set a new high for film rights to stage hits by paying $255,000 for *Room Service* as a vehicle for the Marx Bros. The previous record was held by *Broadway,* which collected $20,000 less in 1929. Runner-up was the price for *You Can't Take It With You* —a $200,000 buy by Columbia. Highest paid writer of Hollywood in 1937 was Ben Hecht, whose annual take from Goldwyn was $260,000 a year.

The Radio City Music Hall enjoyed its biggest week, a $123,700 gross, with *The Prisoner of Zenda.* The Roxy's top for 1937 was $78,000, with *One In A Million.* The New York Paramount hit its high at $62,000, with *Double Or Nothing.*

Better "B's" was the war-cry of 1938, as moviegoers protested against the lower ends of double bills. Thomas E. Dewey's gang-busting in New York inspired a wave of gangster films that rode the tide of the headlines, along with racing and fight pictures. There was also a cycle of newspaper reporter films, portraying the Fourth Estate in the usual Hollywood manner. Top musicals enjoyed the usual good business.

Top film of the year was Walt Disney's *Snow White and the Seven Dwarfs*. Mickey Rooney scored as main prop of the new *Andy Hardy* series, MGM's bid for the family trade.

still more escapism   The trend in 1939 was for frothier screen fare, as a deliberate reaction to the grim newspaper headlines of the day. The emphasis on escapism was so strong that many war stories, particularly those anti-Nazi and anti-neutrality, were chopped from shooting schedules.

There were the usual screwball comedies, gangster, prison and G-Man films, seasoned by straight whodunits and family-trade "B's." American history was dusted off and presented in Errol Flynn in *Dodge City*, Cecil B. DeMille's *Union Pacific* and Henry Fonda in the title role of *Young Mr. Lincoln*, all of which were given special premieres in appropriate cites. Producers footed the bill for getting critics there and back by train.

As though the imminence of war had destroyed any illusions Americans of the 1930s may have had, Hollywood began to de-glamorize its oomph girls. In *Hollywood Cavalcade* it showed Alice Faye being hit in the face with a pie. In other films, Marlene Dietrich was allowed to mix with barflies, and Clark Gable dragged Joan Crawford through a very muddy bed of mud.

The big deal of 1940, highly touted in the industry's most successful and expensive campaign, was *Gone With the Wind*. Among the other five top-grossing films—*Boom Town, Northwest Mounted Police, Rebecca, The Fighting 69th,* and *Strike Up the Band*— not one was an accurate or vital reflection of the world then in flames. The fact that these six were the top-grossing films lent weight to Hollywood's claim that Americans wanted escapist entertainment, not realism.

The year's six top stars were Gable, Mickey Rooney, Spencer Tracy, Errol Flynn, Bette Davis and Gary Cooper. Abroad, the best-rated stars were Gable and Garbo, followed by Deanna Durbin, Flynn and Cooper.

During the era, Hollywood ran the emotional gamut in its attitude toward radio. Suspicion of radio as a boxoffice competitor was gradually replaced by co-operation and actual participation. In 1933 many exhibs were demanding that producers prohibit stars under contract from appearing on the air between noon and midnight, so as to stifle their microphonic "opposition."

But it wasn't long before Hollywood convinced exhibitors that radio was helping to sell pix, rather than hurt the b.o. Since commercial radio depended heavily on film stars, more and more broadcasts began to originate from the Coast. In 1937 fully 95 per cent of the top radio shows originated in Hollywood. Metro went one step further—the studio went on the air under a $25,000 package deal. Certainly filmusicals, having their scores radio-exploited, were being benefited at the b.o. And with the years there were instances where even a theme- or title-song of a picture could add as much as $1,000,000 onto a film's gross.

A decade later history was to repeat itself with TV. The picture business, at first scared of the medium, realized that trailers over the iconoscopes into television homes were one way to prove to the video viewers that there was better film product available at their theatres than the 10-or-more-year old crop of pix being videocast at them.

42

'Flash! We Interrupt This Program to . . .'

★

A CBS survey in 1933 counted over 60,000,000 listeners, and over 16,000,000 sets in operation, throughout the country. In addition, 300,000 drivers were tuning in on auto sets. Network balance sheets for the following year showed a revenue of $42,900,000, up 37 per cent over 1933. Of this sum $25,000,000 represented talent costs.

The money in radio continued to climb fantastically throughout the era. The gross shot to $86,000,000 in 1935. A 1937 survey showed that the public was shelling out $900,000,000 for radio equipment, spare parts and service. In 1939, radio reported a net profit of fully $19,000,000. And the following year, with 35,000,000 radio sets tuned in, weekly air shows cost $490,000 a week in talent.

At the beginning of the era, radio was still fumbling the ball in entertainment. Most programs were dull, despite an influx of headliners from other branches of show business. The tendency of imitation was so strong that Variety in 1933 introduced a "Protective Material Department" for radio, as it had done years before for vaudeville. Little came of it, however, because, for all practical purposes, Variety always counselled idea creators that the best common-law protection—lacking a copyright on unpublished literary material—was mailing one's self a registered letter, with the idea intact, and not unsealing the envelope until some court issue arose. It's preferred that it be mailed across a state line, and of course the Post Office mark is the barometer for priority. In the heyday of vaudeville, the Vaudeville Managers Protective Assn. working closely with the N.V.A. and Variety's Protective Material Dept., was better able to police any infringements. Then, too, there were always the friendly stagehands in every key city who could psychologically "control" a copy act when the plagiarism was flagrant. In later years, however, with the speed-up of communications, such as radio, plus the Broadway columnists' habit of "crediting" this or that comedian with "the newest gag," in short order that "newest gag" was quickly "adopted" by callous, hinterland comics as their own.

Amos 'n' Andy were still the top stars of the year, radio having developed no new personalities. They did smash b.o. everywhere on their 1933 personal appearance tour, and animated cartoons using their voices mopped up.

Ed Wynn, rising to the top of radio as Texaco's "Fire Chief," decided to give the two major webs some competition in 1933. Throwing in almost $250,000, he organized a new broadcasting network—the Amalgamated Broadcasting System—with 6 stations and 27 sponsors in his pocket. Lack of advertising revenue killed it in a few months.

The big event of the year was the debut of the Kraft Hour with

Al Jolson, Paul Whiteman and Deems Taylor. "Good as any show's Broadway premiere," Variety reported. Jolson had signed at $5,000 a week for 40 weeks; Whiteman, $4,500 a week.

The audience—"strictly Woolworth people"—was separated from the performers by a thick glass curtain, with audience mikes picking up their cued applause as desired. Jolson's big hit of the opening night show was the theme song of the depression, "Brother, Can You Spare A Dime?"

Other big hit shows of the year were Rudy Vallee on the Fleischmann Yeast variety show, and Jack Pearl as Baron Munchausen on Lucky Strike. Pearl's rise in radio was meteoric—going from $3,500 to $8,500 a week in the short space of five months.

Major Bowes, managing director of the Capitol Theatre in New York, introduced amateur nights to radio in 1934. Some branches of show business, nostalgic for the lost proving grounds of vaudeville, were enthusiastic about the trend. It offered possibilities for discovery of new talent. Show biz gamblers figured the odds against an amateur clicking on Broadway at 200,000 to 3.

By 1935, Bowes was the heaviest earner in show business, grossing $1,000,000 a year for his radio show, amateur units, film shorts, and management of the Capitol. His amateur units toured the nation, supposedly arousing new interest in vaudeville among hinterland theatregoers. As many as 20 Bowes units were traveling at one time, until they dwindled to only five in number by 1937. Vaudeville was too dead for even Major Bowes to bring it back to life.

Among the curious attractions of 1933 was the broadcast of radio's first millionaire "canary"—Harold F. McCormick, of the International Harvester Co.—who came to the mike to unveil an unsuspected talent as a whistler. Negro circles applauded a Chicago station for hiring 15-year-old James Mitchell, radio's *only* Negro actor of that date. The cheers were short-lived; a companion stabbed Master James, who was carted off to the Cook County Hospital for repairs.

those catch-phrases   By 1934 it was axiomatic in radio that if you wanted to stamp your personality unforgettably into the consciousness of listeners, you had to develop a trademark— just like soap or coffee—and hammer it over the airwaves mercilessly. It was the rare star or show of that year which didn't have its aural mark of identification.

For Amos 'n' Andy it was their famous theme song, "The Perfect Song," and Andy's catchline, "I'se regusted." Joe Penner popularized, "Wanna buy a duck?" and "You nasty man, doncha ever *doo-ooo* that!" Wendell Hall's hallmark was "It Ain't Gonna Rain No Mo'." Then there were the "moon" theme songsters: Ruth Etting's "Shine On, Harvest Moon"; Morton Downey's "Carolina Moon"; and Kate Smith's "When the Moon Comes Over the Mountain."

Ben Bernie greeted his fans with "Yowza" and signed off with "Pleasant Dreams." Crosby came on with "boo-boo-boo," Rudy Vallee with "heigh-ho, everybody" and Ed Wynn with "so-o-o-o." Norman Brokenshire caught ears with "How *DO* you do, everybody, how *DO* you do." Tony Wons made "are you listenin'?" famous. Phil Baker's trademark was the yell of his stooges, Beetle and Bottle—"Get off the air!" Gracie Allen's tagline for George Burns was, "Oh, George! I bet you say that to all the girls!"

Paul Whiteman made Gershwin's "Rhapsody In Blue" his own. Jack Pearl's famed "Vos you dere, Sharlie?" was varied with mentions of his "Cousin Hoogo." Jimmy Durante became famous to radio fans with "colloseal!" and "I got a million of 'em!" Jack Benny's "Jello again" was as standard a Sunday night greeting as Winchell's "flash!" and "Good evening Mr. and Mrs. America." Jolson always had his "mammy" and "you ain't heard nothin' yet!" Almost all of these catchlines found their way into the conversational slang of the day. However, in time, they wore out their welcome for reasons of corn or monotony and only an occasional upcoming sportscaster like Mel Allen ("how do you like *that?*"), or Clem McCarthy's hoarsely exciting "They're off!", or Winchell's trademarked excitement and staccato style of news flashes, have survived.

Entertainment highlight of 1934 was the dramatic re-emergence of Broadway's one-time great star, Maude Adams (the original *Peter Pan*), who spent 44 hours rehearsing for a broadcast of Sir James M. Barrie's *The Little Minister* for Pond's Cold Cream. NBC presented a rebroadcast from BBC—a program called, "What the Fairies Know," which NBC lost no time in changing to "Fantasy for Midsummer Eve." Joe Penner was the outstanding comic to climb up that year, taking only six months to go from $950 to $8,000 a week.

By 1935 it was generally accepted that radio's policy of overlapping all other branches of show business was permanent. Stars from films, opera, the concert, vaudeville and the legitimate theatre all gravitated toward the airwaves—most for the publicity of guest appearances; many to stay, with programs of their own. Only one star of Hollywood could not be tempted, even with an offer of $25,000 for one show—Greta Garbo. Eddie Cantor's radio appeal shot up so remarkably that he won the first unique bonus contract in radio history. Bristol-Meyers agreed to pay him a $200 bonus for every point over 20 he scored on the Crossley tabulation of radio listeners.

a bad commercial　　And the first belch to be released over a national network, to amused and shocked listeners, was broadcast in 1935 by Melvin H. Purvis, ex-head of the G-Men, when he put in a guest appearance for Fleischmann's Yeast. The association of Purvis' ad-lib performance with the product understandably made the J. Walter Thompson executives highly sensitive.

The Chicago Cubs became the first baseball club to buy radio time, when they took an hour in 1936 to re-enact the games played on the days of the broadcasts.

Although radio was still developing no new stars of its own during 1937, it did take two mildly well-known personalities from outside and build them into headliners. The two were Edgar Bergen, whose showcasing on the Vallee show jumped him from $300 a week in 1935 to $10,000 a week in 1937, at the Los Angeles Paramount; and Red Skelton, whom the Vallee program boomed from $400 a week to a $2,000-a-week contract from RKO. The "Vallee Varieties" also cradled Bob Burns, the bazooka man.

The distinctive contribution of 1937 radio to American mores was the emergence of a new phenomenon—the disk jockey. The term was coined by Variety to describe announcers who held down dull midnight-to-dawn time by spinning (or "riding") records (or "disks"). Listeners, mostly women, sent in requests for their favorite numbers.

The stunt spread rapidly, and a sizable Lonely Hearts bureau was soon in operation. The ladies' requests were played—along

with their names and addresses. The songs they chose were a cue
to interested male listeners, many of whom picked up phone books—
"I'm Lonely," "Melancholy Baby," "I Ain't Got Nobody," "Lover,
Come Back To Me," and "All Alone Blues." In some localities it
was a cue for vice cops too.

Another development that year was the appearance of experimental Mr. & Mrs. "breakfast" shows in radio time slots that were
once tossed to religious services and calisthenics. These proved an
effective medium for plugging sponsors' products more heavily
than any show dared to do during the evening hours. From then
on America's habit of breakfasting in private became a lost cause.
Prior to this, the predawn platter-chatterers and later the calisthenics
cheer-up boys (usually under insurance company auspices) filled
the A.M. kilocycle void. Ed and Pegeen Fitzgerald are trade-credited
for creating the Mr. & Mrs. pattern.

In the cautious but constant search for novelties in program
material, radio tried freak celebrities in 1937, of the kind which
once rejoiced the heart of the great Willie Hammerstein. Brought
to the microphone were the white wife of the Rajah of Borneo;
the wife of the vanished Judge Crater (on Ripley's "Believe It
Or Not"); and the lone survivor of a Greek ship that sank (on
"Radio Newsreel.") Station KGFF in Oklahoma topped them all
by broadcasting a World War I shell victim, whose head ticked like
a clock.

l'affaire mae west   Mae West gave radio officials heart-
burn toward the close of 1937 when she appeared on the Chase
& Sanborn program. She delivered a Biblical story—West style
—of the fall from grace of Adam and Eve. Clergymen all over
the country shrieked protests. Newspaper editorials were headlined, "Mae West Pollutes Homes." Other newspapers rushed to
her defense, and the general defense of radio. The controversy
bubbled for months, hastening NBC's closing of a deal with Toscanini to win back some of its tarnished prestige.

While it helped her pix b.o., understandably there were no sponsors risking further Maewestian versions of "Adam and Eve"
or anything else. [*Sime* once observed in a review of Miss West
that "she has a way of making clean lyrics sound dirty."]

Gracie Fields arrived in America that year and promptly was

offered $5,000 for a guester on the Jack Benny show, which she turned down. That same weekend, at Palm Springs, she sang at a barbecue for an hour—for free. Eventually, of course, Miss Fields did plenty of United States commercial radio.

In 1938, Bob Hope's radio star shone brightly, along with Edgar Bergen and Charlie McCarthy. The Rudy Vallee show, showcase of so much new talent, started to slip, however, because of its familiar pattern. Other radio faves of the year were the usual old faces— Amos 'n' Andy, Benny, Cantor, Whiteman, Burns & Allen, Easy Aces, Fred Allen, Penner, Crosby, Spitalny, Bernie, Lombardo and Jolson. A surprisingly large quota of these was still going strong at the half-century mark.

Following NBC's Toscanini scoop—at $4,000 a performance—the year's second cultural triumph was the radio debut of Paderewski. A new twist in quiz shows made its debut—"Information, Please!"—which pleased its sponsor as a low-cost, high-prestige, and influential package. The success of the Fadiman-Kieran-Levant-Adams quizzer caused a rash of quiz shows, ultimately leading to the type of programs inaugurated by "Stop the Music" 10 years later. The original idea, of course, was nothing more exciting than the old-fashioned spelling bee; or a step further, classroom examinations.

awesome orson   Along with Clifton Fadiman, only two other names emerged in 1938 radio to cause Variety to pause and note. One was Frank Morgan, who became the first radio actor ever to take his pants off for a laugh before a studio audience. The other was the *enfant terrible* of show business—Orson Welles —who introduced some of his Mercury Theatre ingenuity into the airwaves. Welles finished by scaring the United States out of its wits when he staged the unforgettable radio "Invasion from Mars."

Ex-Mayor of New York Jimmy Walker suddenly showed up as a radio entertainer in 1939, broadcasting off the cuff each Sunday for 12 weeks over WMCA. The Modern Industrial Bank paid for the time. With his other hand, Walker wrote his second song in 25 years, collaborating with Jimmy Hanley on a tolerance number called "In Our Little Part Of Town." Walker sang it with George Jessel at Madison Square Garden's "Night of Stars" benefit. To make this conversion to show business complete, Jimmy Walker became prez of the National Assn. of Performing Artists, a group sparked by Fred Waring. The bandleader's then manager got Walker in as "front" man in a move to collect from jukeboxes and radio disk jockeys every time a certain artist's waxing is performed for profit. The courts ruled that since this constitutes a supplementary property right, the organization is without redress under the existing Copyright Act of 1909. (It's an open secret that this now obsolete statute, in view of the advances of the electronic forms of show business, will have to be considerably revised in time.)

After a hitch as the impartial arbiter of the ladies' garment industry, acting as umpire in management-labor relations, Walker resigned that $20,000-a-year post to become president of the ill-fated Majestic Records, Inc. He had a stock interest in the disk subsid of the Chicago parent firm, Majestic Radio & Television Corp., and as he often told us at Toots Shor's, later to become his favorite New York eatery, "At least this deal (the Majestic stock) should give some protection to my children." (This never came to pass, of course, with the bankruptcy sale of Majestic Records assets.)

the hucksters   In 1940, with America tense and poised on the brink of war, radio took the lid off slightly. The election brought forth a flock of Republican jokes—"Are you a Republican?" "No, I'm just naturally thin"—and cracks with international overtones. Sex was also allowed to rear its head, at least up to the eyebrows, with gags like, "When that girl jockey was racing, one of her shoulder straps broke, and the horse finished wearing a camisole."

There was little doubt in anyone's mind—at least, those behind the scenes—as to who controlled radio in 1933. That year, food products, cosmetics, drugs and tobacco provided 70 per cent of the networks' revenue.

One NBC announcer that year received a remembrance gift from his grateful sponsor—a 60¢ jar of cold cream. This generous gesture was rivaled by a network efficiency expert, who placed half-dollars under studio radiators to test (1) whether the janitor was thorough and (2) honest.

The men who made ulcers famous later in Frederic Wakeman's *The Hucksters* were getting set for their milk diets in 1933. Sponsors switched their accounts from one ad agency to another with a fairly monotonous regularity. The old school tie equation and nepotism (such as a favorite nephew just out of college) usually figured in these ad agency maneuvers. It was considered a good batting average to hang on to a sponsor as long as 18 months.

Sponsors were protesting that year against unfair competition by "one-lung" stations which would spin platters offering stars like Ben Bernie, while Bernie in the flesh would be holding down the next wavelength on a fancy paycheck from Blue Ribbon Malt.

The late Jack Kapp, founder-president of Decca Records, however, had a visionary theory about this. He even encouraged broadcastings of Bing Crosby records, arguing that that was another step in making the singer "the best known voice in America," which he set out to do and achieved. Many years later, talents like Crosby, Guy Lombardo, Arthur Godfrey, Leopold Stokowski, Tommy Dorsey, Deems Taylor, Walt Disney, Igor Cassini (Cholly Knickerbocker), Vallee were to become glorified disk jockeys with their own shows, plugging not only their own pop and longhair platters, but those of contemporary artists, while merchandising this or that product.

The leading ad agency of 1934 was Blackett-Sample-Hummert, Inc., which bought $4,104,000 worth of air shows that year for Bayer's Aspirin, Ovaltine, College Inn Food Products, and others. Tailing B-S-H was J. Walter Thompson, with radio accounts like Chase & Sanborn, Fleischmann, Cutex, Carter's Ink, Eastman Kodak and Kraft-Phenix. In the third slot was Lord & Thomas, which boasted the Lucky Strike program. Nine other agencies each spent over $1,000,000 in 1934 radio.

The Government was prodded into action during 1935 by the below-the-belt promises, menacing and offensive huckstering that cluttered the airways. It indicated too careful an interest in radio advertising copy for both sponsor and network comfort. As a result, while NBC stood pat, if apprehensive, CBS dropped the other shoe. It booted out medical accounts and medical copy, publicized a long list of must-nots for advertisers, and pledged to cleanse the air of the medicine show aura. Listeners cheered, and CBS prestige zoomed.

A sponsor craze—more for reasons of prestige than entertainment —put big names on a radio pedestal. General Mills was the leader in the drive to dazzle dialers by packing shows with celebrity appearances. The move led to the origination of more and more shows from the Coast, where the names were more easily gathered around the mike. By 1937, radio won social recognition at Hollywood, with sweatshirts absolutely taboo at radio show premieres. Admen moved to the Coast with their shows, found the social routine and sunshine quite heady, and did everything they could to anchor radio in Hollywood.

United Fruit was the first commercial shortwave sponsor in 1939, picking up the check for a musical show with Spanish dialog beamed to South America over NBC. That year radio won another unique sponsor, also in the fruit division, with the Oregon apple growers, whose usual English market was cut off by war. Faced with apple-dumping to hold up prices, the Oregonians drummed up a war chest, sank it into radio, and kept doctors away from coast to coast.

Radio cracked a particularly satisfying nut in 1940 with the addition of department stores as sponsors. For years the stores had put all their eggs into the one basket of newspapers, refusing to entertain any notion that radio could do a better or cheaper selling job for them. In 1940, suddenly, department stores opened the door to radio, and newspaper executives from coast to coast snarled in unison.

press-radio feud   The battle between radio and the press was waged hotly on every front throughout the decade. In 1933, newspapers curtailed radio publicity to an absolute minimum, in some instances banning any mention of radio whatever. CBS poured fuel on the fire by organizing its own newsgathering bureau along newspaper lines. NBC followed suit.

Hotheads on both sides of the fence were brought together for a conference. A compromise was reached whereby both networks agreed to disband their own news services, in return for which the wire services agreed to feed the nets with news. Meanwhile, newspapers were secretly jubilant over the return of many radio advertisers to the printed medium, on the theory that they were dealing with many less tangible factors in newspaper ads.

The following year, radio ran into more opposition when stations in Denver and Omaha put microphones in police courts and broadcast proceedings. The New York Bar Association voiced a protest, stating it considered the move prejudicial to justice. The organization moved into action when New York's WMCA broadcast a three-week hearing of the Morro Castle disaster. The Bar Association succeeded in getting WMCA banned for the balance of the hearings. Insiders stated the real reason the ban had been allowed was that the broadcasts had resulted in heavy criticism of the Government's steampship inspection methods, and also of the Ward Line for incompetence. In 1951, television's spotlight on crime (the Kefauver investigation) and kindred telecasts of other Congressional committee probes cued the new order of things under this medium.

The clash between press and radio that year was highlighted by the law suit filed by two radio writers of the New York *Daily News* against Eddie Cantor. Cantor had declared, during an interview, that in his opinion radio editors were dishonest. The suit was later dropped for lack of grounds, because Cantor hadn't mentioned any names.

Variety inspired its own uproar by coming out in 1934 with its "Showmanship Ratings." Everyone in radio who placed lower than No. 1 squawked, and for a while in radio circles Variety was less friend than "another network."

The press-radio feud broke out afresh in 1936, when Gabriel Heatter's 35-minute ad-lib broadcast of the Hauptmann execution far overshadowed anything the papers were able to come up with. To heighten color to the event, the newscaster's marathon gabbing was made necessary by the fact that something went awry with the electricity that circuited into the Lindbergh baby killer's death chair, and it was quite a feat of emergency radio showmanship and savvy. The broadcast lifted Heatter to the top, which didn't endear either him or radio the more to the press.

As the decade drew to a close, newscasts became radio's most important achievement. They were so highly regarded for attention value that one cigar manufacturer of 1937 offered extra pay for one-minute spot commercials between newscasts of flood rescues. To the credit of radio that year, he didn't get it.

The press, realizing that it couldn't stop the competition of radio, moved by indirection in 1937. By the end of the year newspaper interests owned 25 per cent of the radio industry.

Radio's contribution was recognized by the Government in 1938 with the setting up of a United States radio studio at the Department of Interior. It was the occasion of America's first attempt at official broadcasting, designed especially to strengthen ties between North and South America. Eventually shortwave radio propaganda to our World War II allies and enemies, via the BBC (British Broadcasting Corporation), the AFN (Armed Forces Network), and the "Voice of America" programs, were to become important in the world struggle against totalitarianism.

The press, which had been licking its wounds and biding its time, jumped on radio hard when the occasion presented itself in 1938. That occasion was the Orson Welles "War Of the Worlds" broadcast. The background of the broadcast, of course, was the war abroad —and the war-jittery nerves of Americans. It was an hour show, and many who tuned in after the opening announcement were under the illusion that they were actually listening to on-the-spot news reports—cleverly handled, even to ad-lib asides, awkward pauses and offstage noises—of an invasion from Mars.

The show undoubtedly alarmed or baffled millions of listeners who heard it. And many did rush into the streets, or into the attic for rifles. But the newspapers joyfully pounced on the story and made it seem as though every American in the land had gone crazy. By exaggerating to the hilt, the press was able to bring down severe reproach on the heads of CBS executives—and all of radio—including crippling restrictions as to the use of news-type techniques in dramatic programs. No single broadcast in radio's history received more press publicity and general notoriety than this one. It, of course, catapulted Welles to stardom—and Hollywood.

Most newspapers that year took another punch at radio by cutting down space devoted to radio to a minimum. But the war eventually swept radio to such a pinnacle of American interest that the pin-prick was hardly felt. As Variety summed it up in 1939, "Radio has capacities possessed by no other channel of communication. Its place in the lives of everyone becomes more intimate."

Radio not only had to slug it out with the press, but with opposition from many other sources as well. In 1933 the networks were waging internecine warfare over the question of spot broadcasting by individual stations of the nets. The Federal Radio Commission —now the Federal Communications Commission—was gunning after radio scalps for unethical advertising. And all of radio was fighting the music unions.

In 1934 the Tugwell bill hit out at radio advertising, and Mayor

LaGuardia contemplated junking New York's municipal-owned WNYC. In 1935 there was national revulsion and Government action against offensive air advertising. In 1936 name orchestra leaders tried to stop the broadcasting of platters, on grounds that this cut into their disk royalties; and the F.R.C. handed down adverse decisions against a number of stations for code violations.

Lawsuits against radio comics, who ad-libbed unfortunately, and their sponsors, were more of the headaches that dogged radio. In 1939 the Preferred Accident Insurance Co. helped out by offering to insure both against the consequences of these nuisance suits.

radio vs. ascap—again   In 1940 radio was once more battling vigorously with ASCAP over music fees; RCA-NBC television was in hot water with the F.R.C.; the two major nets were busy fighting off a Government investigation of monopoly charges inspired by the Mutual Broadcasting System; the Federal Radio Commission was pressing the case for F.M.—a new system of Frequency Modulation broadcasting, as distinguished from AM (Amplitude Modulation).

Radio was in trouble up in Canada during 1934, when an actor named Art Joseph aired his criticism of the Governor-General, the Earl of Bessbrough, for an alleged slight to Mary Pickford. Joseph and radio both were scored off for their temerity. There was no official censorship in Cuba that year, either, but soldiers stood on guard in all radio stations as a hint to anybody with ideas about criticizing the regime.

In 1936 the first Jerusalem radio station began transmitting, inaugurating with the words, "This is Jerusalem calling," and broadcasting in English, Arabic and Hebrew. Free radios were distributed in small towns to make the broadcasts effective. This inspired Milton Berle's crack, "Star of stage, screen, and Tel Aviv."

And that year, in France, radio won a signal distinction when Cardinal Verdier designated a patron saint for radio—Saint Genisius.

The first television note of the New Deal was made by the Don Lee Television Station on the West Coast, which televised a Paramount film, Pathe News and a trailer. In 1935, A.T. & T. asked for an experimental license for "voice and picture transmission," and was scored off by the F.R.C. for attempting to monopolize the new coaxial cable field.

The German Olympics of 1936 were televised, but with blurred and general unsatisfactory results. Television boomed that year in London, however, when films were telecast in the summer. At the end of the year, tele was demonstrated on an 8 feet high, 6 foot 6 screen (1949 American home tele screens were still only 10 by 8 *inches*) at the Dominion Theatre, London. Inventor John Baird, from a studio in the building, talked to newspapermen seated in the theatre audience.

Philadelphia had a Philco tele demonstration in 1937, which Variety chalked down as bad. When the New York World's Fair was televised that summer by NBC-RCA, Variety complained, "It was an exposé, rather than a demonstration—pics flickered much too much." The Federal Radio Commission thumbs-downed television schools beginning to spring up, promising to train recruits for "highly-paid" tele jobs.

RCA-NBC produced the first televised drama in May 1938—"The Mummy Case," starring Tom Terriss. Terriss had been on the King Tut expedition. For several months that year RCA-NBC ran regular five-hour weekly tele shows, beamed from studios in the Empire State Building, booming a sale of television sets at eight New York department stores. RCA-NBC finally decided to call it quits—the venture had been experimental—until later in the year. Set owners in New York were stranded with nothing to look at but the mahogany on the expensive sets they had bought from the eight stores.

The same year, the British Broadcasting Corp. in London televised a full-length play directly from the St. Martin's Theatre—J. B. Priestley's *When We Are Married*. It was the longest single-stretch video show of that date, running two hours and 25 minutes. Set-owners reported the mechanical end had been perfect, but the eye-strain for so long a period had been too great.

some video firsts   Variety began to review television shows on June 14, 1939. It also carefully compiled a list of television firsts, in its capacity as historian of show business. The first President to be televised was F.D.R. The first governor, Herbert H. Lehman of New York. The first mayor, LaGuardia. The first name band, Fred Waring. The first jugglers, the Three Swifts. The first film cartoon, "Donald's Cousin Gus." The first take from a Broadway show, "Mexicana." The first fencer, Nadi. The first midgets, Paul Remos

& His Toy Boys. The first magician, Robert Reinhart. The first tap dancer, Ann Miller. The first harpist, Margaret Brill. The first Negro team, Buck & Bubbles. The first ventriloquist, Bob Neelor. The first comic drunks, Frank (Fritz) and Jean Huber. The first skaters and skiers, the Sun Valley Show. The first hillbilly act, Judy Canova. The first composer, Richard Rodgers. And the first King and Queen, George and Elizabeth.

The outbreak of war in Europe set television back sharply. In 1939, England called all bets off. In New York City, there were no scheduled broadcasts, and less than 500 purchasers of television sets, at $600 apiece, plus a $50 installation charge. The main progress made during the year by television was in publicity, with the magazines painting rosy pictures of things to come—things that no longer sounded like Buck Rogers copy.

Set-owners were jubilant at the televising of the Max Baer-Lou Nova fight at the Yankee Stadium on June 7, 1939. There had been an earlier attempt to televise a sporting event—the Columbia-Princeton baseball game at Baker's Field in New York in May—but the fixed camera and blurred image were heavily disappointing. The only tele transmitter licensed in Chicago in 1939 was the Zenith station, W9XZU, which operated daily. But if Zenith was ready, television was not, and their sets had to be loaned out instead of sold to viewers.

Singers from the Metropolitan were telecast from Radio City in 1940, but the results were not inspiring. The big news of the year was a private preview by CBS, for trade and press, of something new —color television, invented by Dr. Peter Goldmark. It was kept carefully under wraps, for fear of upsetting black-and-white television. Rumor had it that there was inner warfare in tele circles between color enthusiasts, and the black-and-white men who opposed it because it would mean scrapping millions of dollars worth of expensive equipment as junk. RCA opened experimental TV in 1928, and for the next 20 years poured $50,000,000 into television. At the opening of the N. Y. World's Fair in April 1939, David Sarnoff made the first commercial telecast with, "Now, at last, we add sight to sound."

43

Legit Bounces Back—Ditto Longhair

★

For the first time in theatrical history, 1933 saw every Broadway legitimate show in the cut-rates. Post-rumblings of the great crash of 1929 were still being heard. The New Amsterdam Theatre, once the fortress of Klaw & Erlanger and Flo Ziegfeld, was surrendered to the Dry Dock Savings Bank. Three years later the Gaiety and Fulton passed to the banks also, and the last of the Erlanger houses vanished from Broadway.

The bank holidays of 1933 crippled Broadway. Theatre managers implored actors to accept salary cuts. Equity reluctantly okayed the cuts, then changed its mind when stagehands and musicians refused to go along. The stagehands finally agreed to reduce the number of men backstage at each show—rotating the work among union members—but would not allow a slash of union scale.

Many theatregoers offered checks at the boxoffice, during the bank holidays, and these were accepted. Incidentally, very few bounced. Some managers did the noble thing and maintained salaries and full staff, operating at a loss, until the banks once more opened.

For the Shuberts, 1933 was a remarkably fine year. They bought back out of receivership all their properties, worth some $16,000,000, for $400,000. Playing their cards closer to the chest, they gradually eased out of the producing field, concentrating on being theatre-owners, and only occasionally investing in shows.

Many stage actors were entraining back to Broadway from Hollywood, in 1933, as it became apparent that Broadway was slated for a boom via Hollywood money. Film producers were bidding for Broadway hits, and trying to buy a winning ticket by backing dark horses for win, place or show. In 1934, Hollywood dished out $800,-000 to Broadway for screen rights to hits. By 1936, the ante had risen to $1,000,000, and Hollywood was the acknowledged backer of at least one out of every four Broadway openings.

In 1929 there had been over 200 stock companies in the United States. Then, when *The Jazz Singer* introduced talkies to the road, the stocks fell by the wayside. By 1939 there were only five Equity stock groups left in the United States. Film theatre chains which shuttered some of their theatres kept these shut, rather than rent them to stock outfits. Hollywood believed in boosting legit on Broadway—for their own purposes—but not on the road, where legitimate shows represented competition to films. In 1940, Hollywood paid Broadway $1,200,000 for screen rights, two-thirds of that going for plays produced during the 1940 season alone.

Something new in legit was introduced in 1934 with the debut of the Center Theatre, a Rockefeller Center-RKO-RCA project. The vast showplace opened with *The Great Waltz,* which played to capacity throughout a year which boasted only 13 clean-cut hits. The explanation was a mammoth publicity campaign which had as its links radio (via NBC), film trailers (via RKO), and outdoor billboards at Standard Oil gas stations. Despite the average weekly take of $43,000, the production never got all its money back.

As Thousands Cheer, a top-grade Irving Berlin-Moss Hart musical, with Marilyn Miller, Helen Broderick and Clifton Webb, before he turned baby-sitter for Hollywood, finished a 49-week run in 1934 with a total gross of $1,200,000, at $4.40 top. George S. Kaufman-Moss Hart's play "Merrily We Roll Along" (with Jessie Royce Landis and Walter Abel) was also current. The road, ostensibly dead, came through nobly for Katharine Cornell who played 75 towns in 29 weeks, doing *The Barretts of Wimpole Street* and *Candida* for a total gross of $650,000. Lillian Hellman, a $35-a-week script reader for Metro, scored on Broadway with her first play, *The Children's Hour*—and promptly demanded $1,000 a week from Metro to go back on the lot.

Faces were bright on the Broadway of 1935. The number of chorines working in legitimate were counted as 390—the highest since the crash. With the general recovery of the nation, New York recovered; and when New York recovered, legitimate producers rejoiced. The year provided the comedy, *Sailor, Beware,* which so shocked a visiting lawyer from Minneapolis that he sued the management for $4 and expenses. And from Boston came word that the critic of the Boston *American*, George Holland, had hit upon a novel idea to keep himself from being barred from theatres whose plays he rapped. He had himself appointed Deputy Fire Commissioner, and as such could not be denied admittance to any theatre.

The boom of W.P.A. shows in 1936, Broadway estimated, had kept hundreds of actors off the street. Managers didn't fear the competition of the W.P.A. shows, because their content and prices appealed to a different type of clientele than the legitimate's regular trade. But they were worried about the possibility of a permanent Federal Theatre, which might raise new problems.

Back in 1932, when *The Green Pastures* had played in Washington, special Sunday performances were given for Negroes—who were not allowed, in the capital of the United States, to attend the regular performances to watch a cast of their own race perform. The Washington atmosphere, under the New Deal, was vastly different. For the first time in 100 years, racial barriers were dropped for the 1936 Washington run of *Porgy and Bess* at the National, and Negroes were accorded their Constitutional rights as both theatregoers and citizens. The National, in the next decade, again became the stormy center of the race question, the management again refusing to admit unsegregated audiences stating it was compelled to comply with local customs regardless of its own personal feelings on such an issue. Eventually the capital, where the Constitution's principles are administered and interpreted, was to be without a legit house because of Equity's edict not to permit its members to participate in a policy which was so discriminatory. Some strange things have happened at D.C. boxoffices, among them the necessity of colored Americans to simulate foreign accents or demand *deux billets, s'il vous plait,* and thus gain admission in white houses which, adhering to the principle of diplomatic courtesies to foreign nationals of maduro tincture, felt it was OK for them, but not OK for native colored Americans.

With the boxoffice in a flowering condition in 1936, productions became more lavish and spectacular. Three Broadway shows alone used a total of 169 stagehands. These were *The Eternal Road, White Horse Inn* and *The Show Is On*—incidentally all costly flops.

the bard—and george m. cohan   Shakespeare came into his own with a 1936 duel of Hamlets. The rival Melancholy

Danes were Leslie Howard and John Gielgud, and the two Hamlets over Broadway were regarded as an histrionic joust between Broadway and Hollywood. Broadway won. Gielgud stayed, and Howard suffered the slings and arrows of the road.

As though there weren't enough Hamlet to go around, Eva Le Gallienne did it again the following year, in stock at Dennis, Massachusetts. On Broadway, Maurice Evans scored with *King Richard II,* grossing $21,000 a week. *Anthony and Cleopatra* (Tallulah Bankhead-Conway Tearle) was less successful Shakespeare, losing $100,000 for its backers. But the Bard was boffola b.o. with Orson Welles' surprise version of *Julius Caesar* in modern dress at the new Mercury Theatre, where Welles was attempting also to give Broadway a lesson in lighting effects.

George M. Cohan, after knocking them dead as an actor in the 1933 presentation of *Ah, Wilderness,* turned up again in 1937 with songs and dances in *I'd Rather Be Right.* Highlight of the Gershwin musical was Cohan's impersonation of F.D.R., which the President enjoyed heartily. *Ah, Wilderness* was Cohan's first thesping under a management not his own, and so was *Right* which also set a precedent for the Theatre Guild in billing a star above the production.

Pulitzer prizewinner of the year was Moss Hart and George S. Kaufman's *You Can't Take It With You* (Josephine Hull and Henry Travers), which scored a long run with 103 weeks, although the Critics' Circle award went to Maxwell Anderson's *High Tor* (Burgess Meredith). Incidentally, Anderson's personal choice for the season's "best" play was *Johnny Johnson,* by Paul Green and Kurt Weill, which ran a meagre nine weeks with Russell Collins and Morris Carnovsky in the cast. The distinction of the critics' scallions as "the worst play of a decade" went to something called *Bet Your Life* which ran briefly at the John Golden Theatre. There was also a revival of *Abie's Irish Rose,* for those who cared.

Thornton Wilder's *Our Town,* with Frank Craven and Martha Scott, took the Pulitzer for 1938, although the New York critics again dissented by giving John Steinbeck's *Of Mice and Men* (with Broderick Crawford and Wallace Ford) the nod. It was about to folderoo when the award gave it an unexpected lease of life.

Another 1938 theatre note was provided by the newly-founded Mercury Theatre, Orson Welles' repertory established in the old and almost-forgotten Comedy Theatre on West 39th St. Welles' staging, direction and lighting, as well as his new conception of old classics, won him applause as an "uplifting" force in the theatre. Welles followed *Julius Caesar* with Dekker's Restoration classic, *Shoemaker's Holiday,* also a click.

Looking forward to the highly-touted New York World's Fair of the coming year, Broadway got out its brooms in 1938. Cooling systems were installed in almost all theatres that didn't have them, to catch the overflow summer crowds from Flushing Meadows. The opening of the Fair was a crippling event for the legit during the first month. But by June Broadway's expectations were being realized, and the Main Stem enjoyed a wonderful and unusual summer boom.

Olsen & Johnson's *Hellzapoppin,* with a strong hypo from Winchell, shook the 1939 World's Fair visitors for $31,000 a week. *The Philadelphia Story* (Katharine Hepburn), *Streets of Paris* (Carmen Miranda, Bobby Clark, Abbott & Costello), and *No Time For Comedy* (Katharine Cornell) were also socko b.o.

The most costly production of the year was Max Gordon's patriotic spectacle *The American Way* by Kaufman and Hart at the Center Theatre in Radio City which, despite the cast presence of Fredric March and his wife, Florence Eldridge, was too heavily budgeted to pay out. It just about broke even when Hollywood bought the screen rights, but never filmed it because, by then, the subject matter had become cliche. If legit patrons wouldn't buy propaganda, certainly film fans wouldn't.

Howard Lindsay and Russel Crouse's *Life With Father* settled down at the Empire Theatre to a run that was to make theatrical history, and the bellicose *Man Who Came to Dinner,* Kaufman & Hart's opus, launched Monty Woolley to stardom and a new Hollywood career. The critics were unable to agree on the best show of the season, so no Critics Circle award was made.

garment workers over broadway   Big surprise of the year, however, was furnished by the International Ladies Garment Workers Union. This union, which had thrived and grown under the kindly aegis of the New Deal, decided to introduce a realistic note into the theatre by staging a labor union musical.

The show was *Pins and Needles,* presented at the Princess Theatre, off Broadway, which promptly became the "Labor Stage." The show began as a weekend affair, then went daily when critics threw their hats up in the air. It clicked so solidly that the very people it mocked and ridiculed—the carriage trade—came in droves.

In 1940 the critics were able to make up their minds—and were slightly embarrassed to find themselves in agreement, for the first time, with the Pulitzer Prize Committee. The unanimous choice was the unpredictable William Saroyan's *Time Of Your Life,* with Eddie Dowling, Julie Haydon, Gene Kelly, Celeste Holm and William Bendix. Saroyan promptly threw the Pulitzer Committee into confusion by rejecting the prize, becoming the first to do so since Sinclair Lewis handed back his Pulitzer award for the novel *Arrowsmith.*

The road was reportedly prosperous in 1940, as a result of the steady increase of the national income through the union-active years of the New Deal. That year Variety found that it was offering 735 playing weeks, and accounted for an annual legitimate gross of $9,000,000. The era came to a close with the return to Broadway, after an 18-year absence, of John Barrymore. When the great Barrymore had played last in New York, it was as Hamlet at the Harris Theatre, which had since become a movie grind house. Barrymore's return vehicle was *My Dear Children,* a light comedy which sat heavily on critics' stomachs. To some of the old-timers on the aisle, it was painful to see one of the world's formerly great artists destroy memories with a performance that all but caricatured himself. The play staggered along on the Barrymore reputation, and round-the-town gossip that Barrymore's ad-libbing could be expected to provide unexpected entertainment.

longhairs' upbeat too   The New Deal, with its tremendous changes in the national fabric, also stirred new life into the opera and concert field.

The first sign of this New Deal in longhair was the emergence during 1934 of, not one, but three native American operas—a record for show business. The first was the world premiere of Howard Hanson's *Merry Mount* at the Metropolitan. The second was Gertrude Stein's baffling but intriguing *Four Saints In Three Acts.* The third was *Helen Retires* by John Erskine and George Antheil. Of the three, the Stein opus received wide national attention, and opera was suddenly amazed to find itself in the popular limelight.

Opera stars could be seen rubbing elbows in Lindy's with radio comics. Stokowski was an enthusiastic audience for Benny Goodman's swing sextet. "Minnie the Moocher," sung in tights, was presented on a concert stage. Baritones sang traditional Wagner at the Met and 24 hours later were swinging pops with a radio or disk fave on a coast-to-coast hookup.

New York's Town Hall pulled a Hammerstein and offered an armless pianist. The Philharmonic Symphony chamber group suddenly went berserk and played "hotcha" music at one session. Salmaggi offered Wagner at the Hippodrome for 99¢, complete with an advance apology. Radio tenors went into concert. If not highbrow, America's musical tastes certainly were getting more middlebrow.

a male striptease   The Met's standout hit of 1936 was Col. Wassily De Basil's Ballet Russe de Monte Carlo which overfilled its 3,500 seats and played to standees, grossing the Met $8,500. Star piece of the ballet was "L'Apres Midi d'Un Faun," presented for the first time in the United States in 20 years. "A male striptease done in six minutes," according to Variety.

The big news in the longhair field of 1938 was Yehudi Menuhin, who at the age of 21 was the year's top concert draw. With 38 playdates, Menuhin played to a gross of $500,000, of which half was his personal share.

Variety noted in 1940 that "the opera and the concert are doing quite nicely in the United States, without national, municipal or other official subsidy." During the year, over 20 opera companies toured the nation. There were between 500 and 600 performances given in some 100 large cities, at prices ranging from 25¢ to $7 a seat. The total annual gross was estimated at $5,000,000, with the Met alone grossing almost half that amount in New York and on tour.

This accounted for Variety's headline that year: NAME SINGERS FIND GRAVY TRAIL IN HINTERLAND—STIX, NOT OPERA, PAYS INCOME TAX.

Lawrence Tibbett was the best-paid among concert singers, at $2,500 per performance, although Grace Moore got between $2,500 and $3,000 in some spots. Richard Crooks, John Charles Thomas and Kirsten Flagstad all averaged around $2,000 a night. Gladys

Swarthout commanded between $1,500 and $2,000, while Nino Martini slumped to about $1,500.

Among violinists, top billing was shared by Jascha Heifetz and Fritz Kreisler, each receiving about $2,000 to $3,000 a performance. Yehudi Menuhin, who used to average that in his prime, slipped to about $1,750 a performance in his hoary dotage of 23. Serge Rachmaninoff and Vladimir Horowitz led the pianists, with the pianist-composer drawing $3,000 and Horowitz slightly less. Josef Hofmann held down third place with an average fee of $1,750.

Tickets were also quickly sold out whenever Benny Goodman decided to appear as a concert clarinetist, and Alec Templeton as an exponent of classic and jazz.

1940 also found the face of opera vastly changed. The change was wrought by the gradual disintegration of its old audiences, the box-holders, whose coffers had been cut into by the New Deal; and who regarded with contempt the singers offered by the opera to replace the golden voices of the Carusos, Gadskis, Galli-Curcis, Pattis and De Reszkes. The greats no longer were being supplied by Europe, where opera patrons had largely been decimated by two wars, and sponsors of new operatic personalities were now few and far between.

With the passing of the old guard, the Met decided on a fresh approach. Its herald was Edward Johnson, Canadian-born tenor, ex-musicomedy chirper who had to Romanize his name into Eduardo Giovanni in order to impress the Met with his singing prowess. New York would now have an opera house, Johnson declared, which would get support from the general public. He tied up with a radio network for a kilocycle subsidy, to which many of the die-hards mumbled deprecations, hollered "communism," and cursed That Man In the White House. Years later Billy Rose was to cate-chize the Met and Johnson for the outmoded methods, and eventually Rudolf Bing was brought in as impressario with even more advanced production methods and "modern" ideas.

44

Vaude: *Corpus Delicti*

★

In the deepest year of the economic drought, the odds were heavily against vaudeville surviving even in tatters. Films and radio were the cheap popular entertainment of 1933. These media had hardened the theatregoers to the corn which was too often the stock in trade of vaudeville. Some circuit theatres still offered vaude acts, but only—as usual—to bolster bad films, or because competition made a plus value necessary. Most stage shows were dropped to cut expenses.

Vaude's booking time fell to a new low in 1933. From 179 weeks at the start of 1932, it slipped to 46 weeks of scattered playdates. To play them all, an act would have had to make a grand tour of the United States and Canada, with the vast bulk of its time spent in traveling. Loew's offered 15 weeks of playing-time; RKO 13, Fancho & Marco 10, Paramount 5, and Warners 2. As the exception that proves the rule, the Winter Garden was offering Sunday night vaudeville concerts at $2.50 top, and doing well.

Most of vaude of 1933 was cast in the shape of unit shows, featuring scenery and costumes above the bands and talent. Many were tabloid versions of old legit musicals and revues, with props out of the warehouse. Some played theatres on percentages and guarantees ranging from $5,000 to $8,000 a week.

The year's outstanding vaude presentation was Mary Garden, who appeared for the first time at popular prices at the Capitol in New York. She shared top billing with the Mills Bros. Grace Moore, scheduled to play the Capitol later, was vastly disturbed at this "humiliation" to ofay artists. She insisted upon a "no-colored-act" clause being written into her contract. The Loew management called the deal off rather than agree.

Miss Moore's attitude had its counterpart in the early 1900s when Walter C. Kelly, the Philadelphia-born "Virginia Judge," refused to play a Hammerstein's vaude bill with Williams & Walker. It caused much excitement at the time, and resulted in a big gross for Kelly, and ditto on the week when the great colored comedy team played there. It was subsequently suspected that the showmanly Willie Hammerstein engineered this one too.

The trade in 1934 indulged in lachrymose recriminations about the demise of vaude—"Did it fall, or was it pushed?"

Hollywood took most of the blame, but the profilm fans pointed to the fact that vaudeville thrived—and still does—in Great Britain, and the English are just as ardent pix patrons as the Yanks.

In 1934 vaudeville's principal excuse for being was as a peg on which stars from other fields could hang their hats for brief personal appearances. Earl Carroll's Casino Theatre, on Broadway, made a vain attempt to hypo vaude by presenting *Casino Varieties,* at a 75¢-$1.50 scale, with George Jessel and Walter O'Keefe as twin M.C.'s. It died in three weeks. The United States Patriotic Society—which hadn't been told vaude was dead—backed "Flashes," a hodge-podge at the 42d Street Lyric. This, too, was quickly draped with crêpe.

columnists' 'benefits'   The only innovation of the year was the appearance on vaude stages of Broadway columnists. The bookings were awarded on the basis of a curious kind of boxoffice draw—the ability to entice top talent on stage as "guest stars" at no cost to the management. Influential, syndicated columnists naturally have a way with talent which depends on year-round publicity.

Although the rest of show business made a comeback in 1935, vaude stayed put or slipped further. Variety noted that the hands which had once been outstretched to it, out of sentiment, were now conspicuously absent. "The dollar sign still speaks louder to theatre operators," it pointed out. Films came in convenient cans, while vaudeville meant booking problems, stagehand and musician worries.

All that was left of vaude was 24 weeks in the hinterland. In New York there was only Loew's State and Capitol, RKO's Tilyou Music Hall stage shows. The Palace was playing straight films— (Coney Island) and the 14th St. Jefferson; besides the Roxy and double features. Most of the vaude acts playing the one- and two-night stands of the road made the jumps by car. In unit shows, $75 was tops for comedians, $20 to $27 for chorus girls.

Vaude had fallen on such evil days that when an English booking agent came to New York to look over American acts, there was no place for acts to "show" for him. William Morris arranged for a special showing of 20 acts at the Biltmore, a Broadway legit theatre.

Headliners were scarce. The few theatres that still played vaude turned to radio mostly for their talent. Major Bowes took his amateur units onstage, and Jack Benny was another radio figure whose name went on marquees. Small towns which couldn't afford Bowes units staged their own amateur nights—giving their theatres a "stage show" at practically no cost. And with no Willie Hammerstein to give him a stage, Jafsie Condon, the celebrated Lindbergh case witness, accepted a booking at the Capitol, Lynn, Massachusetts, where he also appeared for an hour in the store window of the Kane Furniture Co. to demonstrate—aptly—ladder models, nails and chisels.

Vaudeville, sinking fast with amateurs and units as its last props, found that its props were termite-ridden. The am shows began to pall, turning more and more audiences against stage entertainment. And the unit shows became tawdry, with nudity entering the ranks of vaudeville for the first time.

Unit show producers with short bankrolls and shorter ideas went in for burlesque types of production. It was vaude on a shoestring— and dressed about the same—with units playing for about $150 a day. The bubble dances, fan dances, veil dances and flame dances all had one motive—epidermis display. With this descent into strip-tease, vaude lost its last vestige of respect, its last distinction as "family entertainment."

The lone bright spot of 1936 vaudeville was the success of the New York Paramount with a new pit band and stage show policy. Otherwise the downbeat trend continued to be emphasized. Even the stubborn Chicago Palace threw in its chips and joined its New York namesake in a straight pix policy. The Cleveland Palace deserted vaudeville for five weeks, but business fell off so badly that the management was forced to return to it. Eventually New York's Jefferson and Tilyou Theatres closed, leaving no RKO vaudeville in Gotham for the first time in history.

Vaudeville, no longer in the theatres, went underground, and emerged chiefly in the more hospitable fields of hotel and nitery entertainment. Variety recognized this fact by merging the vaudeville and night club departments.

Eddie Cantor, proving once again that top talent did not have to worry about prevailing conditions, chose 1936 to set a new vaudeville record by getting $25,000 for a six-day week at the RKO Boston, with only a payroll of six in his act. This topped the record of Ed Wynn and Al Jolson at the New York Capitol.

But despite this, vaude was so dead that Edith Maxwell, the Virginia farm girl who was twice convicted for killing her father, couldn't win an engagement while out on bail, though every vaudeville booker in New York was approached. Vaudeville was dead, and Willie Hammerstein was dead. Appropriately, Variety reported that Baltimore burial ground salesmen were booking acts for "the cemetery time."

In the hands of the burly operators, vaude took another lacing during 1937. Vaude-burly was nothing more than burlesque with its face washed. And, as Variety caustically noted, dirty burly was bad enough, but dull, albeit clean burly was worse.

Many units were thrown together in an attempt to imitate the success of the Broadway Paramount and its bandshow policy. These tabloid musical shows, some costing between $3,500 and $5,000 weekly to mount, failed to find enough playing time to pay off costumes and transportation. The few theatres offering stage shows couldn't even win headliners from Hollywood for a few brief weeks, because the stars were eschewing personals to hold down their income taxes.

And while vaudeville cried in its beer, from overseas came the report that a headliner who had once flopped with a two-week engagement at the Palace in 1930—Gracie Fields—had grossed $760,000 that year. If vaudeville was dead, England hadn't heard about it.

Vaude didn't sink much further in 1938—because it couldn't. For the first time in several years, there wasn't a single tab show—boiled-down version of an old Broadway musical—available. Nor was there one night club troupe, such as the French Casino flash revue, which had played the major circuits a few years back. The heavy losses of unit producers had frightened off new tries. And theatres were refusing to play unit shows on anything but a straight percentage basis, with no guarantee of any minimum.

B. A. Rolfe and Jack Horn tried to give vaude a boost via a shoestring device called "Vaude-Vision." This dispensed with sets, scenery and live music, projecting the scenery via film with a musical soundtrack, to which acts synchronized their turns. It was introduced at the RKO Hamilton, but was stopped in its tracks by a firm thumbs-down from musicians, stagehands and film operators' unions.

Boston was entirely without a single stage show until the end of the year. In Cleveland, RKO tried a few feeble weeks of vaudfilm at the start of the season, quickly reverted to straight films, and swung back again to vaudfilm in November, after four solid weeks of film flops. Minneapolis, Pittsburgh, Detroit and Indianapolis continued to offer stage shows in support of films—because most films needed support.

jitterbug craze   The jitterbug craze in 1938 helped vaude by making bands big headliners for the year. Although the average band commanded $7,500 a week, it was a cheap stage buy for many theatres offering stags shows, which otherwise would have had to pay between $3,500 and $7,500 for a name act, plus the cost and trouble of booking four or five other acts. In most cases, the bands provided the entire stage show.

On Broadway, the Paramount was making its name band policy pay heavy dividends. The Strand, setting its band on the apron instead of in the pit, as the Paramount did, likewise found a goldmine in "hep" audiences. The Roxy and Loew's State also went in heavily for the bandstand policy.

A form of vaudeville received another chance—and a big one—when Billy Rose opened his lavish theatre-cabaret, the Casa Mañana. Actually it was nitery entertainment. For a while it flourished, arousing speculation over a possible vaude revival via the Rose technique. Henny Youngman cracked that he could remember "all the way back" when a vaudeville career meant 40 weeks of work a year instead of a Sunday night at Billy Rose's Casa. But when 1939 rolled around, there wasn't even that Sunday night.

1939 dipped United States vaudeville to a total of 11½ weeks playing time. A wave of bad films gave vaude a temporary lifeline, with nine New York theatres adding acts two or three days a week for a brief period. RKO put one-a-day vaude bills in some of its neighborhood theatres. The Brandts tried to revive straight vaude at the New York Audubon and Carlton, Jamaica, L. I., quickly giving it up.

The downbeat of vaudeville was best summed up by a Variety reviewer's summation, "In place of variety entertainment is the bandshow. In place of humor as the backbone of a stage layout is the percussion acrobatics of a drummer, or a trumpeter's hot licks. . . . What little soul vaudeville had left has passed out." Musicians had become comics, hoofers and chirpers.

Some succor for talent came with the hot weather on the Borscht Circuit, as the Catskill Mountain and Poconos (Pennsylvania) resorts got to be known. The "Sour Cream Belt" was spending $75,-000 to $100,000 a year for talent. The resort inns had grown up; it was no longer a case of "we had to dance with the customers," as in the pioneer life-of-the-party era in the Borscht Belt. Actors, in short, were doing a lot better at the 20 to 25 class and middle-grade hostelries in the Catskills than in all the other theatres east of the Alleghenies.

Even the splendid surroundings of Radio City's Music Hall couldn't sell straight vaudeville in 1933. The Music Hall tried it for two weeks, but was quickly forced to feature films plus stage show. The old Roxy won a court decision which made Radio City take Roxy's name down from its marquee. Roxy himself stepped down from his $50,000-a-year job as managing director of Radio City Music Hall the following year, after a dispute with the Rockefellers over high costs. To beat the $78,000 a week overhead, Roxy wanted to hold films over for runs of longer than a week. Rockefellers refused . . . but later came to see it Roxy's way, after Roxy had left.

To rival Radio City's Center Theatre, which had turned to legit in a big way with *The Great Waltz* in 1934, the Hippodrome introduced another spectacle in 1935. It was *Jumbo* and cost Billy Rose's backers—John Hay (Jock) Whitney and friends—some $300,000. Even with Jimmy Durante, Paul Whiteman, a Rodgers & Hart score and elephants it flopped. It grossed $18,000 opening night but nosedived thereafter, causing a Broadway crack, "You just can't mix silk and fertilizer." The Hipp, a white elephant, was still trying to find a place in show biz when, in 1938, it converted into a fronton for jai-alai. In the Hipp tradition that soon flopped too.

The Center's career was checkered, mostly in red ink. A musical, *Virginia,* spelled a $250,000 loss, in 1938. This was preceded by one of the most costly failures in show biz history—the pageant, *The Eternal Road,* at the Manhattan Opera House in 1937, which wound up over $500,000 in the red. And the year before that saw an American version of *White Horse Inn,* with a strong cast including William Gaxton, Kitty Carlisle, Carol Stone, Robert Halliday, Buster West and Billy House, go for a quick $160,000 loss. Size and spectacle were not boxoffice insurance quite obviously. *The Eternal Road,* a religioso theme, was not expected to turn a profit, having been heavily underwritten as a morality play.

The Center Theatre eventually was to become a fairly paying proposition in the heyday of the Sonja Henie-Arthur M. Wirtz ice shows, but eventually succumbed to television and became an NBC-TV house.

45

Blue Blood Blues Singers and Cuffo Society

★

The quickest pickup of New Deal show business was in the night life branch, particularly for the large places. The hotels, emerging from receivership, began to compete with the niteries for an increasingly lusty Broadway trade, using name bands and acts as bait. The average tariff was $2.50 to $3 for a table d'hote dinner, which rose to $4 on Saturdays.

The big clubs were going in for mass business. They offered semi-nude shows, sans cover charge, at a $1.50 to $3 minimum check, which included dinner. Their shows cost as much as $9,000 a week, but their average 1,000-seat capacity meant weekly gross receipts of $20,000 and upwards.

The old speakeasies with small capacities were forced to hike prices to stay in business—and had little to offer for the increase in tariff. The mobster element of the speaks largely disappeared, to be replaced by suave front men who represented the change of the speak from a fleeting racket to an established and courteous business.

Billy Rose, with a generous bankroll from "the boys," set the pace for the new style in night club entertainment with the Casino de Paree, formerly the Gallo, and later the New Yorker Theatre on West 54th St. The entertainment was along music hall lines, patrons afterward mounting the stage to dance to the music of two bands in stage boxes. The raised dance floor-cum-stage gave exhibitionistic patrons a vicarious feeling of being spotlighted. The Manhattan Casino, formerly Hammerstein's Theatre, followed suit, and Ben Marden renovated the Palais Royal along the same lines. Clifford C. Fischer's French Casino, on the site of Earl Carroll's Theatre, was the most successful operation of this type later.

Repeal gave the hotels their opportunity to swing from the conservative patronage of their residents to the more lucrative trade of the transients. In 1934 they offered "cocktail hours" as a means of dramatizing themselves as centers of social life. The end of Prohibition definitely proved the salvation of the Waldorf-Astoria, where the management had formerly shut off several floors at a time to trim overhead. By 1934, the Waldorf was 85 per cent rented, and bolstered its income with revenue from its various bars, cocktail lounges and other social rooms.

The various hotel "rooms" quickly became an integral part of upper-class night life. Women liked the respectable and pleasant atmosphere; men had more confidence in the food and drinks. The hotels were quick to respond by adding suitably appealing talent and name bands, as well as by decorating their social rooms in what was considered the latest and smartest manner, à la Joseph Urban. Some even went so far as to install cabaret floor shows and ice revues to the horror of a few more fossilized guests—but OK b.o. for the bonifaces.

The Rockefellers, who had already made show business sit up and take notice with Radio City Music Hall and the Center Theatre, also stole the night club show in 1934 by opening the Rainbow Room on the 65th floor of the RCA Building. "A night club in the clouds," Variety called it, "in a natural setting of beauty and magic which not even the Rockefeller financing could conjure up were it not for the gratis aid of Nature."

Among the remarkable features of the new club, as Variety noted them, were glass walls; the first super-organ ever installed in a nitery; a revolving dance floor; every seat a ringside seat; and imported talent. "The nut for the Rainbow Room really doesn't matter, as the Rockefellers couldn't break even if they turned 'em away every night. Which places the oil tycoons in the category of show biz philanthropists rather than show biz investors."

The cover charge was $1.50 and $2 on Saturdays. Reservations had to be made in advance, and formal dress was a must at first, but later relaxed. For those who just wanted to see the view and relax on top of Radio City, a 40¢ cocktail paid the way in the afternoon via the more informal Patio cocktail lounge. During the day both the Rainbow Room and Rainbow Grill merged into a membership luncheon club, still operating, for the convenience of Rockefeller Center tenants.

Business was generally lush for most of the night spots in 1934. Popular prices, no cover charge, and an elaborate floor show were the magnets—drawing mass patronage which had never been possible in the days of the Club Lido's $5 couvert and Texas Guinan's $20-$25 "champagne." Now customers were attracted by the advertised $1.50 dinners; came to find that $2 bought a better dinner, and a $2.50 minimum check assured ringside tables. The longer the floor show, the longer they sat, the more they ordered and drank. Drinks at 75¢ a throw gave most clubs a very neat margin of profit.

Billy Rose's Music Hall offered $1 dinners, and employed 100 hostesses and 100 singing waiters. Rose, who was only the front man for the Hall and Casino de Paree, was soon ousted by the shoulder-holster boys who controlled them when he had the temerity to ask for a bigger share of pie.

Among the reformed speakeasies which made the grade by dressing for dinner were El Morocco; Leon & Eddie's, which took in between $11,000 and $12,000 a week in 1934; "21"; Joe Zelli's; and Hector's Club New Yorker. The Stork Club debuted at its present 53d St. site. Several have become Gotham institutions.

On Broadway, Morton Downey and Dan Healey were pulling them into the Palais Royal. Rudy Vallee was the attraction at the Hollywood Restaurant. The Paradise was baited with Sally Rand and an N.T.G. revue. The Broadway segment did well, but kept an anxious eye on the east-of-Fifth Avenue clubs and hotels which were shaping up as sharp competition.

the debs go hildegarde   1934 was the year which saw the first influx of society debutantes into show business via the night clubs. The first to start the vogue was Eve Symington, daughter of Senator Wadsworth, who earned $1,000 a week for warbling at the Place Pigalle on 52d St. off Broadway. Her salary went to charity at first, then it became a career. Lois Ellman, daughter of a wealthy realtor, sang for the Club New Yorker. The Embassy Club had blueblooded Adelaide Moffatt, who later took to the air via CBS.

The trend was inspired by the Social Register aura given night clubs with the bow of the fashionable Rainbow Room. Cafe managers encouraged it, considering a Blue Book background more valuable than top professional talent in drawing the trade from which the socialite songbirds stemmed. And it was good newspaper publicity.

Sally Rand, who had started at the Chicago Fair in a sideshow called "Streets of Paris" for $125 a week, was drawing a $6,000 weekly paycheck from the Paradise in 1934. To discourage competition, she copyrighted her bubble dance. And did the dance behind a specially-constructed screen, to keep her modesty intact by preventing any playful contact of patron's cigarets with her big balloon.

With the revival of east- and west-side night life in New York, the vogue of Harlem went into decline. The Ubangi Club, formerly Connie's Inn, made its principal bid to a specialized trade of jazz addicts. The Cotton Club, which called itself in ads "The Aristocrat of Harlem," dropped its aristocratic $2.50 cover charge and ballyhooed the absence of same. The following year, however, Harlem was exerting its old lure of the 1920s again, although Connie's Inn decided to move downtown into the stand of the old Palais Royal.

1936 and 1937 were such boom years for Harlem hotspots like the Cotton Club, the Kit Kat, the Harlem Uproar House, Ubangi, Small's Paradise, Plantation, Black Cat, Dicky Wells and others, that there was a shortage of sepian talent for the Negro theatres, which had to hire ofay actors to round out their bills.

america's montmartre   The French accent came into vogue in 1935. Variety observed, "New York today is more Frenchy than the Paris boulevards." There were about 25 niteries of all types, prices and ranges congested within one block on West 52d, between 5th and 6th avenues, reminiscent of the bistros, bars and boites of Paris' hilltop, Montmartre. Patrons were demanding vintage wines. Even Schrafft's served Scotch with whipped cream, while the Paramount Theatre Bldg. Childs' restaurant installed an emcee and swing band.

The fan dancers of 52d St. were a little more restrained, if not any more clad, than the Montmartre brand. One near New York gambling casino-roadhouse, à la the Riviera version and as part of the French lure, had the double-zero removed from roulette wheels for two hours each day to give players a better chance. Broadway's French Casino (Clifford C. Fischer's elaborate theatre-restaurant) was in the chips, grossing $50,000 weekly.

The hotels, with one eye on the Rainbow Room, wanted to achieve the same stratosphere by insisting upon formal dress but they found business slipping. A compromise of a split policy—formal dress only if on the ringside—also flivved.

The 25th cafe opened on 52d St. in 1936, when the sector became known as "Swing Street." Variety reported that the top night club city in the nation was not New York, as most supposed, but San Francisco, which had the largest number—1,252.

The revival of night life, and the glittering social tone lent by the evening wrap trade, brought about a resurgence in popularity of the dance team—always a pet with society. In 1936 the top teams were Tony & Renee De Marco, Veloz & Yolanda, Ramon & Renita, Rosita & Fontana, Dario & Diane, Lydia & Jeresco, Fowler & Tamara, Minor & Root, Gomez & Winona, Stone & Collins and David & Hilda Murray.

Nobody was quite sure why, but in 1937 night clubs were badly dented. Most fingers were pointed at the new International Casino, a vast and spacious nitery which opened at popular prices and catered to mass patronage. There was no denying that the International sent the Hollywood into bankruptcy by practically kidnapping all of the latter's trade. The International was strategically situated in the heart of Times Square, directly opposite the Hotel Astor, on the site now occupied by the new Criterion Theatre and the giant Bond clothing store. The Hollywood, further up Broadway, at 48th Street, was a cleanup with its mass-capacity, super-floorshow to a "no cover" policy that started at a theoretical $3 minimum tariff.

Meantime the French Casino, which enjoyed a brief revival, went into the discard and was picked up by Billy Rose who relabeled it the Casa Mañana.

Some of the class spots, wondering what had hit them that year, decided to revert to a Prohibition technique—make it tough for the customers to get in. One or two found that it worked, as customers damned the owners, headwaiters and captains . . . and *demanded* admission. The Stork and "21" still employ that technique for unknown or "undesirable" patronage.

To prop sagging business, some niteries began to throw in free dishes, much as the movies were doing. They also offered bingo, lucky number contests and rhumba contests. Even the Rainbow Room, along with El Morocco and the Versailles, smeared honey on the boxoffice via "champagne dance contests." The Stork Club tied up with 20th Century-Fox in a film-talent contest.

Leon & Eddie's tried five acts, with a $1 table d'hote lunch. The Paradise threw in Rudy Vallee. But the trend was downward, and a number of 52d St. clubs folded. The summer slump made some clubs desperate. These ordered their girls to mix with the customers. A few even descended to straight honkytonk tactics, and some had arrangements for a 25 to 50 per cent split with female "steerers." The cops came.

As the b.o. dropped, so did the clothes of some nitery performers. Strippers didn't mind the ogling, but many strongly resented the sudden candid camera fad. The issue was solved when the New York License Commissioner stepped in with a stern ban on all nitery stripping.

An old escapist theme, the hula vogue, entered night life in 1937, resulting in the Lexington Hotel's Hawaiian Room, and Leon & Eddie's $15,000 Pago Pago Room, with windstorm and rain effects. There was also a new dance craze—"The Big Apple"—which made its debut in the Rainbow Room. Originated by Gullah Negroes around Charleston, South Carolina, who danced it barefoot, it was described by Variety as "requiring a lot of floating power and fannying."

The year saw America once again dance-crazy . . . or in Variety's terminology, "hoof nutty." The trend was more toward audience-participation. Besides swing and the jitterbug vogue, the Lambeth

Walk craze started. There were also the Little Pear and Little Peach.

In 1937 ice-skaters and saucy songsters both suddenly found themselves in demand by night clubs. Dwight Fiske, whose risqué entertainment had been barred from London, found delighted fans at the Savoy-Plaza, in New York. Sheila Barrett was another 1937 favorite, while Hildegarde—still to make her giant success of the 1940s—sailed for Europe. With the irony of which only show business was capable, Charles King—only a few years before a top-priced film star—was discovered to be one of a trio singing at tables in the Victoria Hotel, New York. He also did a stint at Bill's Gay Nineties spot, that New York haven for old-time troupers.

Society was still in the spotlight in 1937 with "Junior League Follies" and similar amateur theatricals.

The Savoy-Plaza introduced what it thought was a smart new note by inviting audience-participation, via a mike, which recorded the conversation for an immediate playback. Russell Swan, the magician, asked the guests to recite some toasts. Some debs promptly gave out with strictly stag toasts. Swan hastily found some excuse for not playing the record back.

The drought on Broadway continued in 1938. Among the clubs that "parlayed themselves into 77B," or went bankrupt, were the Paradise, Hollywood, International and La Conga, which had enjoyed a brief boom on the wave of the still then new Latin American cycle.

Variety noted a letdown in tone of some clubs on the "Park Avenue circuit." The St. Regis' Maisonette Russe booked a Negro band; and the Waldorf let its august walls shake to Benny Goodman, installing a milk bar for the jitterbug trade.

But the debs were still in there pitching. Cobina Wright, Jr. went into the Waldorf's Sert Room. Sally Clark, a Roosevelt in-law, tried out at the New York Plaza, then decided to get married, with popular approval. Eleanor French and Lois Ellman were doing vocals with bands. A socialite amateur contest won a regular job at Le Coq Rouge for Annee Francine. And Adelaide Moffatt shocked her sister debs by announcing, at Harry Richman's Road to Mandalay, that she was making show business her career.

Billy Rose opened his Diamond Horseshoe in the basement of the Paramount Hotel. Jack Dempsey opened his new Broadway Bar, flashing films of his early ring triumphs for the customers to ogle, eventually foregoing the Dempsey's Restaurant on 8th Ave. and 50th Street, directly opposite Madison Square Garden, which he never quite put over. Another nitery venture in that socially conscious era was Cabaret TAC (for Theatre Arts Committee)—the first American night club which appealed to the politically-minded trade. European capitals like Paris and Berlin, particularly the German capital, in the 1930s spawned the political nitery where the conferencier spoofed the mores of nations.

cuffo society   Variety spilled the beans that year on the why-and-wherefore of the heavy socialite attendance at niteries. It pointed out that most of this was strictly on the cuff, with the management taking a beating in order to staff his club with the proper "tone," to win society and gossip columnist mentions and photos, and to lure the subway trade which liked to go where it was "smart to be seen." When the chips were down, it was plain Joe Doakes who paid for the bluebloods' entertainment— including their choice seat locations and special catering.

The type of night club represented by the International Casino, and Midnight Frolic (the erstwhile Paradise) went heavily into decline in 1939. The International, $250,000 in the red, went on the auction block. But business boomed for the hotel rooms, and most clubs switched from lavish to nostalgic entertainment. The leaders in this field were Bill Hardy's Gay Nineties, Billy Rose's Diamond Horseshoe, the Sawdust Trail, the Brown Derby, and Joe Howard's Gold Room in the Hotel Ambassador.

The bar of the Sherry-Netherland went in for old Chaplin films, along with beer and pretzels. Other spots featured old-time silent newsreels, along with current news clips. The season's most interesting personality was Alec Templeton, the blind pianist who rose from a $350-a-week turn in the night clubs to a concert personality commanding $1,000 a night.

1940 proved a generally desultory year, tolling the Midnight Frolic and Jack Dempsey's Restaurant (the one on 8th Ave. and 50th St., not the Dempsey Broadway Bar) among the principal foldees. With business off, a return to clip-joint practices was noted.

46

'Don't Take Off Your Panties'

★

Burlesque started the 1930 season with 37 shows and 37 theatres. It ended ignominiously with 27 shows and 24 theatres. Burlesque—and not the depression—was to blame. While the Columbia Circuit had operated, it was possible for burlesque to defend itself against accusations that it was unclean. When Mutual took over, burly was roughed up to give the public "what it wanted" . . . or what Mutual considered would turn a fast buck.

Nudity and outright crudity have little fascination . . . at least for any protracted length of time. Dirt dished wholesale tends to bore and that means chasing 'em. Lana Turner in a sweater, shapely gams, a chantoosey with a slightly tilted eyebrow can pique the male trade more than a chorus of nudes.

That was burlesque's big mistake. Having gone the limit in dirty dialog, Mutual frantically tossed in strippers. But the strips were all alike.

The more lowdown burlesque was forced to get, the more, too, it invited trouble. Civic authorities won convictions in city after city. Burlesque was caught between two fires. If it cleaned up, it was too late; if it didn't, patronage slipped anyhow, and the cops came besides.

Some shows tried to grasp at straws by adding vaudeville acts, but vaudevillians couldn't stand the degrading atmosphere. The competition of cleaner and better entertainment made burly's $1 and $1.50 top prices impossible. In 1930, the name "burlesque," once so enticing to the male trade, was enough to murder the boxoffice of any theatre which flaunted it.

Mutual Burlesque died in 1931, to be replaced by another try of the Columbia Wheel under I. H. Herk, who collected $500 apiece from producers wanting to tie in. Stock burlesque settled down to a dreary routine which emphasized strippers on runways, comics filling in between strips with bawdy jokes long enough for the strippers to change costume. "They can't get any hotter," Variety noted wearily, "or the police would interfere, and they can't cool off because the customers would drop off. No cleverness—men just go to see nakedness, and that's all they get. Save to the degenerate and moron, there is little to attract in burlesque but mere nakedness."

In a desperate effort to drum up business for the burly show at the Gaiety, the manager opened the front doors facing Broadway, so that passersby could get an eyeful of the strippers on the runways. The stunt attracted crowds—outside. Minsky's stock burleycue on 42d Street advertised "Fannie Fortson From France—dances at all shows." The Minsky diet included "strippers, tossers, hip-heavers and breast-bouncers."

the old no. 3 routine   Road burlesque developed a carnival twist in 1931 with one burly traveling in its own train. At towns where it gave shows, the girls would be "auctioned" to the audience—highest bidders winning the privilege of after-show dinners and dates. The suckers, anticipating a delicious evening, were delighted when the girls suggested that—since there was usually no place to go in the small towns—they go aboard their special train. Once aboard, the suckers were further delighted by being taken to the "privilege car," where they could order drinks and play cards. At midnight, when the suckers began to have ideas, a fake raid would be pulled by some of the men in the show, claiming to be railroad detectives, and ordering "strangers" off the train. The suckers went home, and the girls went wearily to bed.

When New York authorities sternly said, "Clean up—or else!" in 1932, burlesque actually didn't know how to go about obeying orders. Especially the Minsky shows, which had become infamous even outside New York as the dirtiest theatre in the big city. But the Minskys realized the city authorities meant business—it was either clean up or get out.

They thought of Sam S. Scribner, who had represented everything that was clean about burlesque—he was one of the founders of the original Columbia Burlesque Wheel—and who had quit when it turned dirty. Scribner agreed to become the censor or czar of burleycue, and was influential in getting City Hall to OK re-opening Minsky's Republic, with the explicit understanding Scribner would bluepencil all shows. Instead of strips, the Minskys turned to such sensational marquee items as Kiki Roberts, sweetheart of the notorious gangster, Legs Diamond. She got $1,500 a week.

The bits and routines of the average burly show were as inflexible as sewage drains. Comedy scene; strip; comedy scene; strip; intermission curtain and the aisle hawkers. Most customers yawned and read their newspapers between strip numbers.

There was practically no competition in 1934 burly, with the exception of a brief show of fight by a new eastern wheel. The two principal wheels of that year, Supreme and Independent, together served a total of about 15 cities. Only in one city did they play in opposition—Philadelphia. Variety summed up the situation, "The conflict is over who is going to get those six customers in Philly."

The same set of boxoffice conditions prevailed in 1934 as in most years. In cities where the authorities could be persuaded to look the other way, and stripping went the limit, the company didn't starve. Where the lid was on, the show echoed over empty orchestras. Yet burly executives kept mouthing the sentiment—as though they believed it—that it was time to cut down on stripping and emphasize comedy.

The New York police made their usual number of raids in 1934, with the Irving Place Theatre making the wagon again. Convictions were rare, however, which encouraged burly managers to believe their lawyers who told them there was no urgent need to mend their ways.

ann corio and gypsy rose lee The top personality to emerge from 1934 burly was stripper Ann Corio, who had scored such a personal success that she was about the only name in burlesque known to other branches of show business, with the exception of producer Allan Gilbert, who won attention by staging some novel "flash girl numbers" at the Apollo and Irving Place theatres.

"I don't like to be called a stripper," Miss Corio told Variety's Cecelia Ager. "In fact it absolutely galls me. But as long as they give me the money, that's all I look forward to. . . . Why should I give up my percentage of the gross for $100 a week and glory? . . . Where are all the Broadway beauties now? When I finish I'll have a bankroll."

She explained the secret of her success. "Make yourself as feminine-looking as you can. Go in for a lot of frills, furs, ruffles and parasols. Always put everything you have into your work to put it over. . . . Don't take off your panties; it makes a girl's figure look prettier to have those little gadgets on."

The road, said Miss Corio, was lovely territory for strippers. Apart from the 15 to 25 per cent of the gross she was paid, compared to the $750 a week straight salary she drew in New York. "I love the road. They don't expect so much from you. New York audiences just want to see how much you'll take off . . . I love New England best of all. It's so easy to please. You don't have to do much in New England because they haven't had it."

She was also conscious of the "better" type of audiences. "I love the two-a-day houses best, where the audience is such a different class. In the four-a-day lots of the customers sit through two shows, and by the time the second show rolls around they're exhausted. That doesn't inspire a girl to do her best work . . . They're too tired to care what you're hiding."

In 1940, Miss Corio apparently had enough in the bank to take a flier in less remunerative fields. She appeared in strawhat versions of *The Barker* and *White Cargo*. A newspaper reporter asked whether she considered what she was doing art. "Art?" replied the indignant stripper. "I should say so! Why, I've been to the bank twice to draw money to eat on!"

Another Irving Place graduate, who soon eclipsed Miss Corio in the national spotlight, was Gypsy Rose Lee. Her first break came in 1936, when she jumped into the Shuberts' *Ziegfeld Follies* at the Winter Garden . . . still as a stripper. Her debut in legit rated more newspaper space in two months than all of burlesque had received in the previous two years. Miss Corio also received legitimate offers that year, as in other years, but until 1940 persisted in doing her undressing in burlesque, where she took top money as burly's No. 1 stripteuse.

Gypsy Rose Lee was unique because she put the accent on her IQ as well as s.a., later demonstrating her versatility by turning novelist. She was also clever enough to show far less than almost all the other strippers, and yet get the boys out front applauding wildly. She proved that strippers could draw for burlesque without stripping down to their skeletons.

london finally falls for strips   Other top strippers
of that year, who carried what was left of burlesque on their G-
strings, were Evelyn Meyers, Margie Hart, Carrie Finnell (an ample-
sized performer whose stock in trade was her mammary St. Vitus),
Countess Nadja, Hinda Wassau, Georgia Sothern (a redhead who
practically tore down the curtains with the violence of her grinds),
Jeanne Carroll, Betty Howland, Toots Brawner, Maxine De Shon
and Gladys Clark. The following year stripper Diane Rày left for
London, to export the new American art into the British Isles. It
must have taken a while to register, because not until 1940 did
Variety report, "London Goes For Strip-Tease."

The Minskys, who dominated three of the five burlesque stands
in the Times Square area, were primarily responsible for bringing
down on burly's neck the fiery breath of Mayor Fiorello H. La-
Guardia. After outlawing of the word "burlesque" in 1937, the burly
operators did everything but promise that it would be as pure as
Shirley Temple. The mayor relented to the extent of permitting
them to reopen as "Follies" shows—no filth, no strippers.

Burly—or "Follies"—in New York dropped from 40 weeks of
playing time at the start of 1938 to 12 by the year's finish, with
only two summer weeks in New York. The rest of burly was
handled by 10 stock companies operating throughout the country.
One burlesque operator conceived an idea for defeating the La-
Guardia ban, in the manner of the floating speakeasies, via a burly
show offshore. He chartered the S. S. Yankee, a Hudson River
showboat. License Commissioner Paul Moss got wind of the plan,
and New York's finest were at the pier before the S. S. Yankee
could get up steam. The sailing was held up on a docking technicality, with intimation that the technicality would last indefinitely,
and that kayoed that idea.

All that could be said for burly in 1938 was that it was the last
spawning ground of new talent since vaudeville had died. Burly,
desperate for any kind of entertainment, often opened its arms to
genuine, if untried, talent, which soon left it for greener pastures.

great cradle of talent   "Peanuts" Bohn jumped from
burly to English music halls. Abbott & Costello left to go with
Kate Smith on the radio and subsequently their own radio and
Hollywood stardom. Joey Faye went into legit with *Sing Out the*

News, and of course subsequent television stardom, as did Sid Stone into *The Fabulous Invalid,* legiter, before clicking on the Milton Berle video show. Rags Ragland and Phil Silvers joined Rudy Vallee. Sid Kent graduated to Eddie Cantor's writing staff, and Joe Yule went to Hollywood to appear in a film with his son—Mickey Rooney. The upsurge, through the years, from such cradled-in-burlesque talents as Bert Lahr, Fanny Brice, (Bobby) Clark & (Paul) McCullough, Leon Errol, Jim Barton, and Jack Pearl has given rise to periodic grievance among showmen that that great school of the future funny men and women—among the greats on the American stage—is no more.

While the State Street (Chicago) honkytonks are still running, and there are still 35 burlesque shows in the United States at this writing, the twilight of burlesque was a combination of spurious economics and no talent.

When Izzy Herk conceived the Mutual Wheel idea of a stationary line, with the principals only traveling from city to city, as a measure to cut down traveling expenses, the choristers in short order became local favorites, but soon thereafter palled on the steady clientele.

Meantime Herk had acquired a fresh bankroll via a Toledo concessionaire who urged more turnovers and intermissions as a bolsterer for his candy butchers and comic-book salesmen. The 4- and 5-a-day burlesque thus came into being, plus midnight shows, Sunday shows, and the like.

Variety was still scratching its head over the fact that burlesque was still around in 1940. "Burlesque's survival—in fact, its prosperity," it confessed, "can only be based on the greatly underestimated lunatic fringe in this country. Though a family-type entertainment, such as vaudeville, can barely keep what head it has above water, the dirty slapstick and sloppy G-stringers manage to keep going, and very profitably in most instances, without the buying public first asking what picture is playing."

Getting down to cases, Variety attributed burly's resurgence in 1940 to the industrial boom under way, which created greater defense spending, and also gathered together burly-ripe audiences at Army and Navy reservations.

Vaudeville acts of 1940 had tough sledding to book 20 weeks a year. But burlesque had two new, and separate circuits routing shows for a total of 25 weeks' playing time. One was the Midwest Circuit, a co-operative group, and the other was the Izzy Hirst Wheel.

Asked Variety, almost plaintively, "And how many legit road companies get 25 weeks outside of New York?"

47

Hep to the Jive

★

During 1933, Americans in the depths of the depression mournfully sang "Stormy Weather," "Are You Makin' Any Money?," "I'll String Along With You" and "Who's Afraid of the Big Bad Wolf?" Lachrymose romance was in vogue with "It's The Talk of the Town," "Sophisticated Lady," "Smoke Rings," "Don't Blame Me," "It Might Have Been A Different Story" and "Trouble in Paradise."

As counterpoint, swing was struggling to set a to-hell-with-it note by offering "Jive Stomp," via Duke Ellington, and "New Basin Street Blues." The natural setting was featured in "In the Valley of the Moon," "Under A Blanket of Blue," "Shadows On the Swanee," "My Moonlight Madonna" and "Down the Old Ox Road."

Love, pure and very simple, was offered in "Sweetheart, Darlin'," "My Love," "Love Is the Sweetest Thing," "Don't Blame Me," "Here You Come, Love," "Close Your Eyes," and "Ah, But It's Love." Top novelty number of the year was "Lazy Bones," and Bing Crosby crooned "Learn to Croon" to fame.

A key song of the year, "The Old Spinning Wheel," touched off a nostalgic series of songs about old things in 1934—"By the Old Wheel Pump," "The Old Covered Bridge," "The Old-Fashioned Girl," "The Old-Fashioned World," "The Old Trunk in the Attic" and "The Old Grandfather's Clock."

Billy Hill, composer of "Spinning Wheel," sparked still another 1934 cycle with "The Last Round-Up," which provoked a score of Western numbers on the order of "Wagon Wheels" and "Night In the Desert." Hill was awarded a special $1,200 prize by ASCAP for "Spinning Wheel," and publishers fought for numbers which he had sold at $25 apiece before clicking with "Round-Up."

The year also brought an eye cycle, with "I Only Have Eyes For You," "With My Eyes Wide Open," "I'll Close My Eyes," and "It Happened When Your Eyes Met Mine." Some smash hits came via the filmusicals of the year, which offered "Love In Bloom," "Beat of My Heart," "Cocktails For Two," "A Thousand Goodnights," "Did You Ever See A Dream Walking?" "Love Thy Neighbor," "The Very Thought Of You" and "I Never Had A Chance." An ineffectual attempt to revitalize the waltz tempo was made by the legit musical *Great Waltz*.

The hit song of 1935 was "Isle of Capri." That year a number of old tunes were protested as derogatory to Negroes by the Society for the Advancement of Colored People. Among these were "That's Why Darkies Are Born," "My Old Kentucky Home," "Swanee River," "Muddy Waters," "Carry Me Back To Old Virginny," "River, Stay Away From My Door," "Without A Song" and "Underneath the Harlem Moon."

Indicative of the new festive feeling of the nation, and heralding the swift advance of swing by 1936, was the comedy number, "The Music Goes 'Round and 'Round." Its earnings exceeded those of the fabulous "Yes, We Have No Bananas," and launched a new cycle of "Round" numbers, including "The Merry-Go-Round Broke Down," which inspired a subcycle of its own with "Love Is Like A Merry-Go-Round" and "The Girl That I Met On the Merry-Go-Round."

The South Seas vogue of 1937 was reflected in music by a revival of Hawaiian numbers, and new popularity for the ukulele. The vogue prompted O. O. McIntyre—for whom Meredith Willson had written "The O. O. McIntyre Suite"—to remark that, "Those Hawaiians always say goodbye—but never go."

"Blue songs are the rage among bluebloods," Variety noted that year—a spectacular year for swank night clubs. "Songs have dirty lyrics, framed in semi-polite language, and are put across in the fashionable cafes by beautifully-gowned chanteuses or immaculately-groomed gents who conduct themselves like members of a London regiment. Swells delight in the indigo, and the later the hour becomes, the more outspoken the lyrics."

Less sophisticated, but with the same basic appeal, were the records offered to wayside rests which couldn't afford live talent. Known as "operator's specials," these disks included such titles as "Pool Table Papa," "Four or Five Times" and "Give It To Me, Daddy." They were infinitely more popular than the poor crop of 1937 numbers turned out for the standard field.

The floods of 1937 inspired a Mills number called "Flood Waters," while a number exalting the gloved victory of Joe Louis called "Joe the Bomber" was composed, arranged, rehearsed and recorded in 24 hours. The recording artist was "Billy Hicks and His Sizzling Six." Other timely numbers were songs woven around radio catch-lines of the day—"Vass You Dere, Sharlie?" "Today I Am A Man," "Oh, You Nasty Man"—all of which rated zero in popular favor.

The biggest hits of 1938 were the songs from *Snow White*. With the advent of swing, songstresses began to use the tempo on Scottish classics, and then on nursery rhymes. The vogue inspired swing versions of "Tisket-A-Tasket," and "All Around the Mulberry Bush." Other top tunes were "Ti-Pi-Tin," "Thanks For the Memory," and "Bei Mir Bist Du Schoen," adapted from a Yiddish song, a surprise hit. Orders for the latter number poured in to baffled music dealers as "That new French song, 'Buy A Beer, Monsieur Shane,'" "My Mere Bits of Shame," and "Mr. Barney McShane."

musical echoes of the war drums   America was too prosperous and happy in 1938 to want to be reminded of war in the outside world. But they were glad to sing Irving Berlin's "God Bless America," an old number he wrote and discarded in 1917 as puerile until Kate Smith rediscovered it. Another topical number was "Wrong Way Corrigan," celebrating the insouciant flier who took off from Brooklyn without permit or passport and landed in Dublin.

Songwriters in Europe, however, were very much aware of the war. Hermann Leopoldi wrote an Austrian "youth song" called "We Are On the Dolfuss Road To Better Times." Then came Anschluss, and Leopoldi landed in a Nazi concentration camp for writing the wrong song. Austrian composers quickly took the hint, and one of the first songs turned out after Hitler's Austrian putsch was "Soldier From Berlin, Girl of Vienna."

England gave America its best songs of 1939—despite the war—with "Penny Serenade," "South of the Border," "My Prayer," "The Beer Barrel Polka" and "Boomps-A-Daisy." Broadway replaced Hollywood as the feeder of hits that year with "South American Way," "Comes Love," "Are You Having Any Fun?," "Get Out of Town," "I Didn't Know What Time It Was" and "Do I Love You—Do I?"

More and more tunesmiths were discovering wonderful melodies —in the tunes of previous centuries. As Variety dryly reported, "Refugees coming over observe, 'My, what a wonderfully musical nation America is! They even whistle Mozart, Tschaikowsky, Debussy and Chopin in the street!'"

Among the numbers which owed more than inspiration to the classics were "Our Love" and "My Reverie" (Debussy and Larry Clinton); "Moon Love" (Tschaikowsky and Andre Kostelanetz) and "How Strange" (M.G.M. and Prozorovsky).

Escapism via juvenile songs came with "Little Sir Echo," to be followed by "Little Mischief Maker," "Little Skipper," "Little Genius" and "Little Lad." This in turn touched off a "cute" cycle—"Oh Johnny," "Chatterbox," "Baby Me," "Goody-Goodbye" and "Three Little Fishes."

Swing was represented by "Hold Tight," "Well, All Right," "T'aint What You Do, It's the Way Thatcha Do It," "I Want the Waiter With the Water." Benny Goodman introduced "Sonata to ASCAP," "Opus Local 802" and "AC-DC Current." Woody Herman offered "Woodchoppers Ball," "Neurotic Goldfish," "A Deb's Diary" and "Weekend of A Private Secretary."

By 1940 "God Bless America" had risen to the status of a new national anthem, and there was a strong movement on foot to replace "The Star-Spangled Banner" with it. Some newspapers criticized Berlin for "making money" out of patriotic feeling, apparently unaware that a committee comprising Col. Theodore Roosevelt, Gene Tunney and Herbert Bayard Swope, at Berlin's own request, were administering all the song's profits and royalties, divided equally between the Boy and Girl Scouts of America. Whereupon Bucknell University awarded Berlin a Doctorate of

Music. Berlin purposely placed a high royalty on the song in order to swell the fund which has realized over $130,000.

With England fighting for existence, and the rise of anti-Fascist feeling in America, war songs began to make their appearance in 1940. There were "Thanks America," "Let Freedom Ring," "What Will I Do If I Marry A Soldier," "Your Homeland and My Homeland," "Liberty Bell, It's Time To Ring Again," "What Are You Doing For Your Uncle Sam?" "Is It Love—Or Is It Conscription?," "Who'll Take the Place of Mademoiselle From Armentieres?," "Give the Stars and Stripes A Permanent Wave" and "He's A Typical American Boy."

How can you have a war without war songs?

dance vogues   For its dances of the 1930s America turned at first to foreign and pseudo-foreign styles—notably the rhumba, the Carioca and the Continental, the latter two made popular by Fred Astaire and Ginger Rogers via their filmusicals, *Flying Down To Rio* and *Gay Divorcee* respectively. In 1934 Gene Edwards introduced a new idea at Sherry's Park Avenue—a dance orchestra composed of half Negro, half white musicians—"to blend natural Negro syncopation with the more restrained white dance rhythms." Bing Crosby was the top creator of song hits, with Rudy Vallee leading on the air, and Dick Powell first warbler of the films via Warner Bros. musicals. Tin Pan Alley was enthusiastic about two English music maestros—Ray Noble and Jack Hylton.

Swing began to develop on two levels in 1935. On the top level was "musician's music"—or bands whose most enthusiastic audience consisted of other musicians. In this bracket were Benny Goodman, Louis Armstrong, Fats Waller, Louis Prima, Wingy Manone, Farley-Reilly, Red Norvo, Red McKenzie and Adrian Rollini. On the lower level were the popular swing bands, whose popularity was based on less complex renditions of swing for dancing and listening.

Among the up-and-comers were Hal Kemp, the Dorseys, Kay Kyser, Eddy Duchin, Dick Haymes and Ted Fio Rito.

Guy Lombardo still held his tremendous following, explaining that the secret of his success was, as a radio band, playing for listening rather than dancing. "He believes," Variety reported, "that despite the misguided conceptions of some ad agencies that folks in the sticks roll up their carpets and dance to the radio, what most of 'em really do is just listen. Hence Lombardo's smooth, reedy music is 99 per cent patterned for ear-appeal. Most listeners either just recline, some lie down, others play bridge or read with the radio going."

birth of swing   The first swing contest took place in 1936 at the Imperial Theatre, New York, with 17 orchestras swinging it for three hours. Variety, sidestepping any "best" label, handed out adjective awards. Glen Gray was "most elegant"; Stuff Smith, "most personable"; Bunny Berigan, "most jam"; Paul Whiteman, "most finished"; Louis Armstrong, "most penetrating"; Artie Shaw, "most arresting soloist and clarinet." Mildred Bailey won the laurel of "most compelling chanteuse."

Variety's editor asked top swing musicians for their definition of the new brand of music. "It's jam," said Mike Farley, "but arranged." Wingy Manone declared, "It's a livelier tempo, you know —swingy-like." Red McKenzie was more explicit: "It's an evolution of 'The Dixie Style,' that is, the Original Nick La Rocca's Dixieland Jazz Band's style. It's the difference between the old and the new music. It's definitely the music of the future. Swing dates from 1914, with the 'Livery Stable Blues' and the 'Original Dixieland Jazz Band Blues.' That's only 20 years or so ago. Swing is carefully conceived improvisation. . . ."

According to Red Norvo, "It's a desire to achieve a definite, livelier rhythm, and only advanced musicians can do that. It's a tempo that inspires the listener to accelerate in rhythm with an ultramodern swing. You know, they *swing* with you."

The contest between swing and sweet music for American favor was still going strong by 1938. To establish swing's right to be considered as serious American music, Benny Goodman gave a recital at Carnegie Hall, where, as Variety noted, "the longhair crix didn't savvy his jive." Paul Whiteman also appeared at Carnegie Hall and found the welcome warmer—as official spokesman for jazz who had made it respectable at Carnegie Hall and Town Hall 15 years before.

Swing influenced dancing among the younger generation, which found its expression in jitterbugging. The vogue at first amused, then dismayed older generations which found themselves literally kicked off the dance floors of the nation. The adolescents of 1938, thanks to swing and jitterbugging, were vastly different specimens from the serious, depression-conscious youths of the early 1930s who had taken their revolt against their elders out by joining unions, and various "progressive" movements. These youths, now in their late twenties, regarded their adolescent successors with undisguised contempt.

Even in 1938 swing was having its moral repercussions, through the association of "muggles" or "reefers," as marijuana cigarets were called, with "cats," "alligators" and "ickeys." The use of drugs by swing musicians—a vice which later spread to juvenile swing addicts—was a private but not yet public scandal in 1938.

Swing made the nation so band-conscious that in 1940 bands were the top stage entertainment. Some high-rating bands playing film houses even were able to get away with specifying the type of "A" films to accompany their engagements, a function "old-fashioned" acts usually left to theatre managers. The latter also strongly resented the stiff price tags on name bands. The average good orchestra rated only $1,400 weekly in night clubs and hotels —because of radio hookups which made these engagements profitable—but rarely asked below $6,500 from the theatres.

Vaude's oldtimers further resented the bands because of "lazy stage habits." Musicians frequently refused to wear makeup, and band singers thought nothing of doing their solos in street attire . . . sometimes in sweaters. As Variety pictured the bands in vaudeville, "Nearly all of them have jamming, jaw-grinding trapmen; wide-stanced, wooden-faced singers; pale-faced and blue-jowled musicians (all without makeup); and an always-smiling leader, to whom none of the musicians pay any apparent attention. That's now the core of what was once vaudeville."

one of ascap's major fights   The musical world of the 1930s was stirred behind the scenes by a running battle between ASCAP—undisputed spokesman for America's composers, lyricists and publishers—and the National Association of Broadcasters. The battle actually dated from a first skirmish in 1925, when the American Society of Composers, Authors and Publishers won a court verdict against Station WLW of Cincinnati which set the precedent that radio stations would have to obtain licenses from

ASCAP, and pay fees, if they wished to broadcast ASCAP-controlled music.

ASCAP, not fully appreciating the extent to which radio was destined to grow, was content to collect only nominal fees from radio under this arrangement until 1932. Then, realizing that radio was the biggest and most important consumer of music in the nation, the Society demanded in addition to its fee a share of radio station revenue. Its argument was that since ASCAP music was largely responsible for radio entertainment—and hence the money paid in by sponsors—it should be rewarded accordingly.

Independent radio stations protested vehemently, but the networks signed a contract giving ASCAP 2 per cent of sponsor revenue for 1932, 3 per cent for 1933 and 4 per cent for 1934. Independent station owners continued to denounce "the oppression of the music front" at each annual convention of the National Association of Broadcasters.

In 1934 NAB was prevailed upon to get the United States Department of Justice to haul ASCAP into court on charges of violating the anti-trust law. The case wes suddenly shelved after a few weeks of trial because the Government's special counsel, Andrew Bennett, found that he did not have enough evidence to go ahead.

Frustrated, NAB then instructed its managing director, Jimmy Baldwin, to insist upon a special clause in its next contract with ASCAP. That clause would compel the Society to collect its fees directly from the networks, on network commercials. But while Baldwin cooled his heels in a suite at the Hotel St. Regis, New York, waiting to hear from ASCAP's president, Gene Buck, the networks shrewdly worked fast and signed a five-year contract with Buck that raised the payoff of ASCAP to 5 per cent annually. The first that the astonished Baldwin heard about this was when the networks sent out wires to their affiliates announcing that all, because of the new contract, would have to be licensed by ASCAP.

Furious, NAB hired Andrew Bennett away from his Government job to become the spearhead and strategist of a campaign of harrassment against ASCAP. The campaign resulted in lawsuits in eight state courts; hostile legislation in every state where it was possible to get it; and three tussles before the United States Supreme Court. The fight cost ASCAP almost a million dollars, not including the loss of revenues from the states of Washington, Montana, Nebraska and Florida, where NAB had won out. Despite these headaches, ASCAP cleared $6,950,000 in 1939, of which $4,300,000 represented radio revenue. By 1951 *ASCAP's* music license fees from all sources, including television, was nearer the $14,000,000 mark.

Neville Miller succeeded Baldwin as managing director of the NAB. After examining the fruits of the organization's struggle with ASCAP, he then let it be known that he was prepared to sit down with the Society and discuss a new contract. But misunderstanding of the arrangement for such a conference led to no conference—and mutual recriminations. ASCAP let it be known that its next contract would include a direct fee derived from all network revenues, rather than just sponsor income.

bmi vs. ascap   CBS decided to pitch its lot in with the predominantly independent-run National Association of Broadcasters. It suggested to the NAB that the only way to lick ASCAP was by building a musical reservoir of its own, which radio could draw upon. And it lent one of its lawyers, Sidney M. Kaye, for the purpose of forming a rival to ASCAP called Broadcast Music, Inc., yclept BMI. The first step in this maneuver was the leasing by BMI of the Edward B. Marks Music Publishing Co. catalog for $1,250,000.

ASCAP watched with amused contempt, confident that BMI would prove a flop. ASCAP had the nation's top tune writers, publishers and songs in its pocket. BMI had nothing but third-string songs and talent, and classics like "Jeannie With the Light Brown Hair," which was played several million times during 1940. But NBC, after hesitating, joined CBS and the NAB in boycotting ASCAP tunes from sustaining shows.

Variety stayed neutral, running battle stories in which both sides were given equal space to tell their stories, to make and answer accusations. Among the accusations made by ASCAP prexy Gene Buck was his charge that NAB had, out of spite, engineered his arrest as a fugitive of justice from the state of Arizona—"a state I had never visited in my whole life"—an example of the legal persecution and skullduggery being carried on against ASCAP. The outcome of the battle was still undecided when the curtain rang down on 1940.

payolas—again   Songplugging with bribes, the bane of the industry since Variety had come on the scene in 1905, was still a headache throughout the 1930s. Pluggers themselves realized, in 1934, that if publishers could get their songs plugged merely by sending along a $10 bill to orchestra leaders or singers, there would be no need to employ songpluggers for the same work.

So the music "contact men"—fancy for pluggers—themselves set fines of between $1,000 and $2,000 for any plugger or publisher found guilty of bribery to obtain plugs. Lou Diamond, head of Famous Music, Inc., a Paramount subsidiary, used the raw knuckles approach, threatening that if any competitor tried bribery, he would subsidize a bribery campaign of his own to the extent of $100,000.

Variety presented a composite picture of the songplugger at work in 1937. "Every new song becomes 'the greatest ballad we ever had,' or the 'greatest score Berlin ever wrote.' . . . That's where the personality comes in. That's where nights of carousing, days of golfing, sessions at a beach club, great manifestation of care and worry about this or that radio act or band's welfare, stand the personality song contact men in good stead."

Plugging also called for "gigoloing on the side." As Variety explained, "The gal warblers may cotton to this or that contact man who knows how to buy them an interesting lunch or dinner, and manages to step a nifty dance set as a coincidental social grace . . ."

That payoffs were still very much in evidence by 1938 was indicated by the sudden interest of the Federal Trade Commission in the problem. The FTC advised ASCAP that bribery for plugs was definitely an unethical business practice, and that the close ties between Tin Pan Alley and Hollywood entailed "subsidies" which were in effect paid for plugs. FTC pointed out another subtle method of bribery—the appearance of bandleaders' names on music as "co-authors." This obviously gave bandleaders a financial interest in the success of certain songs. ASCAP promised to check up on name-singer or bandleader "co-authors" to ascertain whether the collaboration was genuine, or just a cut-in.

The growth of the American Society of Composers, Authors & Publishers was a reflection of the boom in music through post-1933. In 1934 Decca of London invaded the American market with Jack Kapp, former general manager of Brunswick, as its president. The music business began to move uptown into Radio City. First Tin Pan Alley resident on Rockefeller soil was Marty Bloom, who became the first music publisher in the business without a piano. The Rockefellers wanted no disturbing noises on their dignified premises. But as more and more of Tin Pan Alley moved in, the ban was broken, and pianos banged merrily from Remick and Witmark, Marks, Chappell, Fox and Harms.

ASCAP, the Music Publishers Protective Assn. and the Post Office joined hands to war against mail-order racketeers who were swindling some $2,000,000 annually from would-be songwriters. ASCAP's guns were also trained on the peddlers of 5¢ song sheets containing unauthorized reprints of song lyrics. The situation became confused when the M.P.P.A. made a separate deal for "authorized" lyric sheets.

Variety reported the musical favorites of Japan that year, finding Beethoven on top of the list, followed by geisha songs and Japanese jazz. But two years later Variety was gratified to note that the best-selling record in Tokyo was "St. Louis Blues," trailed by "Sweet Sue." Japan was getting more "American-minded."

Something new entered the American music world in 1935 with "Muzak"—or wired radio. The process was developed as early as 1922 by a Belgian engineer. By the time it was introduced into America, it was already serving 66 per cent of the populations in Belgium and Holland by home subscription. The foreign service fee was high—$20 a year.

Muzak agreed to pay ASCAP a 4 per cent split of profits, and began to rent out its "wired music" to restaurants, niteries and hotels, which paid for the service on a basis of customer capacity. For home set owners, the tariff was set at between $1.50 and $4.50 a month, depending on the type of channel desired. Its big attraction was that it would offer continuous music, with no advertising and only the briefest of announcements.

During 1935, piano sales shot up 40 per cent—prosperity was returning—and sheet music sales zoomed accordingly. Royalties for the performance of music were estimated at $4,000,000 for the year. From then on until the close of the decade, music was a seller's market, with a climax reached in 1938 through the *Snow White* songs. The Disney numbers sold over 1,500,000 disks and 1,000,000 copies of sheet music.

In the next decade the music business was to experience more new trends. For one thing, ASCAP suffered a second Consent Decree, this time at the hands of a group of New York exhibitors known as the ITOA (Independent Theatre Owners Assn.) They balked at paying a double music tax, i.e. for the film synchronization and a seat tax for their theatres, and the Government upheld them.

Meantime, however, new horizons via television asserted themselves and by midcentury ASCAP had exceeded the $10,000,000 gross annual revenue, and AA writers saw $18,000-$20,000 annual dividends. For a topnotch songsmith this was tantamount to a $1,000,000 annuity at a 2 per cent yield. As Billy Rose once told the editor of Variety, "Of all the worldly goods I have and can leave Eleanor (Eleanor Holm; Mrs. Rose) is my ASCAP income. It pays out like a gold mine."

With the second Consent Decree there were new mathematical hurdles for the songsmith in that the "current usage" of a work became an important method for calculating income. Thus the "country club set" within ASCAP, as some of the old-timers were labeled, could not rest on their laurels but had to return to creating or reactivating their old and new songs, because their compensation was so closely tied to a payoff predicated on a continuing current usage of their songs. In turn, the new "payoff on performances" system skyrocketed the dividends of Irving Berlin, Cole Porter, the Gershwin Estate, Richard Rodgers and Oscar Hammerstein, 2d, to $35,000-$45,000 a year.

Meantime BMI moved forward and in the post-World War II era, where nostalgia and a yen for the folksy music asserted itself, many an obscure BMI publisher enjoyed the top hits, and both the big league ASCAP writers and publishers found themselves eclipsed.

Dance band styles, too, reverted to the smooth and sweet; bebop died aborning; balladeers like Bing Crosby, Vic Damone, Frank Sinatra, Perry Como, Frankie Laine, Gordon MacRae, and smooth songstresses like Dinah Shore, Doris Day, Jo Stafford and Margaret Whiting sold records into the millions.

48

World's Fair—and Overture to War

★

Chicago opened its Century of Progress Exposition in May of 1933. Costing $38,000,000, it ran for two years, with an interruption between November and May of 1934. Chicago show business enjoyed a boom, with night clubs and beer gardens spending $150,000 weekly for talent. The 16,000,000 visitors enabled the Exposition to pay off all of its bondholders.

Top gravy of the Exposition went to the Greyhound Bus Co., which took in $1,647,000 with its sightseeing "yap wagons." The Union News Co. earned $1,301,000 with souvenir postcards. And the rest-room concession, with the fee set at a nickel—to the outrage of out-of-towners—earned $862,000 in five months.

There was a spree of expositions in 1936, with an estimated $200,000,000 being spent by Dallas, Fort Worth, San Francisco and New York. Overseas the following year, the International Paris Exposition was the outstanding tourist draw of Europe.

In 1939 San Francisco beat New York to the punch and opened the Golden Gate International Exposition in February. But the big expo event of the decade took place two months later on the 1,216 acres of Flushing Meadows—the New York World's Fair, which opened to a first day's business of 600,000 payees.

New York hotels and theatres, which expected a tremendous boom in business as result of the Fair, were dismayed by results of the first few months. Tourists weren't arriving in the expected numbers. Most came with thin wallets, staying at the Fair all day, and returning to their hotels too tired to do anything but rest their feet or sleep. The few who had enough reserve energy to patronize night clubs were quickly voted by waiters as the "two bit" trade.

Broadway night life was further hurt by the flocking of its usual patronage to the fancy restaurants in the foreign "pavilions" at the Fair for dinner. This trend didn't last long, when New Yorkers discovered that the French, Belgian, Italian, Brazilian and other pavilions charged exorbitant prices for inferior meals. They were further antagonized by poor, and frequently insolent service.

Not until June did Broadway feel any of the promised benefits of the Fair. Then the New York *Daily News* editorialized, "The Fair, which at first almost knocked the props out from under the New York theatre and night club business, is now pulling in enough customers from outside to furnish encouraging gate receipts to both the Fair and Broadway. We're more than glad to note this justification of the confidence of those who always said the Fair, for all its $150,000,000 investment, would be a paying proposition for New York City in the long run . . . It was admittedly one of the greatest shows ever put on in the world."

The most successful attraction at the Fair was Billy Rose's Aquacade, which earned $1,000,000 net profit during the Fair's first year. The aquamarine amphitheatre seated 10,000 at a price scale of 40¢-83¢-$1.10. Variety called the show, which starred Johnny Weissmuller, Eleanor Holm, Morton Downey and Gertrude Ederle, with a cast of over 500, "the greatest spectacle in the history of show business."

The biggest show of the San Francisco Exposition was Sally Rand's "Nude Ranch," which did $40,000 a week, top-grossing attraction of the Fair midway.

growth of outdoor show biz When the nation began to have some money in its pocket, and moved outdoors again in 1934, the outdoor show business rejoiced. State and county fairs showed increased grosses of between 50 and 85 per cent, while circus receipts rose 33 per cent over 1933. The growing boom revived hundreds of carnivals, and pitchmen were once again barking their way into three squares a day. Small truck and wagon shows began to roll through the countryside.

The Tom Mix-Sam B. Dill show, moving in General Motors trucks, grossed handsomely. Al G. Barnes brought his show back to California with $150,000 in profits. Ringling's show had one of their best years, contributing heavily to the $75,000,000 record chalked up in 1934 by all of outdoor show business. Even the fake

Cardiff Giant, which had earned $200,000 before being exposed as a hoax made of gypsum rather than an exhumed ancient giant, returned after 20 years to tap the cash customers.

Two new notes were introduced in 1936. "Auditorium circuses" gained a four-months' winter route—playing special organization dates for the Shriners, American Legions and others. And at Dobbs Ferry, New York, an outdoor showman borrowed a rodeo stunt: baseball played on donkeys.

In 1937, a banner year for circuses, the Ringlings paid off the Manufacturers Trust Co. to regain control of the Big Top. There were 350 carnivals in action, scooping an annual $100,000,000 at beaches, parks and fairs. Madison Square Garden, however, guessed wrong that year with a Carnival of Champs, offering four fights for the price of one. The loss tallied $30,000.

The Garden was soothed the following year when Sonja Henie opened her ice revue, clicking profitably with an opening night audience of 16,000. When she returned there in 1940, the advance sale was $200,000, with the Garden jammed every night. In 1939 the Garden offered something new in Rodeo—cowgirls, most of whom were the daughters of well-known ranchers. And in 1940 the Ringling-Barnum & Bailey circus racked up the record boxoffice of $52,000 in a single day.

more commercials   Show business found a strong new route opening during the 1930s—the private enterprise circuit. More and more, business firms found that by utilizing the glamor of show business, they were able to attract crowds to their goods and services.

In 1934 Macy's opened a talent booking bureau for parties. Hearn's department store booked a Fancho & Marco unit. Standard Oil of New Jersey paid Guy Lombardo and his band $10,000 a week for a tour of big city auditoriums. The price of admission was simply a driver's license—Standard Oil charging the stunt off to select-group advertising. Theatrical pressure forced Standard Oil to call it off. The theatres feared that it would set a precedent for other big corporations to offer free shows as part of their advertising budgets.

In 1935 Philip Morris Cigarettes hired Marshall Montgomery, a vaudeville ventriloquist, to tour the better hotels and cafes as an innocent-looking guest, while putting "Call for Philip Morris" into the air. The new Liggett drugstore on Broadway and 42d Street turned its opening into an all-star show, with Benny Leonard as emcee.

Almost every United States department store today goes in for Christmas showmanship; in fact merchandising is another name for showmanship. Today there is more cheesecake in intimate apparel and depilatory advertising than would be countenanced in connection with out-and-out show biz attractions. The brassiere industry is a good example. But in that era Gimbel's was pioneering when it toured a reproduction of Barnum's Museum, freaks, animals and all. Macy's annual parade is now a New York civic institution.

In 1936 a Los Angeles brewery presented a vaudeville show, charging bottle caps for admission. And in 1950 the latest 20th-century style medicine show booked was the $350,000 one toured by Louisiana Senator Dudley J. LeBlanc, headed by Mickey Rooney and Connee Boswell, admission, one Hadacol boxtop which nostrum the Senator manufactures at Lafayette, Louisiana. For more limited spots, where Hadacol invades a new potential market, Senator LeBlanc has booked such "extra added attractions" as Jimmy Durante.

The depression years gave industrial (or commercial) films their biggest hypo. Automotive, oil, tobacco, harvester and kindred industries paid film exhibitors on a basis of per-1,000 seating capacity, per performance, for exposing their audiences to pix plugging certain products. Sometimes these films were one-minute celluloid commercials, and sometimes they were well-made industrial shorts so sugarcoating the trademark or the commodity being exploited as to be downright educational and entertaining. Lucky Strike made 1937 a big year for commercial shorts by producing some that were good enough to be shown in some of the country's best theatres. By 1938, industrial films had 6,000 playdates, and were a $20,000,000-a-year business.

A grocery chain in Hollywood started using vaudeville acts in 1937, offering "two-a-day" with stars. Variety pondered this phenomenon as the possible beginnings of a new "carrot circuit." Wholesale grocers and food distributors, in time, borrowed this idea with real name acts to glamorize their conventions. One New England food distrib paid Amos 'n' Andy $12,000 and Edgar Bergen $10,000.

This same grocery wholesaler was eventually to go in for a glorified banknite or giveaway, with automobiles as door prizes, in lieu of the talent lure.

Among the other oddities of show business noted was the first rooftop skating rink on Broadway, opened in 1933 by Philadelphia Jack O'Brien above Roseland. In San Francisco that year, the Tai Chug Wah Theatre on Jackson Street was still going strong after 66 years, dramatizing current events in China at $2.50 top. The Walnut Street Theatre in Philadelphia, America's oldest legitimate playhouse, was reopened in 1937 for Yiddish films. The Morro Castle wreck in 1934 was turned into a performance by Asbury Park, which sold postcards, peanuts and popcorn to visitors who came to gaze at the hulk.

the church and show biz   Church figures played their usual active role in show business of the 1930s. Aimee Semple McPherson started the ball rolling with a personal at the Capitol Theatre, New York, for which she received $5,000 the week of Sept. 26, 1933. Covering the event, Variety remarked, "She wears a white satin creation—sexy but Episcopalian." Despite the gown, the Capitol dropped $20,000 on the week's business.

The church's heavy hand made itself felt that year through the act of the New York censors in clipping the Fox short, "Pirates of the Deep." The scene objected to was the love life of the clam —and the film had to be released with its romance scissored.

The church, which had been fulminating against the immorality of films for several years, blew up in 1934 and went into action. "Undesirable" films were placed on blacklists, and pledges solicited all over the country for membership in the newly-organized Legion of Decency. In Philadelphia, the Catholic Church slapped a boycott on all film theatres, regardless of their attractions. Alarmed, Hollywood producers began to scrap or re-shoot films. The Motion Picture Producers & Distributors Association took stock of the situation, and decided that no film would be released unless it had been certified 99 44/100 per cent pure by Joe Breen, the industry's censor.

But the church refused to call off its watchdogs. Throughout the decade there was constant friction between the theatre and church over what was art—and what was smut. In 1936, Oklahoma

City, which had never banned or blue-penciled a play or film in its history, balked at the touring *Tobacco Road* company.

The following year the church, needling the New York legislature, succeeded in sneaking through the Dunnigan Bill, which would have given one man the power to decide what New Yorkers should or should not see. All of show business became suddenly aroused and united behind the cause of defeating the bill. Every New York newspaper editorialized against it, influencing Governor Herbert H. Lehman finally to veto and kill it. The only organization fighting hard for the bill was the Knights of Columbus.

The church had its axe out in 1938 for the Mae West burlesque of the Adam and Eve legend over NBC. The red-faced network made meek apologies, although the skit was actually the brainchild of the J. Walter Thompson ad agency. But when the church shot arrows at Eugene O'Neill's *Beyond the Horizon,* so many respected names in literature and the drama came angrily to its defense that the church discreetly dropped the hot potato.

In 1939 the church joined parents in attacking radio's programs for children, taking a sideswipe at the same time at films—both for exciting youngsters with crime stories. A decade later this campaign took an encore with television.

Radio's biggest headache with the church was centered in the figure of one cleric—Father Coughlin. Radio found itself caught on the horns of a dilemma—how to shut up Coughlin without being accused of denying him freedom of speech, and without alienating a large, if lunatic fringe, following. In 1939 Coughlin was finally banned by the National Association of Broadcasters, which cited his word-for-word parroting of Nazi propaganda.

sime dies in 1933   The era was marked by the passing of some truly show business greats. When the founder of Variety, possibly the most influential and best-loved man in the amusement industry, died in 1933, the nation's press eulogized Sime Silverman.

A relatively unknown great, because he so shunned the limelight, the dailies ran laudatory editorials on his integrity, courage—and the unique living monument that he left as a perennial reminder of his special journalistic genius.

That same year saw the passing of that unique product of the Prohibition era, Texas Guinan; scenic artist Joseph Urban (who designed most of the opulent Ziegfeld musicals), Fatty Arbuckle and at age 73 the great matinee idol of an earlier era, E. H. Sothern. Death also took author Ring Lardner, and from the sports world, Jim Corbett, William Muldoon and Jockey Tod Sloan.

In 1934 show business lost producer Charles B. Dillingham and Otto Kahn, who had angeled many Broadway productions. The year also saw the passing of Rockefeller's top publicity consultant, Ivy Lee, who originated the idea of John D.'s dime giveaways. At the age of 77 death took Maggie Cline, once known as "The Irish Queen" and "Brunnhilde of the Bowery," whose most famous song was "Throw 'Em Down, McCloskey."

Will Rogers was killed in 1935 while flying with Wiley Post in Alaska, his death mourned deeply and personally by all of show business. De Wolfe Hopper also died that year, at 77, the same span of years which claimed the New York *Times'* Adolph S. Ochs.

The movies led the obituary list of 1936, with the deaths of Metro's production genius, Irving Thalberg, at 37, and its one-time great star, John Gilbert, at 38. The great showman Roxy passed on at 53, and Alexander Pantages at 65. Marilyn Miller died at the age of 38, Madame Schumann-Heink at 75. (The great opera star was accorded a military funeral.) Other deaths of the year included John Ringling, last of the seven famous brothers, and Alexander Glazounoff, composer of "The Volga Boatman."

gershwin and ravel   Music lost George Gershwin, at 38, in 1937, and Maurice Ravel, composer of the "Bolero," at 62. The theatre lost playwrights Samuel Shipman, John Drinkwater and Sir James Barrie; stage stars William Gillette and Mrs. Leslie Carter, and producer Winthrop Ames. The films lost actress Jean Harlow and oldtimer Joseph Jefferson (J. J.) McCarthy, who started film road-shows by touring *Birth Of A Nation* at a $2 top. Vaudeville lost S. Z. Poli, pioneer New England vaudeville man, and James McIntyre, of McIntyre & Heath, most famous of all oldtime blackface acts. Tom Heath died one year later, at the age of 85. Other deaths of 1938 included the widely syndicated columnist O. O. McIntyre, at 54, and Ben Harney, pioneer of ragtime music, at 66.

In 1939 the films lost Douglas Fairbanks, who died in his sleep at the age of 55, Alice Brady at 47, Carl Laemmle at 72 and Ford Sterling, an original Keystone cop, at 56. The Fourth Estate lost

Heywood Broun at 51, and Floyd Gibbons at 52. The stage lost Fay Templeton at 74 and noted Jewish actor Boris Thomashefsky, whose death at 71 was the occasion for wide East Side mourning. Ernie Hare died at 55, evoking memories of 1921 when, as "The Happiness Boys," Billy Jones and Ernie Hare, were radio bywords. The year also saw the passing of noted magician Horace Goldin, at 65, novelist Zane Grey, at 74, and musician Hugo Riesenfeld at 60.

The opera was the greatest sufferer through deaths of 1940. Gone were Giulio Gatti-Casazza, impresario of the Metropolitan for 27 years, who died at 71; opera star Luisa Tetrazzini, at 65; Italian tenor Alessandro Bonci, at 70; and violinist Jan Kubelik at 60. The films lost Tom Mix, who died in an auto accident at 69, leaving an estate of less than $115,000; and film pioneers Dick Turpin and Flora Finch, both at 71. Vaudeville lost a pioneer, Martin Beck, at 73, and the stage its "grand old man of show business," Daniel Frohman, at 89. Other deaths of the year included Dr. Paul Nipkow, television inventor who conceived the idea over 50 years before, at 80; and Ernest Thayer, author of the famous "Casey At the Bat," at the age of 77.

the roll of drums   Throughout the 1930s, the muffled overtone of war could be heard "offstage." The noises grew more disturbing each year, but America, enjoying a resurgence of prosperity and new security under the New Deal, preferred to concentrate its attention on the home front—until the bombs of the Fascist nations were too loud to hear the strains of "God Bless America" in comfort.

In 1933 Hitler, then the new Chancellor of Germany, was a curse at the American boxoffice. An anti-Hitler film made in Belgium was offered to New York exhibitors for three months, but nobody wanted to touch it. *Kultur,* a play ridiculing the German aversion to culture, laid a quick egg on Broadway. *Germany In Flames,* a Jewish production with a star cast, fo'ded in five days. In that year of depression, the American people had too much trouble with the wolf at the door to worry about the wolf at other peoples' doors.

Nevertheless, the first Hitler gags began to sneak into vaude and night club turns. A typical bit of business called for one actor to put his hand on his hip effeminately, while the other cracked, "Ah, a Hitlerite!," a reference to the notorious homosexuality rife in top Nazi ranks.

In 1934, Variety reported that night life in Nazi Berlin was at a standstill. Drinks at $1 and cigarettes at $3 a pack spelled no tourists—and no tourists spelled no night life. Ben Beyer, an American comedy cyclist, booked a month's stay at the Scala, Berlin, in 1936, explaining that he expected the Hitler regime to be defunct by that time.

In 1936 Mussolini, who had appeared three years earlier in a Columbia release called *Mussolini Speaks,* appropriated several million dollars for films that glorified war. The following year, with the Japanese end of the Axis alienating Americans by slicing into China, Hollywood stopped using Chinese villains—or at least used Chinese actors, but labeled them Japanese.

1938 was radio's big year—the year of the Anschluss in March, and Munich in September. The growing significance of political events in Europe began to dawn upon most Americans, who turned to their radios for enlightenment. Radio, sensing what was expected of them, turned from straight newscasts to political analysis. Commentators such as Fred Bate in London for NBC, and Ed Murrow for CBS were rapidly catapulted to fame.

War scares and excitement speeded the tempo of radio's growth from an entertainment medium to the nation's watch-tower. H. V. Kaltenborn, at the mike all day and all night, sleeping on a cot at CBS, became a household name. Max Jordan, Maurice Hindus, William Shirer and others sent their voices 3,000 miles across the Atlantic to inform an anxious American public.

Hitler's Nuremberg address of September 14, 1938 broadcast and translated over the networks, caused a nation-wide sensation. Radio's first-hand reports helped inspire the resolution of leading theatrical organizations and stars calling for a boycott of all trade with Germany. Concessionaires cashed in on the rising tide of anti-Fascism by putting Hitler's face on the old African Dodger game, and did a huge business with Americans who itched to bean Der Fuehrer with a speed ball.

Because of America's jumpy state of nerves—for which radio was unwittingly responsible—the Orson Welles radio scare succeeded much more brilliantly than radio executives expected. It also pointed up sharply the trust and reliance the American public had grown to place on radio, which made it now a kind of quasi-public service.

radio's new stars   The outbreak of war in 1939 placed newscasters and commentators in the category of show business stars. Each had a tremendous following, which tuned in faithfully for its own favorite. Undoubtedly much of the commentary was flash stuff, and even misleading, but on the whole the American public was well informed. Aid to England would have been a dubious American possibility if the nation's sympathies and horror had not been aroused by overseas broadcasts.

War news came so fast that year, one station's announcer actually said, "We interrupt this flash to bring you another flash!" Short-wave listening increased vastly, with newspapermen among the more eager dialers. The increasing excitement of the night hours also attracted new sponsors to late time slots which once had been impossible to sell.

It came as something of a shock to the American public in 1939 to hear over their radio some of the distortions and lies being aired from Fascist European capitals. It made United States dialers appreciate their own radio—with all its commercial shortcomings—more than ever before. It also convinced set owners that radio had an obligation to keep off the American airwaves United States counterparts of the poison peddlers rampant in Europe.

The movies joined the anti-Fascist crusade in 1939. Warner Bros. produced *Confessions Of A Nazi Spy*. Fritz Kuhn, head of the German American Bund, fruitlessly sued for $5,000,000 libel, claiming, "We are loyal Americans organized to uphold the Constitution of the United States."

Interest in world events catapulted lecturers into top pay brackets. Mrs. Nicholas Longworth received $1,200 a talk; Eve Curie, $1,000; and Dorothy Thompson was too busy to accept $3,000 for a night's engagement. Hitler had a depressing effect on the business of Arizona Indians, who blamed him for a sudden drop in the sales of Navajo blankets, which bore old Indian designs that too closely resembled the Nazi swastika.

In the London of 1939, the Cocoanut Grove Night Club issued handbills announcing, "Open as usual. Approved air raid shelters. Refreshments and dancing from 10 p.m. by special request. Special arrangements for officers in uniform of H.M. Forces. P.S.—The safest niterie in London."

Radio was the show business standout through all of 1940—the crucial year of the Battle of Britain. It was radio, rather than news-papers, which kept a tense American public informed—almost at the moment of happening—of the collapse of Holland, Belgium, France; of the fall of Neville Chamberlain and the rise of Winston Churchill.

Radio contributed memorable on-the-spot descriptions of historic happenings—an achievement which later gave CBS the idea for its "You Are There" radio series, projecting listeners backward in time as it covered famous events in history, just as radio had covered them in 1940.

The British Broadcasting Corp. recorded a shot-by-shot descrip-tion of the air battle over the Strait of Dover, the climax of the Bat-tle of Britain. Radio covered the evacuation of Dunkirk, the bombing of Coventry, the scuttling of the *Graf See*. And it stimulated Amer-ican recruiting by the shortwaved sounds of gunfire and explosions over London.

Commentators found their jobs growing increasingly perilous. Fred Bate, of NBC's Victoria Embankment offices, was wounded by a bomb fragment. Ed Murrow of CBS was twice blasted out of his London offices. Max Jordan was forced to do more of his broadcast-ing from Switzerland and less from Germany. William L. Shirer, Eric Severeid, Quentin Reynolds, Bill Downs and W. L. White were among the other commentators running the war gauntlet with a mike in one hand.

On this side of the ocean, commentators took the fragments of news pouring in and shaped them into meaningful designs for their listeners. Among the analysts whose names grew more famous daily were Elmer Davis, Raymond Gram Swing, John B. Kennedy, Paul Sullivan, H. V. Kaltenborn, Edwin C. Hill, Gabriel Heatter, and Boake Carter.

The drama of war via radio inspired American film stars to donate ambulances which raced through London bearing the names of their donors. Generosity of a somewhat less admirable calibre was demonstrated by audiences of the film theatres in the German York-ville section of New York City who responded when the hat was passed for the Nazi Winter War Relief Fund.

And then the overture was finished, and the curtain was set to go up on the Big Show—once again.

PART SIX

BIG SHOW
1941 - 1945

49

Soldiers in Greasepaint

★

War work created a vast audience of Americans with a yen for entertainment and the means to pay for it. Booming defense industries made every night a Saturday night for show biz.

The nation buzzed with the noise of workers shedding white collars, and housewives shedding aprons, to pick up blowtorches and fat pay envelopes. To stop the traffic congestion on 6th Avenue, New York City ordered all employment agencies to list their job offerings inside, rather than on boards facing the sidewalk.

Actors on the road found it increasingly tough to get hotel accommodations. They were competing on one hand with defense workers moving into big cities, and on the other with the ever-increasing trade conventions. New floods of profits made their way principally to Miami, which had clothed itself in the garb of the French Riviera. Government funds, disguised as defense contract profits, oiled the gambling casinos, niteries, fashion salons.

While the Japs were mopping up in the Pacific—including American bases—newspaper readers devoured such tidbits that Mae West had won a divorce from Frank Wallace, whose 1911 marriage to her had lasted two weeks; and that Al Jolson's brother Harry lost a suit for $25,000 against Al, presumably representing the $150 a week Harry claimed Al had promised him for staying off the stage. Jolson again made news by marrying Erle Chennault Galbraith, niece of General Chennault, and 40 years his junior. She was an X-ray technician in the hospital where the star convalesced following his serious illness incurred in North Africa where he entertained our troops. It almost cost Jolson his life and cost him his left lung. This was an episode in *The Jolson Story* and *Jolson Sings Again,* both unusual in the rich history-making career of the great American star in that (1), it set a new pattern for filmusicals where a great star's voice was matched to a younger personation of the stellar subject, in this instance Larry Parks, of course; and (2), it was the first time that a pix biog had a sequel. Jolson was to repeat history for the third time by becoming the first big name to fly to Korea to sing for the United Nations troops in the fall of 1950. He died shortly after his return from the battlefront, "as much a war casualty as any GI," said the War Department which awarded him the Medal of Merit posthumously. Jolson's will was a dramatic, democratic document wherein he split his more than $4,000,000 estate equally to Jewish, Protestant, and Catholic charities, after setting up scholarships for needy undergraduates, a $1,000,000 trust fund for his widow, and $500,000 trusts for his two adopted children.

In 1943, the year the Allied forces invaded Italy and knocked Mussolini out of the war, Charles Chaplin's marriage to playwright Eugene O'Neill's daughter Oona also made news.

In 1945, the Allied year of victory, these tidbits further leavened the news: Peggy Hopkins Joyce's fifth marriage and Gloria Swanson's fifth divorce. The latter, five years later, was to make a signal comeback in Paramount's *Sunset Boulevard* film. Shirley Templ' marriage to John Agar made readers suddenly feel their age, although their subsequent divorce three years later was to spell box-office downbeat. George Jessel, who was accumulatively to earn the soubriquet of Toastmaster General of the United States for his yeoman after-dinner speechmaking through the length and breadth of the country, formally notified radio networks that he was "not amused" at the avalanche of radio comedians' gags about his private life and child brides. The only exception, he noted, was that anything Eddie Cantor or Fred Allen quipped about him was OK with him.

winchell vs. isolationists   Meanwhile; Jessel's and Cantor's fellow-alumnus of a Gus Edwards "School Days" act, yclept Walter Winchell, was slugging the isolationists on his broadcasts. Three Montana stations dropped his program, for which Winchell blamed isolationist Senator Burton K. Wheeler. In 1943, the Andrew Jergens Co. ("with lotions of love"), worried about their $5,000-a-week hot potato, tried to tone Winchell down, but he refused. The following year he tore into Martin Dies of the Un-American Activities Committee, then confounded that gent by letting him go on the Winchell program for a 15-minute rebuttal of Winchell accusations.

The power that one man on radio could wield was demonstrated in 1945 when Winchell advised listeners to sell stocks and not get stuck when the crash came. The market promptly broke. Winchell didn't quite mean it that strongly, and thereafter was more cautious about his prognostications. More affirmatively he sparked the Damon Runyan Cancer Fund, collecting $5,000,000 for cancer research, which is still going strong. In turn, fellow columnist Ed Sullivan became active in promoting the Heart Fund, while the Alfred J. McCosker-Harry Hershfield Cardiac Home was a continuing charity, as spark-plugged by the former WOR-Mutual Network board chairman and the veteran newspaper columnist-cartoonist. Incidentally, Jergens' caution about Winchell notwithstanding, it upped his $5,000 fee to $7,500, and successive sponsors, Kaiser-Frazer and Richard Hudnut, with their $12,500 fees made Winchell's $1,000-a-minute the record high compensation on the radio, considering that his 15-minute Sunday night newscast reduces to 12½ minutes net, after opening, middle and end commercials.

The dime-dance-and-romance philosophy, an outcropping of

America's defense program, suddenly froze on the day of December 7, 1941. The news was so stunning that theatre managers and night club owners forgot, for a while, to notice that the boxoffice was dead. It stayed dead for several weeks, while the nation strove to get its bearings. The impact was too strong and overwhelming to escape via entertainment—that would come later.

Top showmen offered their services to the Government as dollar-a-year men: Others, notably Elmer Davis and Robert E. Sherwood, went to Washington to take part in hemispheric defense work. Billy Rose staged a giant benefit at Madison Square Garden to help the United Services Organization (USO) raise $10,000,000. A check for $100,000 went to the USO for troop entertainment, signed by Edward G. Robinson.

Actors readily agreed to managers' plans for paying off 25 per cent of their salaries in Government bonds. Philadelphia film houses charged aluminum pots and pans as the price of admission. Broadway opened the first Stage Door Canteen, a tremendous hit with GI's, and provided free theatre tickets which earned New York the reputation as the nation's "friendliest city" in Army circles.

uso-camp shows   USO-Camp Shows received a $500,000 appropriation, later raised to $800,000, which started nine out of 24 proposed Army shows rolling. Each camp show unit was paid between $2,500 and $3,000 a week for its 28 to 30 members. The first two-hour touring unit opened at Camp Upton, New York, on a percentage basis, with 20 per cent of the gross going to the post exchange fund. This show offered a 10-girl orchestra plus an 8-girl dance chorus. The first legitimate unit for the camps was *My Sister Eileen*. The first Army show produced by soldiers was a satire called "The Wizard of Ord" by soldiers at Fort Ord, California.

England's equivalent to the USO—E.N.S.A.—was supported by Government funds, rather than public subscription. Top salaries paid actors were $80 a week, with the minimum set at $16, plus transportation and board. Prime Minister Churchill drafted Gracie Fields for an American fund-raising tour. In 10 weeks of one-nighters in the United States and Canada, she raised $302,000 for British War Relief. In London during the same year, Bebe Daniels and Ben Lyon introduced a song called, "Thanks Mr. Roosevelt," to convey British appreciation of the President's aid to Britain. *ENSA* stood for the Entertainments National Service Association.

Variety's editor summed up what show biz was doing for the war in 1942 with some unabashed sentiment: " 'Morale,' it is called, from the front line to the home front. Morale means entertainment; entertainment means making a heavy heart lighter—a strained day of work or warfare just a shade brighter. The man at the front is sustained by a song on his lips; the men and women on the home front, ceaselessly twisting bolts and riveting steel, are bolstered by a laugh. To dwell on 'morale' may be something akin to corning a cliché, but whatever its label, it's entertainment—and entertainment is Show Business."

Glum news from the fighting fronts dented the Broadway b.o. during spring and summer, making New York "a weekend town." But the weekends were big, Saturday night crowds reminiscent of New Year's Eve. The war made Sunday performances permanent on Broadway, which helped ease the blow suffered by the blackout of all New York marquees.

Getting around the Main Stem became increasingly difficult. All Broadway traffic lights were hooded in dimout covers, showing only slits of light. Tire restrictions, anti-parking regulations, air raid and blackout precautions, gas rationing all helped to scare away the out-of-town trade. Thursdays were particularly glum because of the blackout tests from 9:00 P.M. to 9:20 P.M. MAIN STEM A GHOST ALLEY, headlined Variety. MAZDA LANE HAS SHOT ITS WATTS.

With war plants going on a 24-hour basis, midnight shows became popular throughout the country. The road, despite all the crippling restrictions and delays in travel, began to enjoy a huge revival.

topical stuff   The gagsters began to reap a harvest of new corn. Old jokes were refurbished with new topics—impudent waiters, gas rationing, the omnipotent butcher, priceless nylons, the vanishing servant, rationed tires, rubber salvage and meatless Tuesdays. Broadway knew it was at war when it saw femme cabdrivers.

Show business continued to furnish a heavy share of the nation's top taxpayers. Out of 3,000 Americans who paid taxes on over $25,000 a year, 800 came from show business. The $25,000-a-year ceiling for earnings caused a minor panic in Hollywood, where some stars conceived the idea to finance their own units to get out from under via a "capital gain."

On the patriotic side of the ledger, Equity announced in 1942 that 25 per cent of its membership was already in uniform. Equity bestowed on each of its soldiers and sailors a subscription-for-the-duration to Variety, which furnished a special rate.

The Stage Door Canteen, set up by the American Theatre Wing in the basement of the 44th Street Theatre (the old Little Club), which the Shuberts donated rent free, became famous in 1942 as the mecca for any man in a uniform. Buttons popped along the White Way when Mrs. Roosevelt declared it was the finest of all contributions toward war morale. Branches popped up in Washington and Philadelphia, and finally the Hollywood Canteen opened in a blaze of klieg lights. Stars came not only to entertain but also to wash dishes.

Theatres helped in the junk salvage campaign, collecting scrap iron, copper, brass, zinc, aluminum, lead, rubber, rags, manila rope and burlap. The United Theatrical War Activities Committee enlisted disaster units of singers, dancers and comics, prepared to rush into any bombed zone of New York to help victims. The Criterion Theatre, on Broadway, turned its lobby over to selling "Crack-A-Jap" cocktails for a dime apiece—the cocktails being glasses of water plus a 10¢ defense stamp.

Abe Lastfogel, Marvin Schenck and Howard Dietz took up an idea started by Winchell, and staged a Navy benefit show at Madison Square Garden. Boxes went for $1,000 apiece, seats at $16.50 top. Sales of a 55-page souvenir program netted $35,000 alone. The one performance earned $142,000, an all-time record for any one-shot theatrical performance. Show business also united in the Army-Navy drive for relief collections, and helped garner the lion's share of over $2,000,000 raised.

this is the army   The show business sensation of 1942 was Irving Berlin's soldier show—*This Is The Army*—sequel to his World War I *Yip Yip Yaphank*. It opened on the Fourth of July for a 4-week date, but the demand for tickets was so overwhelming that it stayed on Broadway for 12 weeks, averaging $47,000 a week.

Yaphank in World War I had grossed $83,000 in its 4 weeks' stay in New York at $2.20 top. It was primed to build a barracks for actors visiting Camp Upton's Liberty Theatre, and didn't go on any road tour. *This Is The Army,* in its three years on tour, plus revenues from the Warner Bros. movie version, turned over to the Army Emergency Relief Fund almost $10,000,000—the most fabulous fortune earned by one show, and easily the biggest private gift ever turned over to the United States Government. In time Uncle Sam honored Berlin with the Legion of Merit.

Canadian Navy Relief had its own service show; the British staged theirs abroad also, although its E.N.S.A. units in Australia and other South Pacific outposts contributed most of the morale entertainment. Moss Hart staged the ambitious *Winged Victory* for the Army Air Force; there was a Coast Guard special musical revue, and others.

uso camp shows—the new big time   The USO Camp Shows circuit of 1943 was the new bigtime—bigger than even vaudeville in its heyday. The combined USO tour offered an act seven years of playing time—if it were possible to play the whole circuit. With a $14,000,000 budget, the USO was spending $100,000 a month for soldier entertainment. Bert Lytell, on a civilian committee advising the organization, drew only $8,000 in expenses for the full-time job. It was largely through his counsel that soldiers at Fort Meade, Maryland, were given a chance to see *Macbeth*—and to the amazement of the camp's top brass, asked for "more of that Shakespeare stuff." Subsequently, Major Maurice Evans' streamlined version of *Hamlet* proved a big hit with the GIs in the Pacific areas.

Kay Kyser was one of the camp circuits' most energetic adherents, giving a record 1,700 shows in service bases. When commended for this patriotic duty beyond call, he cracked, "It's not only fun, but where else can I get meat?"

Mayor LaGuardia unveiled the service flag of show business in Times Square during 1943. It showed 135 gold stars, and 78,808 members in the armed services. President Roosevelt paid further tribute to the patriotism of show business at a Madison Square Garden benefit for the Red Cross.

Show people put on a testimonial show called "Theatre People's Dedication To A Cause" at the Winter Garden, paying tribute to actors entertaining soldiers at home and at the fronts, and to the USO-Camp Shows' victims of that plane tragedy at Lisbon.

During 1943 actors began to perform in factories during lunch hours as a morale stimulant to war production. In San Francisco, film theatres ran help-wanted trailers and slides for shipbuilders; and the Frisco Stage Door Canteen made its debut, as host to over 9,000 service men. The nation's writers sent their scripts to the Writers War Board, and gags, skits and blackouts were made available to soldiers for their own entertainment.

In the 1943 bond-selling ranks, Kate Smith led all the others with a total of $37,000,000 worth to her credit—a good share of which was paid for the privilege of listening to "God Bless America." Ralph Edwards was the next strongest bond salesman, with a radio record of $34,000,000. To help raise $17,000,000 for Camp Shows and foreign war relief, Ben Hecht packed them into Madison Square Garden to see "Tribute to Gallantry," a pageant with 300 in the cast, depicting the struggle of the world's little people against barbarism.

zoot-suiters   There was also a liquor shortage, which led to a 10:30 P.M. curfew of saloons and liquor stores. Harlem had some riots over the early shutdowns. The general dimout of New York itself stimulated crime. Teen-agers, left to shift for themselves by overtime fathers and factory-working mothers. turned to zoot suits, flagrantly loud and overlong costumes introduced by Mexicans in Los Angeles, as a method of winning the attention they were being denied in their homes. Zoot suits soon became associated with juvenile delinquency. Zoot-suiters, aided by "zooterinas," plagued theatre managers by slashing seats and defacing restrooms.

The teen-age crime wave was not limited to New York or Los Angeles. A spree of pyromania broke out in theatres all over the country, almost all of it traced to youthful vandals, who were particularly active in Pittsburgh. So many juveniles were stealing into theatres via side doors and fire escapes that managers were forced to put up signs outside these exits warning that breaking in was a Federal offense, because of the failure to pay the Federal amusement tax.

The boxoffice was so big in 1943 that it completely disregarded the usual seasonal limitations. Grosses for Holy Week, instead of taking its traditional drop, actually exceeded normal biz. There was a slight letdown at matinee performances, but this was attributed to the effects of victory gardens and women going into factories.

The star branch of 1944 show business was legit. The American Theatre Wing, at the request of Army heads, prepared and financed an Army production of *The Barretts of Wimpole Street* (with Katharine Cornell) and turned it over to USO-Camp Shows. This was followed by Ruth Gordon's *Over 21,* and 22 other legitimate shows. They were designed to play both the United States camps and the foxhole circuit overseas. Show business won new applause when famous stars donned the USO uniform and went to the Pacific and the E.T.O. to entertain troops near the fighting fronts.

cantor's 'purple heart circuit'   That year Eddie Cantor created the "Purple Heart Circuit." Actors toured hospitals to perform at the bedsides of sick and wounded soldiers. There were also a large number of "Lunchtime Follies" troupes, which provided noon entertainment in factories for factory workers. Kate Smith stuck to her bond sales division, a year after her 1943 record of $37,000,000, making Washington dizzy by selling $108,000,000 worth in just 18½ hours of singing and plugging. Eddie Cantor's bond drive turned in a total of $40,000,000 sales in 24 straight hours.

Al Jolson, knocking himself out playing bond rallies and hospitals, felt a little bitter about some of his colleagues who continued to "fight the Battle of the Brown Derby" in Hollywood. He felt strongly, as Harry Lauder did that year, when the great Scots entertainer refused a fat offer for his film biography by explaining tersely, "This is no time for private gain."

The O.P.A. travel ban of 1944 hit show business where it hurt. New York theatres were silent, but the city's hotels squawked when Mayor LaGuardia asked vacationists to stay away from New York. The year was one of stringencies—paper shortages for newspapers or theatre programs (many New York dailies had to turn down many columns of advertising); cigarette shortages; and few of the other things Americans had learned to do without since Pearl Harbor. Liquor began to reappear in stores, but a bottle of Scotch was still coin of the realm in buying favors or scarce goods.

Show business, almost to a man, backed Roosevelt for a fourth term, and showed it at a New York rally to urge his re-election. Some show business figures decided to run along with him. In California movie actor Albert Dekker, radio commentator Hal Styles, and Melvyn Douglas' wife, Helen Gahagan Douglas, ran on the Democratic ticket and won state and Federal offices.

Show business was still helping to write American history in 1945, the year of victory. Comedian Joe E. Brown, whose son had been killed in the war, was presented with the Bronze Star for his tireless work in entertaining front-line troops in the Pacific. Abe Lastfogel, head of USO-Camp Shows, received the Medal of Freedom for outstanding service.

Show business put its shock troops once again into the job of putting the 7th War Bond drive over. *Here's Your Infantry,* a pageant put on at the Yankee Stadium, sold over $10,000,000 in bonds. Broadway legitimate theatres—16 of them—arranged special matinees for purchasers of war bonds. The best seats were awarded according to the scale of the bond . . . from $25,000 to $25. The unions contributed their services for the matinee gratis. In New York, 23 department stores took page ads in the New York papers to plug the shows, which chalked up 19,100 individual sales. All of show business that year joined, in honor of the late President Roosevelt, to put over the March of Dimes. Some 13,000 theatres helped raise over $5,000,000 for paralysis sufferers.

With their jobs done, the Broadway and Hollywood Stage Canteens closed their doors, to great applause. Show business also revealed that during three years of war, over 9,000,000 free tickets to shows had been given to servicemen—only 35 per cent of whom had ever seen live entertainment before. Although the gesture was intended generously, there was no doubt but that it had also served as a sampling campaign, whetting the appetite of a new young audience for the legitimate theatre.

V-J Day on Broadway, with all motor traffic stopped by the police, provided a colorful spectacle which even show business at its most ingenious couldn't equal. Four years of worry, waiting and inhibitions exploded in wild jubilation. While in New York harbor the first boats from the Pacific were bringing home troops.

Almost overnight the cry rose all over the land, "Bring 'em all home!" Politicians made hasty promises, but the Army, which knew better, called on show business again to help keep things in hand. It wanted all the second-hand saxophones, trumpets and trombones it could get for use overseas—anything that would blare or bleat.

In one week it garnered 700. If GI Joe had to lay in his foreign bunk, sweating out transportation, he could at least blow his brains out dreaming of a white Christmas.

Radio Goes to War

★

During 1940 and 1941, prior to Pearl Harbor, radio found itself exalted to new heights as the nation's forum for important discussions of our foreign policy. With as many as 30 or 40 million listeners tuned in simultaneously, the spoken word gathered a tremendous new importance. While the world at war waited anxiously for America to make up its mind, Americans turned to their radios to have their minds made up for them.

The networks had to be careful to maintain an unbiased position —that of the owner of a great hall who rents it out for a debate. Hollywood could and did take the initiative in making anti-Fascist and pro-British films. Radio could not—without raising a storm of protest from isolationist listeners. Radio had no legal right to propagandize on the air, which belonged to the American people, and was only allotted to them by the F.C.C. It did the next best thing and offered freedom of speech for all viewpoints—reasoning correctly that the Fascist line was bound to lose out in free competition with the pro-Allied cause.

The events of December 7, 1941 automatically ended "the great debate." But before they did, Charles A. Lindbergh had made the mistake of unpolitic remarks in Des Moines, Iowa, in 1941. Almost immediately, Station WOR refused to give him any time unless he dropped his pro-Berlin accent, an example followed by many other stations. Hard-hitting radio commentators sarcastically asked Lindbergh to prove his disaffection for Hitler by melting down the medal the Nazis had awarded to him in 1938.

The Lindbergh issue, and heated debates over forum programs, led one Massachusetts state senator to introduce a bill dealing with radio slander. It was killed because, explained Senator Blanchard, "slander never hurt anybody."

Radio was the vehicle of many historic broadcasts throughout 1941, up to and including December. In May listeners heard Stephen Vincent Benet's classic, "Nightmare of Noon," and Carleton Morse's "The Case of Robert." In August there was the star-studded "Treasury Hour." On December 2, there was Archibald MacLeish's "Introduction of Murrow." On the 7th, the unforgettable news broadcasts. On the 9th, President Roosevelt speaking on Pearl Harbor. On the 15th, Norman Corwin's "Bill of Rights." And on the 26th, Winston Churchill's address to the United States Senate. This was radio—a new, adult radio—in 1941.

Station WMCA, New York, won commendation that year with its program, "Listen America Now," designed to foster the spirit of fraternity and tolerance among youngsters. The show contained one blue-ribbon line, spoken by a boy: "If you don't like another kid, don't call him dirty names because of his race. Just shout, 'You're a stinker'!" That pretty well summed up the case for democracy.

With radio's new maturity came a growing appreciation by sponsors of the worth of its advertising time. The industry net rose staggeringly from $44,296,000 in 1940 to $107,500,000 in 1941. This despite the cancellations by some advertisers, especially in the cosmetic line, who could not get essential ingredients for their products. Jack Benny's 10th year on radio was celebrated by his friends with a special congratulatory section in Variety.

Major Bowes, after nearly 1,000 weeks on the air starting in 1922, finally bowed out.

All of radio chipped in to plug United States bonds, and were credited with much of the $707,000,000 sales record chalked up by June of 1941.

The war made a number of changes in radio the following year. All request song numbers were dropped by programs, Army brass fearing that the titles might contain enemy codes. Sirens were eliminated on all programs, to prevent any listener's confusion, à la the famous Orson Welles broadcast. Weather reports were eliminated for fear of giving vital information to enemy air forces.

603 radio war shows   A count showed 603 war shows on the networks—202 newscasts, 173 war commentaries, and 54 others with a martial overtone. One program, beamed abroad in collaboration with the Office of War Information (O.W.I.) overseas branch, gave "News From Home"—keeping a small-town flavor, talking about minor league baseball, rural politics, and hot music. It was radio's way of making the small-town boy feel closer to home, wherever he was.

Radio's boxoffice bulged in 1943 with the four networks earning $150,000,000 in billings—an all-time high. The prevailing trend, despite the war—or rather, because of it—was humor. Top comedy scripters, once hat-in-hand as ad agency executives spelled out terms, now dickered like full-fledged stars. Quiz shows came back, with announcers who played them heavily for laughs—Ralph Edwards, Phil Baker, John Reed King, Bob Hawk, Bill Slater, Paul Douglas, Kay Kyser, Parks Johnson, Bill Cullen, Warren Hull and Garry Moore.

The church was not slow to cash in, via radio, on the resurge of religious feeling in the nation, as a result of parental worry over boys in the service. Variety estimated the church collection, via appeals over the airwaves, at $200,000,000 a year, and noted the program listings of local stations as top-heavy with religious shows. "The church," it concluded, "has become big biz in radio." Gospel broadcasting paid the Mutual network its biggest individual revenue —$1,566,130—with programs like "The Pilgrim Hour," and "Old Fashioned Revival Hour" beamed to 211 stations.

Variety itself went radio in 1943, when Philco sponsored its "Hall of Fame," a one-hour show. Variety selected the cream entertainment, a kind of Hit Parade of all show business, with the top names appearing before its mike. Show biz grinned as it turned to the radio reviews in the paper, and while Variety liked its own first show very much indeed, some of the later ones came in for considerable panning. Variety's editor, Abel Green, was co-producer and co-author of the weekly Philco-"Hall of Fame" presentations.

Other radio notes of 1943 included the appointment of Paul Whiteman as musical director of the Blue Network; the bowout of the kiddies' Uncle Don from WOR after 18 years; and Pepsi-Cola's anguished demand of all radio comics to stop using its product as a target for radio tomfoolery.

For its war record that year, radio contributed $6,500,000 worth of free time to plug the Second War Loan. The following year radio shelved millions of dollars' worth of revenue to go all-out for coverage of D-Day, radio's biggest story in its history. This didn't prevent another record-smashing year—$383,900,000 in 1944, of which the $250,000 spent by Republicans and Democrats for vote-snaring was merely pin-money.

Censorship reared its head in 1944 when Eddie Cantor was cut off the air while singing "We're Having a Baby (My Baby and Me)," excerpt from his legit musical, *Banjo Eyes*. The "objectionable" lyrics ran:

GIRL: *Thanks to you, life is bright, you brought me joy beyond measure.*
CANTOR: *Don't thank me, quite all right, honestly it was a pleasure.*
GIRL: *Just think—it's my first one.*
CANTOR: *The next one is on me.*

Sponsors were summarily off the air left and right during 1945, when history claimed their air time. Within several weeks there was news of the atomic bomb, the Russian declaration of war against Japan, and V-J Day. When the Japanese surrender was official at 7 P.M., Aug. 14, 1945, radio was prepared. All of its programs and facilities were turned over to complete and full coverage of the significance of events.

Prior to V-J Day, world news also crowded out paid radio time. There was the death of President Roosevelt in April, with a three-day mourning period. The month also produced the San Francisco Conference, demanding radio coverage, and in May—V-E Day. Commercial radio was blitzed out of its time slots to the tune of $500,000 network loss.

The most important dramatic broadcast of the year was Norman Corwin's V-E Day "On a Note of Triumph," a beautifully-written summation of the war and its significance, and a jewel in the diadem of radio's 25th anniversary.

Variety noted that year the progress made in radio by women entertainers, either solo or in double harness. The lack of male talent, increasingly serious as the war progressed, found the women taking on the burden of network shows, and carrying them successfully. Among the outstanding radio women of 1945 were Kate Smith, Joan Davis, Dinah Shore, Ginny Simms, Gracie Fields, Arlene Francis, Judy Canova, the Andrews Sisters, Fanny Brice, Charlotte Greenwood, Hildegarde, Mary Small and Beatrice Kay. They accounted for much of the $46,864,000 talent cost for 1945, which was $7,000,000 higher than for 1944.

There were no new exciting personality discoveries, although ex-Mayor LaGuardia proved a radio find at $3,000 a week, after first clicking over the municipal-owned WNYC Sunday morning broadcasts by reading the funnies. Ex-Police Commissioner Valentine of New York also took to the airwaves. One wag suggested that before any candidate for New York City office was seriously considered, he would first pass an NBC audition.

video's 1941 brushoff The progress made in television that year was mostly in the words department. "Make every theatre a pari-mutuel outpost," suggested Thomas F. Joyce, vice-president of RCA. "Houses can be connected with racetracks by television so that patrons can see better than if they were in the grandstand. They can open a pari-mutuel window to accept bets, just as is done at the track. It would provide the Government with added sources of taxation."

The New Yorker Theatre, at a cost of $30,000, rented tele equipment, including a 15 x 20 screen to televise the fight between Billy Soose and Ken Overlin at the Madison Square Garden, which used a pink canvas for the event. An audience of 1,200 watched, complained of eye-strain, declared the pictures were not as clear as the newsreels.

The first rate card was issued to sponsors for television in 1945. Charges included $120 for a weekday evening hour, $60 for a weekday afternoon hour, $90 for an hour Sunday afternoon. News, weather and time spots called for $8 a minute evenings, $4 a minute during the day. There was also a production charge of $150 an hour for the use of large studios, $75 an hour for smaller ones. Five years later a *TV* network hour came to $20,000-$25,000, depending on the number of outlets.

First sponsors (for NBC) were Sun Oil, Proctor & Gamble and

Lever Bros., who put their plugs on video baseball games that emerged in a blurry and indecisive manner.

In 1943, Dumont's W2XWV televised entertainment from night clubs under the title: "Wednesday Night Session." The first live show in 16 months for NBC's New York outlet, WNBT, was a video version of the Madison Square Garden rodeo. With only one camera riding with the broncos, the camera work was unimaginative. Reception was clear when there was little movement in the arena—but when the cowboys were letting 'er rip, the result was a series of blurred shadows.

NBC, which had been granted the first commercial tele license by the FCC in 1931, maintained a limited schedule of weekly broadcasts of films, sporting events and modest studio stuff during 1944. Chicago's WBKB that year televised the first video show produced, written and directed by service personnel—a Navy show, to sell war bonds. Variety, seeing the handwriting on the wall—even if it was just the back wall—inaugurated a television department in its format.

The largest audience to view a tele show up to 1945 was on hand for NBC's preview of long distance video hookups. The Curtis Publishing Co. picked up the bill for a telecast of the Army-Navy game in Philadelphia, which went out to viewers in Philly, New York and Schenectady.

But the end result of this phase of the kilocycle era was evidence in plenty that radio had come of age. It did a terrific job for morale, and proved just as vividly successful in projecting direct contact between Government and the people, whether it was President Roosevelt's "fireside chats" or directives and other "messages" integrated into the more popular radio scripts. It set the pattern for information not only within our own borders but around the world whenever a crisis called for beaming direct to the masses. Thought control by totalitarian ideologies can never be wholly regimented under such auspices.

51

New Stars Are Born

★

The first impact of the war on Hollywood was newsreel censorship. The Navy cracked down on shots of naval vessels under construction, forcing their deletion despite newsreel executives' protest that no secrets were revealed.

Senator Nye opened up on Hollywood from Washington, charging —before Pearl Harbor—that the movie moguls were "guilty" of "warmongering." December 7 provided a belated and ironic vindication of Hollywood's allegedly "premature" anti-Fascist stand. Senator Nye had no harsh words for Germany, whose Nazi propaganda film *Lowland Blitzkrieg,* was playing at Yorkville's 86th Street Theatre. While anti-Nazi German-Americans picketed the theatre, anyone showing a membership card in one of the "approved" organizations was offered free admission.

The new high war taxes made stars less ambitious. Many, instead of working for dollars they couldn't cling to, cut their schedules and divided their time between loafing and playing benefits. The new taxes were estimated to be costing Hollywood an extra $55,000,000 a year. Despite this, Hollywood helped raise $2,000,000 for various war charities—20 per cent of the quota for the whole Los Angeles area.

Principal trend of the 1941 films, to relieve the grimness of newspaper headlines, was comedy—low comedy, of which Abbott & Costello were undisputed top dogs. Close behind them as boxoffice favorites were Bob Hope and Mickey Rooney, with Bette Davis clicking in the drama division. One of the year's top grossers was a Technicolor outdoor yarn, *Northwest Mounted Police.*

The year's most unusual film was Orson Welles' *Citizen Kane,* which outraged William Randolph Hearst, who took it personally and forced as many theatres as he could to boycott it. Hearst's rancor against the film was so great that Hollywood feared Hearst would blast the entire movie colony because of it.

Academy laurels that year went to Joan Fontaine for her role in *Suspicion,* and to Gary Cooper for *Sergeant York*. The Academy film award went to *How Green Was My Valley* and its director, John Ford. Other credits were divided among *Here Comes Mr. Jordan* (Robert Montgomery), *Citizen Kane* and Walt Disney's *Dumbo*.

The National Archives in Washington that year received 53,840 cubic feet of historical records—everything from film shots of the Coolidge and Hoover administrations and World War I activities to sound recordings of 60 Indian tribe dialects and sign languages, Amos 'n' Andy and the Columbia Workshop.

During 1942 stars were coaxed out of their "why-should-I-work?" attitude by some sage producer arguments. In the first place, said the producers, stars owed it to their public—were they going to be dollar patriots? In the second place, if the stars refused to go before the cameras often enough, they risked having the public forget them. The stars saw the light, $25,000 salary limitation or not.

peak pix attendance   Film audiences had never been so large as they were in 1942—an estimated 90,000,000 a week, all prosperous on defense paychecks. Hollywood was feeling prosperous, too. The total film gross for 1941 had tallied $1,100,000,000—or just $100,000,000 better than for the preceding year. Calamity howlers among the executives who mournfully predicted that the new 60-hour work week would prove disastrous to the pix biz shut up.

Benefits proved booby-traps to many Hollywood stars. A star who had played perhaps a dozen in one week, and who begged off a 13th, was frequently threatened with stigmatization as "unpatriotic." To ease the situation, a special bureau was formed to "assign" benefits to actors, and all requests had to clear through this bureau.

One of the amusing transformations made by the war in Hollywood was the sprucing up of Russian characters in films. Until 1942, movie Russians were either wild comic characters, evil menaces, or hopelessly inept stooges. With Russia our ally, the Russians shown by Hollywood were quickly shaved, washed, sober, good to the folks, 100 per cent family men, Rotarians, Elks, and 33° wowsers.

Leading the boxoffice parade of 1942 were Gary Cooper, Abbott &

Costello, Betty Grable, Mickey Rooney, Bob Hope, Dorothy Lamour, Spencer Tracy, Jack Benny and Bing Crosby. Greer Garson won acting honors for *Mrs Miniver,* while James Cagney carried off the male Oscar for impersonating George M. Cohan in *Yankee Doodle Dandy*—the first film biography of a then still-living show biz prominent. Jerome Kern also lived to see Metro's *Till the Clouds Roll By,* a more or less loose biopic of his career; and another Metro filmusical, *Words and Music,* was based on the careers of the late Lorenz (Larry) Hart and the very much alive Richard Rodgers (now so successfully teamed with Oscar Hammerstein 2d.) Topping all, of course, was Columbia Pictures' *The Jolson Story.* That, with its sequel, *Jolson Sings Again,* again gave the fabulous Al Jolson the edge on any show biz cycle.

Nostalgia and sentiment about famous or distinguished show business figures inspired a host of filmusical biographicals. Irving Berlin says he'll never have his biopic made during his lifetime since he counts upon that as an important heritage for his family when he passes, although the 20th Century-Fox filmization, *Alexander's Ragtime Band* in 1938, was misconstrued by many to be a loose version of his career. There have been and will be biopix based on the life and times of Paul Dresser, Dan Emmett, Oscar Hammerstein I, Will Rogers, the late Bert Kalmar & Harry Ruby, Eddie Cantor, Marilyn Miller, Sime Silverman (*Mr. Broadway,* written by Abel Green, for Warner Bros.), Nora Bayes & Jack Norworth, Fred Fisher, Texas Guinan, Gus Kahn and Joe E. Howard.

Others winning cinematurgical distinction were Van Heflin for his work in *Johnny Eager,* Irving Berlin for his song, "White Christmas" (part of the *Holiday Inn* score); and Walt Disney for his short, "Der Fuehrer's Face."

By 1943 Hollywood began to feel the pinch of the loss of male talent—stars as well as the men behind the cameras. But to its own amazement the loss did not seem too important. Second-rate films, with second-rate stars, cleaned up. First-rate films continued to set new records. Films without any stars wound up with over $2,000,000 rentals. One of the major companies found it had grossed $16,000,000 on just six fair films.

flock of indie producers   The Hollywood gold mine brought independent producers into action by the dozens. Many reasoned, correctly, that with the $25,000 salary limitation, stars could be coaxed away from major studios by percentage deals and shares in film proceeds, which could be spread out over a longer period. But early in 1943, Congress tossed out the salary ceiling, and the inducement of the independents lost its punch. They went ahead nevertheless, with or without stars.

Hollywood lost 29,000 men to the armed services. Of these, only a handful were important b.o. names, but those few stars represented hundreds of millions of potential ticket sales. To offset their loss, major studios began to pay higher prices for plays and books, as well as studio scripts, to give weaker star names strong support at the boxoffice. Older film stars, whose lustre had faded, were dusted off and thrust before the cameras again. Simultaneously, all studios engaged in a vigorous talent hunt. "God makes stars," said Samuel Goldwyn. "It's up to the producers to find them."

Among the new stars to emerge were a dog, Lassie; a horse, Flicka; and an elderly actor, Charles Coburn, who was to win an Academy Oscar for best support in *The More The Merrier.* The year also produced Jennifer Jones in *Song of Bernadette,* Paul Lukas in *Watch On the Rhine,* and Katina Paxinou in *For Whom the Bell Tolls* (Ingrid Bergman-Gary Cooper), all of whom won Academy awards. William Saroyan's *The Human Comedy* (Mickey Rooney-Frank Morgan), Norman Krasna's *Princess O'Rourke,* Irving Berlin's *This Is the Army* and Frank Sinatra's RKO short, *This Land Is Mine* also got nods from the Academy.

Female stars enjoyed a tremendous war worker and soldier vogue, with their cheesecake photos in high demand. Pin-ups of Betty Grable, Dorothy Lamour, Lana Turner, Jinx Falkenburg, Hedy Lamarr and Donna Drake headed the list of stills, many sold for 50¢ apiece. And their male following packed their films, even when admission prices were boosted an average of 28¢ during the year.

Hollywood's policy of building skyrocket stardom for newcomers, to replace the missing old faces, paid off handsome dividends in 1944. Older stars, who had stuck to their guns about laying off after one or two films a year, because of taxes, began to regard their laurels anxiously as the public demonstrated its enthusiasm for new faces.

Metro's Van Johnson and Frank Sinatra; 20th-Fox's Jennifer Jones; Sam Goldwyn's Danny Kaye; Warners' Lauren Bacall, were the new hot stuff.

Among the new ingenues were 20th Century-Fox's June Haver; Paramount's Diana Lynn and Louise Allbritton.

RKO gave its all to Sinatra (on a split contract with Metro), build-him with *Higher and Higher* and *Step Lively,* and lending him out to Metro for *Anchors Aweigh*. Metro also came up swimmingly with Esther Williams.

Academy honors, however, were reserved for the established stars that year. Crosby walked off with the Oscar for his blithe priest in *Going My Way,* and Ingrid Bergman for her slow torture in *Gaslight*. Ethel Barrymore won recognition for her moving supporting role in *None But the Lonely Heart,* and Barry Fitzgerald for his support of Crosby in *Going My Way*.

hollywood's morale job   With the West Coast the important staging area that it was for the GIs going to the Pacific fronts, Hollywood and San Francisco had an important function in the war entertainment formula, particularly the glamor-loaded Hollywood. The Hollywood Victory Committee did a particularly laud-able job in rotating top names to Veterans' Hospitals as well as training camps. Shows ran from the portable jeep variety—a mobile stage on a jeep, with portable mike, an emcee, guitar player, comic and/or singer, and the like. Sometimes a harmonica player substituted for the guitar. Writers mobilized by making plays and playlets, comedy skits and joke files available to one and all—the touring professionals and for self-entertainment by GI talents in the camps.

Hollywood was also winning recognition that year for its morale service in supplying films for the fighting fronts. Many a GI was tickled to reflect, as he sat on an oil can in a coconut grove in the Pacific, that he was watching a film premiere before it had even reached Broadway. GIs sent home amusing stories of the reactions of island natives who watched the first films they had ever seen with a mixture of awe, terror and fascination.

In recognition of Hollywood's service, the Government issued a special postage stamp, honoring the 50th anniversary of the industry. The design showed GIs and WACs looking at an open-air screen on a South Pacific island.

Films played an historic role throughout the war in helping train raw recruits in record time through Government shorts, which were an integral part of training camp curriculum. At the close of the war they served another Government purpose—evidence at trials of Nazi criminals. Atrocity films were also released for general distribution in the United States, inspiring renewed demands for a tough peace.

Hollywood turned out two fine pieces of work that year, for which the movie colony won handsome recognition. The first was a 10-minute reel called *The House I Live In,* in which Sinatra punched home the lessons of democracy and anti-discrimination to his teen-age following. The second was *The Lost Weekend,* which won the Academy Award, and inspired a new approach toward chronic drinking as an illness, rather than a matter of moral turpitude.

The major studios revealed that they were spending $3,000,000 a year in salaries to employees in the service—including the ubiquitous Mickey Rooney, whom Uncle Sam tapped in 1945.

new film czar   Eric Johnston was appointed the new head of the Motion Picture Producers & Distributors Association, succeeding the original film "czar," Will H. Hays, and Jean Hersholt succeeded Walter Wanger as head of the Academy of Motion Picture Arts & Sciences. Oscars for 1945 went to Joan Crawford as *Mildred Pierce,* and Ray Milland for *Lost Weekend.* Supporting Oscars were won by Anne Revere in *National Velvet* and James Dunn in *A Tree Grows in Brooklyn.*

Hollywood ended the war in its best financial shape. Films were grossing $480,000,000 a year, of which the domestic take was $310,-000,000, with film rentals bringing in $6,250,000 a week. Oddly, despite this sensational showing, and the top money being earned by film theatres, no showplace of World War II could top the record of the old Roxy, back in August of 1929, which garnered $164,600 with the Edmund Lowe-Vic McLaglen film, *The Cockeyed World.*

But Hollywood, at the close of the war, was jubilant at its overall record—with few prophets predicting the downbeat to which the industry would be plunged in a few brief years.

52

Legit and Nitery Boom

★

Defense spending brought a boom to "the road"—the market for the living theatre outside of New York City. Legit's most distinguished ladies lost no time in making tracks through a hinterland newly paved with gold. Helen Hayes, touring in *Victoria Regina,* grossed some $2,000,000, topping the record for the decade past. Katharine Cornell, however, held the record for the most frequent road engagements over the same 10-year period.

The third femme fave of 1941 was Katharine Hepburn, whose tour with *The Philadelphia Story* garnered $753,183 in 32 weeks on the road. This compared impressively with the $961,665 the show had earned during its 52-week Broadway engagement.

Tallulah Bankhead hit the road with *The Little Foxes,* playing 121 stands, of which 104 were one-nighters. For this grueling engagement, the plum was $649,820, or about $25,000 higher than the show's earnings during its hit Broadway run.

Lynn Fontanne and her husband Alfred Lunt took the Pulitzer Prize play, Robert E. Sherwood's *There Shall Be No Night,* on the road for a 40-week cleanup of $800,000. Only the outbreak of the war stopped them short of the $1,000,000 mark. Paradoxically, the play was woven around a pity-poor-Finland theme, with Russia the heavy of the piece. Everybody concerned wanted to forget it hastily when Russia was suddenly our ally, and the Pulitzer Prize choice for 1941 became a national embarrassment.

That phenomenal play, *Tobacco Road,* which confounded the critics to run for seven and one half years on Broadway, finally closed May 31, 1941. During its historic run, it had had about 70 weeks in the red, and 42 during which it broke even. Hitting the road, the show took in three to four times its New York receipts.

George M. Cohan took *I'd Rather Be Right* on the road, after a Broadway grab of $986,904, and rolled up another $691,512 on a limited tour, smashing his own records for the road engagements of *Ah, Wilderness.*

Loose cash was so plentiful in the hinterland that the summer stocks and the strawhats cleaned up some $3,000,000 in 1941. Chicago's Auditorium, formerly the home of the Chicago Civic Opera Co., took in the Olsen & Johnson madhouse, *Hellzapoppin,* and found that uproar paid off much more handsomely than arias.

Although Hollywood was being cautious about putting money into Broadway productions, the pix biz shelled out $2,290,000 in 1941 for screen rights to current and previous season's hits.

Governor Lehman struck a blow at the Shuberts that year by signing a bill forbidding theatre managers to refuse admission to any critics or columnists who bought tickets. New York *Post* columnist Leonard Lyons, himself an ex-lawyer, engineered the statute as retaliation against an old Shubert custom of barring out too captious critics. Alec Woollcott, Heywood Broun, Winchell, Lyons and others have variously been targets of Shubertian spleen.

The New York *Daily News,* for no particular reason in 1941, ran a poll to select the greatest actresses of all time. The poll was taken among 49 leading actors and actresses, and the honored actress was Eleanora Duse. Sarah Bernhardt won five votes, Mrs. (Minnie Maddern) Fiske four, Mrs. Sarah Siddons three, and Ethel Barrymore, two.

Three years later six New York critics were asked to name the First Lady of the Stage. Three of the six, Robert Coleman, Burton Rascoe and Ward Morehouse, nominated Ethel Barrymore. Said Coleman: "Her name is synonymous with the stage." Said Rascoe: "She is the epitome of the theatre at its best." Said Morehouse: "Years of active stardom." He tossed in an illegal, nostalgic vote for Maude Adams as well. Burns Mantle and John Chapman gave the nod to Helen Hayes. Howard Barnes split his vote three ways— Barrymore for voice, Cornell for personality, Hayes for technique.

Perhaps as a result of the war, 1942 was an off-year on Broadway, with 54 flops and only six genuine hits. Hollywood cut down its purchases of screen rights to $1,200,000. Straight plays were given the edge over musicals. The Pulitzer Committee passed up giving any award, but the critics voted Judith Anderson in *Macbeth* and Burgess

Meredith in *Candida* as the season's best performances.

Although Sunday performances on the road were big boxoffice events through 1942 and 1943, the road began to feel the pinch of war in 1943 because of gasoline shortages and travel restrictions. The gasoline ban ruined the one-nighters, as well as stock and straw-hats. Cars stayed in garages, and ticket money in pants pockets.

'oklahoma!' & co.   But Broadway legit went into high in 1942-1943 with the unveiling of *Oklahoma!* which was to be the musicomedy high mark until Richard Rodgers and Oscar Hammerstein 2d were to top themselves eight years later with the phenominal *South Pacific* (Mary Martin-Ezio Pinza). *Oklahoma!* didn't depend on its players as much, although it did project Celeste Holm and Alfred Drake, who went on to new heights in Hollywood and on Broadway with the successive seasons, the latter proving particularly scintillating in *Kiss Me, Kate.*

Other leading 1943 shows were the *Ziegfeld Follies* (Milton Berle-Ilona Massey-Arthur Treacher), Mike Todd's Cole Porter musical, *Something for the Boys* (Ethel Merman-Allen Jenkins-Betty Garrett-Bill Callahan-Murvyn Vye); the anti-Nazi play, *Tomorrow the World,* by James Gow and Arnaud d'Usseau, starring Ralph Bellamy, Shirley Booth and Skippy Homeier as the hateful Nazi youth.

Two revivals in the heavy money class were *Othello* (Paul Robeson-Uta Hagen-Jose Ferrer), and *The Merry Widow* (Jan Kiepura-Marta Eggerth).

The season also saw the dream of every legit manager—a single-set show with a three-person cast, and a smash hit—*The Voice of the Turtle.* John van Druten's comedy had the proper amount of spice for the matinee trade, and Margaret Sullivan, Elliott Nugent, and Audrey Christie made the most of their script opportunities. Moss Hart was represented on Broadway also that year with his war show, *Winged Victory,* the Air Force's answer to *This Is the Army.* Among the GI cast were Lee J. Cobb, Edmond O'Brien, Danny Scholl, Barry Nelson, Marc Daniels, Zeke Manners and Peter Lind Hayes who were to become more prominent in later civilian pursuits in Hollywood, legit, radio and niteries.

The Critics' Circle and the Pulitzer Prize committee were again at odds over the season's best. The former favored Sidney Kingsley's *The Patriots* (Madge Evans was featured in her playwright-husband's play along with Raymond E. Johnson, House Jameson and Juano Hernandez), but the Pulitzer trophy went to Thornton Wilder's *The Skin Of Our Teeth,* which boasted a cast including Tallulah Bankhead, Fredric March, Florence Eldridge, Florence Reed and Montgomery Clift. *Teeth* had a long Broadway run but was a dismal flop on the road; lasted a week only in Boston and folded.

A freak long run was reported from the Coast where an ancient morality meller on the evils of intemperate tippling, *The Drunkard,* was cleaning up by playing for ten-twent'-thirt' laughs—but at $1.75 and $2.25 prices. With an "olio," beer and pretzels, *The Drunkard* at this mid-century writing has lasted 18 consecutive years, almost 6,500 performances, over 2,000,000 customers who have consumed almost 4,000,000 bottles of beer. Jan Duggan and George Stuart of the original cast, along with Jackson Swales, the house pianist, are still with it. Mildred Ilse is the present producer; Gail Bell conceived the "revival" idea on July 6, 1933. *Life With Father* holds the legit long-run record with 3,224 performances. Incidentally, *The Drunkard,* when it was first produced at the Boston Museum in 1844 and ran 140 performances, had this authorship credit: "By W. H. Smith and a Gentleman."

Business was so good on Broadway in 1944 that not even a new Federal admission tax of 20 per cent—twice the old tax—could hurt the b.o., which showed a gain of between 10-15 per cent over the previous season. This was all the more remarkable in an election year, which traditionally cut into theatre revenues.

Billy Rose and Ben Marden took over the Ziegfeld Theatre, and then Rose bought his partner out for $100,000. He livened up the 1944 season with a champagne premiere of *The Seven Lively Arts* at $24 a seat. By shrewd publicity and advertising, the show had $350,000 in advance sales before the curtain went up, almost enough to underwrite it as a hit. But not quite, despite the Beatrice Lillie and Bert Lahr marquee names.

More and more producers began to divide up the risks and profits among a multitude of show angels, starting a trend which is still current. The Howard Lindsay-Russel Crouse show, *The Hasty Heart,* had no less than 41 investors in 1945. *Arsenic and Old Lace* was put on the boards in 1941 by the money of 27 backers.

For some reason both the Pulitzer Committee and the Critics'

Circle passed up *Winged Victory*, despite universal acclaim for the show, and refused to grant any play of the 1943 season the laurel. The Pulitzer Committee did give the nod in the direction of *Oklahoma!*, an unusual tribute since the award is rarely given to musicals. *Winged Victory*, in 27 weeks on Broadway, grossed $1,057,318 for Army Emergency Relief Fund.

$750,000 for 'harvey' pix rights   Boxoffice hits of the 1944 season included Mary Coyle Chase's *Harvey* (Frank Fay-Josephine Hull) which was to fetch the all-time record high of $750,000 for the film rights, spread over 10 years, from Universal-International; *I Remember Mama*, John van Druten's expert dramatization of Kathryn Forbes' *Mama's Bank Account*, with Mady Christians in the title role, ably aided by Oscar Homolka, Joan Tetzel, Richard Bishop and Ottilie Kruger; John P. Marquand and George S. Kaufman's *The Late George Apley* (Leo G. Carroll-Janet Beecher-Margaret Phillips-Margaret Dale); Philip Yordan's Negro play, *Anna Lucasta*, expertly acted by Hilda Simms, Canada Lee and John Tate; and two musicals. They were *Bloomer Girl*, with a cast comprising David Brooks, Joan McCracken, Celeste Holm (who had left *Oklahoma!* for newer horizons), Matt Briggs and Mabel Taliaferro. *Song of Norway*, with a score based on the Norwegian Edvard Grieg's melodies, was one of those rara avis —a hit "from the Coast" of which *Lend An Ear*, in a later season, was to be another. The idea of a West Coast tryout, because of lower production costs, revolved around the Edwin Lester type of California manager who, if he has anything, makes a deal with the Shuberts, or kindred more influential Eastern interests, and brings the show to Broadway.

Despite the boom, 11 musicals flopped badly, running into the red for a total of $1,735,000. The rush for theatre tickets turned the spotlight once again on the ticket agencies. Seven brokers had their licenses revoked within a brief period. Some were put out of business and three or four went to jail for flagrant violations. Most, however, enjoyed such lush business that they weren't tempted to step out of line on prices or short-change on Government tax.

While Mrs. Chase's *Harvey* took the 1944 Pulitzer Prize, besides a $750,000 film sale—also marking vaude-nitery comedian Frank Fay's comeback—the critics selected Tennessee Williams' *The Glass*

Menagerie (with producer Eddie Dowling, Laurette Taylor, Julie Haydon and Anthony Ross in the cast), launching Williams as one of Broadway's most promising new playwrights.

Despite excitement over the close of the war, Broadway enjoyed solid business through the next year. Theatres were at such a premium that the producer of *The Red Mill,* in order to move into Shuberts' 46th Street Theatre, had to pay a 5 per cent royalty on the gross to the Shuberts—a first in the history of theatre management.

Two political figures entered the 1945 season. Mayor LaGuardia stepped in and forced the play *Trio* to close at the Belasco because of the Lesbian theme. Clare Booth Luce left Congress long enough to play *Candida* in a strawhat, her first stage appearance; the drama critics agreed "There have been better—and worse—Candidas."

even vaude upbeats   Wartime vaudeville enjoyed the first upbeat it had known since its sad decline in 1929. In 1941, heavy Government spending filtered down to the public, permitting theatre managers to pay the price for stage shows and charge off increased budget costs to the public in raised ducats. Then, with the rapid spread of Army camps, a new demand for live entertainment caused a stage show revival.

Top headliners, both in theatres and in camps, were still the bands; and novelty vocal groups like the Ink Spots and the Andrews Sisters were knocking them dead via recordings and personals.

Outside of bands and singing teams, vaudeville was without a headliner of its own. The last of the tribe was Milton Berle, but in 1941 he was too tied up with 20th Century-Fox and a radio program. Some night club personalities, like Harry Richman, Jimmy Durante, Sophie Tucker, the DeMarcos and Carmen Amaya, played vaude dates, but only occasionally.

The major circuits were slow to respond to vaude's newly eager face. Loew's offered time only at the New York State and the Washington (D.C.) Capitol, plus a few one-night stands in New York neighborhood theatres. The best time offered was that of an independent booking outfit, the Eddie Sherman office, whose vaude jewel was the Steel Pier, Atlantic City, using name bands and vaude talent for 20 weeks in spring and summer.

Burlesque of 1941 was a monopoly combine of Izzy Hirst and the Midwest Wheel, which controlled 30 houses, booking most of the strippers in the business. Variety noted 35 traveling burly shows, another indication that the factory trade in the hinterland was getting cash in its overalls.

topical gags   Vaudeville gag material of the year was built largely around air raid blackouts, air raid wardens, bomb shelters, the draft, Bundles for Britain and sundry other pre-Pearl Harbor headline currency. A favorite gag among actors was, "I just signed for 52 weeks with Uncle Sam—with options."

War gags were dropped quickly in 1942, by management orders, when the coming of war to America sobered the nation. Comics, desperate for timely material, switched to gags about "General Tim O'Shenko." Bands continued to hold No. 1 stage spot, with Kay Kyser getting $25,610 for a week at Detroit's Fox Theatre. Frank Sinatra, growing too big for the Tommy Dorsey band, left the outfit to go into radio and theatre work. His replacement was Dick Haymes, also destined to go into business for himself.

Vaudeville of 1943 found itself in a dilemma. The routes were there—domestic and overseas—in a copious abundance that was suddenly embarrassing. There just wasn't enough vaude talent to go around. What talent was unearthed in USO-Camp Shows was vaude's to have only temporarily, but not to hold. As soon as a promising new headliner appeared, he was optioned at once by either pix, radio or the big-spending niteries.

Only the bands were left as steady headliners. And they weren't vaudeville, but merely transplanted jukebox faves personaling in a theatre. The bands appealed almost exclusively to juve tastes, leaving vaude with very little ammunition for a genuine comeback.

New York was the focal point of the "comeback," such as it was. The Roxy spent as much as $37,000 for one show, including Danny Kaye, Beatrice Kay and Tommy Tucker's band, showing a handsome profit for the first two weeks. Shortly afterward, the Roxy, Capitol, Paramount and Strand bid high for name bands and headliners. Grace Moore got $20,000 solo at the Roxy; Jack Benny and Milton Berle later got twice that, as did Bob Hope and Martin and Lewis at the New York Paramount. As usual, headliner salaries shot up to impossible extremes, making the stage attractions top-heavy in theatre budgets. And as Broadway went, so went the rest of the nation. It was the same pattern of the vaudeville goose beginning to lay golden eggs—and getting his head chopped off.

By 1945 vaude's brief revitalization was being revealed as a zombie. Two top theatres, the Earle in Washington and the Cleveland Palace, dropped stage shows. Other theatres started to follow suit.

Even the unit producers were laying off. In 1945 the only major unit on the road was Earl Carroll's "Vanities." Lack of talent, as well as the heavy expenses of package shows, made producers unwilling to gamble with that type of entertainment. For what top vaude talent was available, it was a seller's market. The DeMarcos were paid $5,000 a week by the Roxy, a new high for a dance team.

For a few brief years vaude had put on its greasepaint again and pretended that the heyday of the Palace was back. It had knocked itself out, especially in the Army camps at home and overseas, thrilling to the huge roars of laughter, the whistles, the storms of applause. It felt proud that it was welcomed so eagerly by the young men in uniform who had been so apathetic toward it as civilians. It hoped that perhaps, after the war, they would remember. After the parades and the ticker tape, vaude put on its best suit and sauntered confidently toward Broadway—only to find that there was no place to go.

the money boom   The year 1941 was star-spangled for night clubs. Prewar jitters created a widespread urge to "eat, drink and be merry, for tomorrow. . . ." In night spots from New York to San Francisco, merry-makers would exchange the sentiments of the day. "You can't take it with you. . . ." "Inflation's coming" . . . "You're spending Uncle Sam's coin in the form of 'expenses' " . . . "If you don't spend it, you'll pay it in taxes. . . ."

Defense spending, of course, primed the pump. The boom began in the hinterland, then spread over both coasts like the overflow of flood waters. Horwath & Horwath, the rating outfit of the hotel and restaurant trade, revealed that the boxoffice for fancy supping and quaffing increased by 35 per cent in 1941. Successful cafes grossed between half a million to a million a year. Spots like New York's Copacabana thought $45,000 weekly grosses just fair; did over $50,000 a week with a Joe E. Lewis and a Jimmy Durante, the latter hitting a $62,500 mark one week. Straight eateries of a mass and class basis, like Dempsey's and Lindy's on Broadway, and Toots Shor's and "21," in New York, did $20,000 a week on straight food. The Stork jumped from $15,000 to $35,000 a week's take.

The trend in night club entertainment underwent a swift change. Formerly, emphasis had been on providing a lavish background with sweet music and luxurious lighting, against which the customers could make their own fun. Now, once and again there was the demand for flashy, elaborate floor shows and hoked-up gaiety.

The pace was not sweet, but hot. Monte Proser opened the Dance Carnival at Madison Square Garden, offering jitterbugging to triple dance bands—Benny Goodman, Larry Clinton and Charlie Barnett —at a scale of 44¢-66¢-88¢, with reserved seats for the intrigued at $1.10 and $1.40. The first weekend attracted 31,553 admissions for a take of $23,200. But the overhead was too heavy, and the attraction folded in less than a month.

One night club in San Francisco brought police, vice societies, and liquor control authorities swooping down as a result of its ad: "See Tommy Harris' Nude All-Girl Orchestra." Many faces were red when the "orchestra" proved to be one-dimensional, sand-blasted into a bar mirror. But it brought in the customers.

In its notes on night life of 1941, Variety revealed that gin-rummy and bridge corners were being set up in some of the popular boites; Harlem night life was suffering from the publicity given its crime wave; Judge Pecora upheld the legality of compulsory fingerprinting for cafe workers; and a "Friendship Club" in the Bronx was running dances with two restrictions—no one under 28, and no jitterbugging. In 1942 seamier night life items revealed some goings-on—2:30 A.M. curfews in war boom towns like Cleveland had inspired a rebirth of speakeasies; men posing as officers and plainclothesmen were shaking down clubs and personnel—a new racket; and clip-joint ballrooms and cheap cafes were bilking the service men.

The celebration department of show business was still in a gold rush by 1943, despite the difficulties of food ration points, and a new liquor shortage. Hotels shared the boom. Sinatra siphoned a heavy take into the Waldorf-Astoria's Wedgwood Room, while Carl Brisson—"the older girls' Sinatra"— had them fighting for seats at the Club Versailles in New York. Other standout attractions of the year were Hildegarde at the Persian Room of the Hotel

Plaza in New York, and the Hartmans (Paul and Grace) all over the place.

The croon-swoon cycle continued full swing. The Coq Rouge ran a Sinatra contest and came up with Martin Kent, one more to swell the ranks of Como, Haymes and Dean Martin, but little was heard of Kent thereafter. In the Danny Kaye tradition, Danny Thomas was slaying them at New York's La Martinique. The Copacabana was mopping up with Jimmy Durante and Joe E. Lewis. Ted Lewis made his *nth* "comeback" at the Hurricane, on Broadway, which also offered Duke Ellington. The Latin Quarter had Georgie Price. Both Billy Rose's Diamond Horseshoe and Lou Walters' Latin Quarter were in the $30,000-and-over weekly gross class.

The heavy spending in night clubs, bars, and other places of wassail was one of the reasons for the Government's salary withholding tax. "It's a certainty many of these saloonatics have little concern about the morrow," Variety said approvingly. "When mama goes back to washing the dishes, and the $110-a-week driller returns to his $30 white-collar job, they will have memories and a terrific hangover, no doubt, but seemingly, as of right now, that seems to be all right all around."

Night clubs were hit hard in 1944, when the Government clamped a 30 per cent amusement tax on the backs of the celebrators. Business slumped, with night clubs going down like tenpins, putting 20,000 out of work. The Government relented and cut the tax back to 20 per cent, which helped more performers get back to work.

By 1945 top night clubs were definitely in the big business brackets. New York's Copacabana took in an average of $45,000-$55,000 weekly, trailed by the Latin Quarter with $40,000-$45,000, and the Diamond Horseshoe and the Zanzibar with an average of $40,000 each. All groaned at a new midnight curfew for the amusement industry imposed by War Mobilization Director Jimmy Byrnes, who "regretted" the inconvenience. Any ordinance so vitally affecting night life inevitably inspires a flock of wisecracks, most cogent of which was boniface Toots Shor's now historic wheeze, in his own picturesque phraseology: "Any crum-bum what can't get plastered by midnight just ain't tryin'."

The curfew, of course, brought a wave of bottle clubs and post-Volsteadian "speakeasies," prompting Mayor LaGuardia to rule,

"New York is still New York; I don't like the curfew law" . . . and so he extended it to 1 A.M., which made everybody feel a little better. At least it didn't disrupt legit curtains, some having started earlier in order to give theatre-goers a little more post-theatre time for supper, a drink and a dance, à la the London idea of double-daylight time theatre curtains at 6 and 7 P.M., with supping —not dining—afterwards. It also advanced the niteries' "midnight" shows an hour, and thus crowded in some revenue, heretofore impossible under the 12 o'clock deadline.

Anyway, 1 A.M. was OK—it meant that you didn't have to go home on the same day!

53

Paeans of Victory—and Labor Pains

★

Soldiers off to war and workers to defense plants march faster and are stirred deeper with proper musical accompaniments. But World War II was not to produce another "Over There" although Tin Pan Alley rallied to all the Government's requirements—and then some—as they cropped up. Jimmy McHugh and L. Wolfe Gilbert contributed "A Grand Vacation With Pay" as a recruiting drive song. Later, McHugh and Harold Adamson were to prove more effective with their musical salute to the heroes of aviation, "Coming In On A Wing and a Prayer." Irving Berlin fashioned "Any Bonds Today," "Arms for the Love of America" (munitions), "Angels of Mercy" for the Red Cross, "There Are No Wings on a Foxhole" (infantry song), and of course "God Bless America," besides the notable *This Is the Army,* with its nearly-$10,000,000 yield for Army Emergency Relief.

Both the Army's Special Services division and the innate showmanship of Tin Pan Alley soon sensed that war songs, per se, never clicked with the GIs. Songs of sentiment, home, the girl back home, the miss-you theme, the completely happy-go-lucky, or escapist, such as "Hut Sut Song," "Don't Sit Under the Apple Tree," "Three Little Sisters," "I'll Be Seeing You," "White Christmas," "The Last Time I Saw Paris" and others, were the ones that the jukeboxes and the bands on the home front found most popular. There was enough oblique suggestion without punching it too hard on the nose.

The militant type of songs like "Remember Pearl Harbor," "This Is Worth Fighting For" and "Praise the Lord and Pass the Ammunition" occasionally were fraught with embarrassment, especially for 4F or "deferred" maestros. There were too frequent interrogations from pugnacious youths in uniforms and hyper-sentimental femmes who openly were heard to ask the bandleader, "Well, why don't you get into a uniform and fight, then?" Ecclesiastic circles didn't like "Praise the Lord" on the ground that religion and killing were an ungodly coupling, in prose or melody. Frank Loesser's song nevertheless clicked, as did his "Story of Rodger Young." (Loesser and Berlin were the Tin Pan Alley outstanders of World War II, even if never achieving the socko impact of George M. Cohan's "Over There.")

Apart from the personal sensitivities, the bands ducked fighting songs because they found the public generally wanted complete escapology when terping; besides which, the tempos of the "message" pops were poor for dancing and, anyhow, the ballroom was no place to arouse patriotism.

There was heated discussion as to the types of music soldiers preferred. Surveys by the Army's Special Services division showed that popular tunes, sweet or dance, won favor with 95 per cent of GI radio listeners. Swing—hot, scat and jive—was second with a 62 per cent rating. Third place went to old familiar music; hillbilly and Western music won the fourth nod; and lowest welcome was accorded classical music.

escapist hit paraders   By and large, the 1942 pop music crop—which rolled up the biggest sheet music sale in 15 years—was largely escapist. Many songs suggested the war, but slightly, such as "Bluebirds Over the White Cliffs of Dover," "My Sister and I," "The Last Time I Saw Paris" and "A Tulip Garden By An Old Dutch

Mill." Sentiment of a nostalgic order was the popular ring of Tin Pan Alley circa 1942. Hits of this nature were "Till Reveille," "Shrine of St. Cecilia," "She'll Always Remember," "Johnny Doughboy Found a Rose In Ireland," "I Left My Heart At the Stage Door Canteen" and "He Wears A Pair of Silver Wings."

The Japanese, of course, came in for due lyrical trouncing. The day after Pearl Harbor, two songs came out—"The Sun Will Soon Be Setting For The Land of the Rising Sun" and "You're A Sap, Mr. Jap." Later in 1942, Japan was the inspiration for "We're Going To Find the Fellow Who Is Yellow and Beat Him Red, White and Blue," "We've Got To Do A Job on the Japs, Baby," "They're Going to Be Playing Taps on the Japs," "The Japs Haven't Got A Chinaman's Chance," "The Japs Haven't Got A Ghost of A Chance," "Goodbye, Momma, I'm Off to Yokohama," "Oh, You Little Son Of An Oriental," "Wake Island Woke Up Our Land," "Slap the Jap Right Off the Map," "We Are the Sons of the Rising Guns," "To Be Specific, It's Our Pacific" and "When Those Little Yellow Bellies Meet the Cohens and the Kelleys."

The rest of the Axis was thrown in with "Put the Heat on Hitler, Muss Up Mussolini and Tie a Can to Japan," "Let's Put the Axe to the Axis," "Let's Knock the Hit Out of Hitler," "We'll Knock the Japs Right in the Laps of the Nazis" and "We Did It Before and We Can Do It Again."

Songs to stir up patriotic feeling were "Me and My Uncle Sam," a revival of "Ballad For Americans," Fred Waring's "Merchant Marine Song," and toujours "God Bless America," which became the theme song of Milwaukee night clubs where the German-American population liked everyone to think of them as un-questioned patriots.

Two songs were beamed at the wartime factory workers—"Don't Steal the Sweetheart of a Soldier" and "Rosie the Riveter." Another Rose was celebrated that year, "Russian Rose."

Songwriters responded to the call of the Music War Committee in 1943, and turned out a drove of bond-selling songs, including "One More Mile," "Swing the Quota," "The Message Got Through," "Has Hitler Made A Monkey Out of You?," "Get Aboard the Bond Wagon," "Unconditional Surrender," "While Melting All Our Memories" (scrap salvage), "Voices of the Under-ground," "Yankee Doodle Ain't Doodling Any Now," "Have You

Written Him Today?," "I Get That Democratic Feeling," "I Spoke With Jefferson At Guadalcanal," "West Of Tomorrow" (submarine song) and "In Business Since 1776."

Our Allies were celebrated in "My British Buddy" (again Berlin), which scored big in England, and Clarence Gaskill's "Franklin, Winston, Kai-Shek and Joe." The approaching capitulation of Italy was anticipated by "One Down and Two More To Go," which was ready for issue on the day of Mussolini's surrender. Hy Zaret wrote English lyrics to the "Garibaldi Hymn" to celebrate the occasion.

There was no great war song—the kind soldiers marched to—because it wasn't a marching war. The kind of song the soldiers sang was the favorite of the African campaign, "Dirty Gertie," which was cleaned up and offered in the United States as "Gertie from Bizerte." It never achieved its hopes as a second "Mademoiselle From Armentières."

allies adopt 'lili marlene'   Perhaps the outstanding real war song—unlike the patriotic "God Bless America" of Irving Berlin, and the sweet-sorrowful nostalgia of "The Last Time I Saw Paris" (incidentally the only non-musical comedy score song ever written by the late Jerome Kern and Oscar Hammerstein 2d)—was "Lili Marlene." It was "adopted" by the Allies from the Nazis during the North African campaign, and it was from the British that the American GIs picked it up. Originally a German ballad ("My Lili of the Lamppost"), this made it the first time in history that enemy troops both sang and enjoyed the same song.

(Postwar, the German songsmith Norbert Schultze sought an American visa, disclaimed being a Nazi but couldn't quite explain away his alleged "anti-Nazi sympathies" when he was spotlighted as the composer also of the 1941 Nazi victory paen, *"Wir fahren nach England"* ("We're Sailing Towards England"). Curiously enough, under American copyright regulations the Alien Property Custodian built up a sizable chunk of royalties for the errant Herr Schultze from the American sheet music and recording sales of the Anglo-Americanized version of "Lili Marlene." (This was the case, too, in the instance of the late Franz Lehar, thanks to a click revival of his *Merry Widow* on Broadway).

"Annie Doesn't Live Here Any More" suggested the upheaval that war production had caused in the lives of the people at home.

"When You Put On That Blue Suit Again" reflected the growing optimism of both civilians and soldiers at approaching victory, as did "Hot Time In the Town of Berlin," "When I Get Back To My Home Town," "Paris Will Be Paris Once Agan" and "There Will Be A Yankee Christmas."

Among "specific" songs were "The U.S.A. By Day and the R.A.F. By Night" (bombing pattern over Germany), "Johnny Zero (Johnny got a Zero today!)" (indicating a new attention to the Pacific theatre), and "Say A Prayer For the Boys Over There."

The songs of 1944 which made the greatest hit, however, were those in which the war theme was openly implied, with romance paramount, such as "I'll Walk Alone" and "I'll Be Seeing You." In a livelier vein were "G.I. Jive," "Shoo Shoo Baby" and "Victory Polka." Top favorites of all were pure novelty numbers, like "Mairzy Doats," "Milkman, Keep Those Bottles Quiet," "The Trolley Song" and "Don't Fence Me In." Escapist songs commanded the top money.

There was a revival of old sentimental favorites. Among the newly popular oldies were "I'd Climb the Highest Mountain," "I'll Get By," "Inka Dinka Doo," "Me and My Shadow," "Moon Over Miami," "Object Of My Affections," "Rainbow Round My Shoulder," "Whistle While You Work" and "Who's Afraid Of the Big Bad Wolf?" As revivals, the songs sold three times the number of copies they did when they were first published.

The Latin tempo was reflected by "Amor," "Let Me Love You Tonight" and "Besame Mucho." The Andrews Sisters started a whole new cycle of neo-calypso songs by taking an old Frank Loesser tune, "Sing A Tropical Song," out of an old Paramount film. Other off-syllable songs quickly followed, among the outstanding numbers being "Rum and Coca-Cola" and "Come With Me My Honey."

Fortune shone brightly for the music biz. Even the song-sheet sellers were frightened into good behavior, paying some $625,000 a year to the publishers and songsmiths for their lyric reprints. The big money for Tin Pan Alley, however, still came from radio— $7,000,000 for 1944, a new high.

petrillo—again   War or no war, James C. Petrillo was battling to protect the interests of members of his American Federation of

Musicians. As in the 1948 debacle, five years prior thereto he was ranting against the phonograph recording as "the No. 1 scab" of the music business; and in 1943 he banned his AFMers from waxing for the "musical monsters which were killing employment" for the live musicians. But that didn't deter the oncoming of such pop disk faves as Bing Crosby, Perry Como, Frank Sinatra, Vaughn Monroe, Margaret Whiting and Spike Jones. And the combination of "middlebrow" musical tastes, along with the ballyhoo potency of pix and radio, zoomed such longhairs as Lauritz Melchior and José Iturbi into extraordinary platter sales.

In 1945 current events were reflected by "The President Harry S Truman March," "Don't Let It Happen Again" (a message to delegates at the San Francisco conference), "He's Home For A Little While" (furloughs), "I'll Be Walking With My Honey Soon, Soon, Soon" (approaching end of war), and Irving Berlin's peacetime paen, "Just A Blue Serge Suit."

Variety limned some notes of musical interest from abroad. The favorite song of the R.A.F. in England was a ribald ditty called "Roll Me Over In the Clover" by Desmond O'Connor. The United States Army stopped publication of "Berlin Will Rise Again" by Heinzo Gaze, after 20,000 copies had been printed in Germany without authorization by Allied occupation authorities. Berlin, meanwhile, was covered in the latter part of the year with Spike Jones' recordings of "Der Fuehrer's Face," a tune not exactly encouraged there in early 1945.

Bing Crosby tried to hit the 10,000,000 disk sale record that year, but Perry Como nosed him out with a Chopin tune, "Till the End of Time"—the year's best-seller—and "Temptation," "That Feeling in the Moonlight," "If I Loved You" and "I'm Gonna Love That Gal (as she's never been loved before)"—and none of his squealing admirers was under any misapprehension as to what those lyrics suggested. A few years previous, Tin Pan Alley had owed a tremendous debt to Tchaikowsky, giving rise to the musical observation, "Everybody's Making Money But Tchaikowsky," but in 1945 the larceny was perpetrated chiefly against Chopin.

Cole Porter's "Don't Fence Me In" snowballed to a sensational best-seller, the first song since "White Christmas" to go over the million mark in sheet sales. Another click was "Chickery Chick." "Bell Bottom Trousers" was popular, and also "When the Old

Gang's Back On the Corner (singing 'Sweet Adeline' again.)"

The boom in the music business led to an increase in recording companies until they totaled 130. Some counted on a new boom when plastic, nonbreakable records were put out to sell in racks like sheet music on newsstands.

Decca ran a big campaign on Crosby, to offset the Como menace, describing him as "the most-heard voice in the world," with no less than 75,000,000 of his records in private homes.

With the close of the war, songplugging and all its attendant evils began to make itself felt again. As Variety observed, "The manpower easement was manifested fast in the Lindy set. The pluggers are back from the war in droves, with the same ya-ta-ta, the same chiz and angle and dipsydoodle."

longhair goes middlebrow   Edward Johnson, the new managing director of the Metropolitan Opera House, gave full credit to the people's medium, radio, for the relatively lush state of affairs of 1941 opera. The longhair field as a whole took $35,000,000 in receipts that year, with the opera latching on to $5,000,000 thereof. The Met had made one concession to the war in 1942—it dropped *Madama Butterfly,* with its quaint and flattering picture of Japan. It retained Wagnerian opera, indicating that the Met's artistic censorship was not because of the composers' nationality but more because of the libretto subject matter.

The intermingling of longhair and shorthair music continued through the war period. José Iturbi withdrew as conductor of the Philadelphia Symphony Orchestra in 1941 when Benny Goodman was a feature soloist. Iturbi's reason: "Beneath my dignity." Edwin MacArthur pinch-hitted on the cuff, declaring, "It is an honor and a privilege to conduct the Benny Goodman concert."

Longhair orchestras also resented the raids on their bandmen by swing outfits. In 1944 Jerry Wald's band burglarized six string men from the Cleveland Symphony. That year swing again invaded the concert field, when a handpicked group of top jazz musicians, under the baton of Eddie Condon, gave a concert at Carnegie Hall and turned 'em away. Hazel Scott also played Carnegie in 1945—while Artur Rubinstein did his chores before the cameras in Republic Pictures', *I Have Always Loved You.* Lauritz Melchior had long since gone Metro and jived the Wagnerian stuff on Fred

Allen and Frank Sinatra radio programs. Paul Whiteman, Phil Spitalny, Woody Herman, the Andrews Sisters, Mary Lou Williams, Duke Ellington, Victor Borge, Sigmund Romberg, and also Spike Jones, likewise went concert.

Agents began to take a second look at the concert field. Certain bands and acts, dressed with stylish showmanship, clicked handsomely in longhair emporia. And Toscanini, conducting a concert in the Hollywood Stadium, played on and looked with disbelieving eyes as a career-bent girl named Helen Faville, of Los Angeles, jumped onto the stage and danced across it—self-appointed ballerina for a night.

the hottest thing on ice   1941 was a sweet year for outdoor show business. The Ringling Circus went into Los Angeles for five days—10 shows—and left with a $230,000 gross, top coin in its 58-year-old history. Luna Park (Coney Island), offering many of the old New York World's Fair attractions, found the pickings equally juicy.

1943, however, found circuses and carnivals ready to quit because of gas rationing. In New York, two circuses opened at the same time. Ringling presented "Spangles" at Madison Square Garden, a one-ring affair which revived the circus parade in the arena. The Sunbrock Circus with three-rings opened on a lot behind the Roxy Theater, but folded quickly. The following year the Ringling show chalked up another record in New York with a gross of $1,500,000.

But 1944 was a year of disaster for outdoor show business. The Ringling-Barnum & Bailey show playing under canvas in Hartford, Connecticut, suffered a disastrous fire in the main tent. In the stampede that followed, 107 persons were killed and 412 injured. Disaster claims amounting to over $4,000,000 had to be paid off. The same year, both Luna Park and Palisades Park had fires doing $1,500,000 damage. Ringling's wound up 1945 still solidly in the black, however, cleaning up in New York, despite the lack of foreign importations which the war had made impossible.

The single outstanding star in the outdoor field was Sonja Henie, who grossed $280,000 at Madison Square Garden in 1942, and over $1,000,000 via a short tour of the nation's ice rinks. In the lecture field, war scribes and swamis raised the boxoffice in the spiel di-

vision to $800,000 in 1943; one of the outstanders being Burton
Holmes, then 73 and celebrating his 50th season.

sunday legits   Equity, once firmly opposed to Sunday performances, was convinced in 1941 that these had proved a lifesaver
for many shows. It therefore promptly endorsed the proposal that
they be continued through the summer and into the fall season.
Sunday shows continued to draw people into New York for weekends, benefiting film houses as well as legit. Once fearful that Sunday shows might seem a confession of boxoffice weakness, this soon
proved a fallacy.

Frank Gillmore, Equity's head for so many of its turbulent years,
died in 1943 at the age of 76. The organization had a fairly placid
year, owing to the fact that so many of its younger members had
left to play more dramatic roles in the war. The only flurry occurred
during the election of councilors. Paul Robeson, although elected,
refused to accept office, in protest against the slur on the Soviet
Union implied by an anti-Red amendment in Equity's new constitution. There was no mistaking Robeson's Moscow leanings even
then.

There were few jobless actors in 1945, with USO units crying for
more talent, many summer musical stocks and a thriving road.
Many retired actors returned and rejoined Equity, which began to
have a recurrence of "ism" trouble when Frank Fay lashed out at
the organization with cries of "Communism at the top."

A New York newspaper strike in 1945 reduced the size of the
papers and cut out amusement advertising, merely listing the shows.
Incidental music in a production of Shakespeare's *Tempest* (Vera
Zorina-Canada Lee) brought a ruling from the American Federation of Musicians that it rated as a musical comedy, requiring
upped salaries and a minimum of 16 musicians at $92 each, despite
the fact that the music was scored for a 12-man orchestra.

War's unrest created other isms throughout show business. With
labor's power asserting itself, its leaders sometimes abused that
power, as witness the Willie Bioff-George Browne scandal in the
picture business. These Chicago hoodlums, remnants of the Al
Capone gangster tactics and in the worst Capone tradition, threatened to "tie up the entire motion picture industry by pulling out
the boothmen" (projectionists) unless Hollywood "made a deal"

with them. Hollywood was forced to. Between the courageous campaign of Arthur Ungar, late editor of Daily Variety and Westbrook Pegler's general daily campaign, Browne and Bioff and their cohorts, eventually got their just desserts via stiff prison sentences and fines.

Hollywood labor strife stirred anew via a jurisdictional battle between two American Federation of Labor unions—the Illustrators & Decorators Local 1421 and the International Alliance of Theatrical Stage Employees, as to which local would get the 72 screen set designers. This cost the studios many man-hours of time and money and tied up the sundry studios periodically through picketing and cross-picketing, walkouts and other demonstrations which led to much physical harm and other abuses. Although production continued, despite these hindrances, riots in front of studio gates resulted in severe strife, when the Hollywood gendarmerie was charged with siding with the IATSE men.

On a lighter note, the Rockefellers shuttered their glamor nitery in the clouds, the Rainbow Room, atop the RCA Bldg. in Radio City, when labor demands by waiters and cooks made an already unprofitable operation still more so—even for the Rockefellers. They just didn't think it was worth the trouble, and turned the operation over to the Union News Co. which runs the many other eateries, cafes and bars in Rockefeller Center. Incidentally it was something of a sentimental venture, since young Nelson Rockefeller had always fancied the idea of a "super nite club way up in the clouds." While at school he used to confide this to one of his tutors, a Mr. John Roy by name. So when the Rainbow Room debuted, the educator became a bistro boniface and John Roy found himself booking shows, hiring the bands and worrying about cuisine, waiters and service. Not until the fall of 1950 was an attempt made to reopen the Rainbow Room to the public, and then on an experimental cocktail dansant basis although it functioned all the time as a private luncheon club for Rockefeller Center tenants.

many showmen pass   The first year of the war period saw the deaths of three men whose obituaries were a shock to show business. All died in July 1941. They were Sam H. Harris, 69, one-time partner of George M. Cohan and producer of such

Broadway hits as *Dinner At Eight, Rain, As Thousands Cheer* and
You Can't Take It With You; Sam Scribner, 82, treasurer of the
Actors Fund; and Lew Fields, 73, whose partner Joe Weber was at
his bedside.

Joe Penner, born Josef Pinter, died at 36, cutting short a promising radio career that had paid him as much as $13,250 one week.
Another radio personality, Earl W. Grasen, "The Lone Ranger,"
died that year in an auto accident. Over 1,000 people paid him a
last tribute in Detroit.

The music world of 1941 lost Isidore Witmark, 71, founder of
the famous music publishing house; Ignace Jan Paderewski, 80,
who had earned between three and five millions in his 40-year career; Brig. Gen. E. L. Gruber, 61, who had written "The Caissons
Go Rolling Along"; and Bartley C. Costello, 70, author of the lyrics
of "Where the River Shannon Flows," a claim disputed by some.

Other obits of 1941 included Julian Eltinge, 57, greatest female
impersonator of them all; legit impresario Stuart Walker at 53;
Hugh Ward, 70, an American who had large theatre holdings in
Australia; vaudeville's "redhead" Irene Franklin, longtime part-
nered with her husband, Burton Green, in bigtime vaudeville, at
65; actors Eddie Leonard, 70, Richard Carle, 69, and George L.
Bickel (of Bickel & Watson, pioneer vaudeville comedy act), 70.
Playwright Eugene Walter (*The Easiest Way*) passed at 67; nitery
chanteuse and Ziegfeld star of *Show Boat* and the *Follies,* Helen
Morgan, at 41. Another premature death was Marie Saxon, musi-
comedy star at 37. She was married to Sid Silverman, the son of
Sime, who died in 1950 at 52.

Sam Morton, of the 4 Mortons, one of the first great vaudeville
family acts, à la the Cohans and Foys, died in his 70th year. Also
one-time Belasco star Blanche Bates, 69; Wells Hawks who press-
agented everything from circus elephants to battleships, at 71.
Steve Clow, publisher of the illfamed Broadway Brevities, a racketeering sheet which sent him to Atlanta, also died in 1941 at 68.

Among the show business pioneers lost that year also were Com-
modore J. Stuart Blackton, 66, one-time head of the Vitagraph
Pictures Corp.; Henry Burr, 59, one of the first ballad recording
artists; Fred Karno, 75, discoverer of Charlie Chaplin and Stan
Laurel (& Hardy), who worked in his Karno's "A Night In An

English Music Hall"; Mrs. Codelia MacDonald, 94, the original "Little Eva"; and Jenny Dolly, of the famous Dolly Sisters, who suicided at 48. [Whenever the Monte Carlo Casino needed a little publicity the story always went out that the Dollys had broken the bank, always a surefire revitalizer for the gaming tables.]

The outstanding obituary of the following year was that of the Number One man of the American theatre—George M. Cohan, who died at 64, and was laid to rest just 45 minutes from Broadway. The funeral took place at St. Patrick's Cathedral, where "Over There" was played for the first time as a dirge, and, incidentally, the first popular song ever played at the cathedral. Cohan left an estate of $712,393, a modest sum considering that the 10 per cent share he was given in *Yankee Doodle Dandy* netted $500,000.

Another great theatrical figure died that year, John Barrymore, at the age of 60, mourned as possibly one of the finest actors the American stage had ever known, despite his decline into buffoonery during the last years of his life.

Two pioneer radio commentators also died in 1942—Floyd Gibbons, who left an estate of $250,000, and Graham McNamee, 53, who set the pace for exciting sports announcers. Joe Weber, the other half of Weber & Fields, died at 74 only nine months after his partner. Morris Gest, famous producer of *The Miracle* and *Chu Chin Chow*, died at 61.

Other obituaries of 1942 included England's top managing director, Sir Oswald Stoll, 76; another famous legitimate actor, Otis Skinner, 83; Emma Calvé, a Metropolitan standout for 13 years and the greatest Carmen of her era, 83; Pawnee Bill (Major Gordon W. Lillie), who was once Buffalo Bill's partner, 81; Michel Fokine, famous ballet master, 62; and Addie Cherry, one of the famous Cherry Sisters—"the worst act in show biz"—at 83.

Hollywood mourned the death of Carole Lombard (Mrs. Clark Gable) at 32 in a plane crash while returning from a War Bond Drive in Indianapolis. An obscure obituary was Felix Powell, 60, who had written only one hit song in his life; as a staff sergeant in World War I he had entered a song contest with "Pack Up Your Troubles In Your Old Kit Bag."

The music world was hit hardest in 1943. Obituaries included Sergei Rachmaninoff, 70; Lorenz (Larry) Hart, of the famous Rodgers & Hart (American "Gilbert & Sullivan") team, 47—later

celebrated in memorium by Hollywood's *Words and Music;*
Vaughn de Leath, pioneer radio singer known as "The First
Lady of Radio," 42; Ben Bernie, "the Old Maestro" who made his
"Yowza" trademark a radio byword, 52; and Jules Bledsoe, the
Negro baritone who sang "Old Man River" in the original pro-
duction of *Show Boat,* 44.

Other music world obituaries were songwriters Joe McCarthy, 58,
George Whiting, 61, and Fats Waller, 39; film veteran Hobart Bos-
worth died at 76; and Cecilia (Cissie) Loftus, noted mimic and
legit actress, at 67. Writers passing were Stephen Vincent Benet,
44, and novelist Elinor Glyn, 78. Other deaths included producer
Max Reinhardt, 70; Elmer F. Rogers, 72, manager of the Palace
almost from its heyday to its decline; and James Madison, 72, the
"American Joe Miller," who published his gag-filled editions of
Madison's Budget for 40 years.

Actors headed the list of 1944 obituaries. Prominent among them
were Lupe Velez, 36, whose suicide created sensational headlines;
silent pix comedian Harry Langdon, 60; veteran Willie Collier and
one-time Broadway sensation Yvette Guilbert; Richard Bennett, 72,
famous actor in his own right and father of Joan, Constance and
Barbara Bennett; and Wilkie Bard, 70, one of England's great
comedians.

Death at 53 rang down the curtain on the glamorous gospel career
of Aimee Semple MacPherson, who had brought the Mae West
touch to the tabernacle for 25 years. Inactive for five years before
her death, she still derived income from the Los Angeles and
Oakland "temples."

Two famous authors, good friends, died in '44—Irvin S. Cobb,
67, and George Ade, 78, whose first show had been *Sultan of Sulu.*
Novelist Harold Bell Wright, 72, who wrote *The Shepherd of the
Hills,* also passed away. Other deaths included artist Nell Brinkley,
56, and a staunch friend of show business, and Republican Party
nominee for the Presidency in 1940, Wendell Willkie, 52, who was
chairman of the board of 20th Century-Fox at the time of his death.

f. d. r.   The greatest loss for all in 1945 was the passing of
Franklin Delano Roosevelt, who had always had a high regard
for show business, which had an equal affection for him. The night
that he died, radio had its all-time peak audience—38,700,000—

except for the night F.D.R. had delivered his war message in 1941, when 62,100,000 were tuned in.

Theatres cancelled all matinees. On a 56-minute NBC show, almost every famous name in show business went before the microphone to pay a throat-choked tribute to the late President. For complete coverage of the sad event, the four major networks and independent nets cancelled commercial time worth some $10,000,000.

Reviewing F.D.R.'s relationship to show business, Variety recalled that his radio voice had first been heard in 1925, at Madison Square Garden, for Al Smith as the Democratic candidate for the White House, and again at Houston in 1928 for the same Happy Warrior. Roosevelt had always shown keen interest in the legitimate stage, Hollywood and radio. He regularly attended stock company plays, where he gladly talked to actors backstage.

Variety had always "reviewed" his talks from the time he first gave them from the Executive Mansion in Albany to the famous fireside chats of the White House. His physical condition had compelled F.D.R. to rely on the microphone, rather than on personal appearances, to win popular support—a fact which helped make him an outstanding broadcaster.

The three show business figures who missed him most keenly were his close friends Robert E. Sherwood, John Golden and Eddie Dowling.

The music world in 1945 lost Gus Edwards (64), Jerome Kern (60), John McCormack (61), Fiske O'Hara, another noted Irish singer (67), Erno Rapee, conductor of the Radio City Music Hall Orchestra for 12 years, also composer of "Diane," "Charmaine" and "Angela Mia," at 55, Moises Simons, Cuban composer of "The Peanut Vendor" and originator of the Latin-American trend in music, also 55, and Edward B. Marks (80), one of the most famous of all music publishers.

Widely mourned by actors, writers and critics, for he was all of these, was Robert Benchley, who died at 56. Actors who took their final curtains that year included Alla Nazimova (66), great tragedienne; famed film cowboy star William S. Hart, 80; Frank Craven (70), who scored so heavily in Our Town; Doris Keane (63), remembered for her role in Romance; and Charles Evan Evans (88), veteran comedian for 75 years, whose 3,600 performances of Hoyt's farce, "A Parlor Match," ran for 10 years starting in 1884, the longest theatrical run in history. Evans' partner was Bill (Old Hoss) Hoey; together they introduced "The Man Who Broke the Bank at Monte Carlo" and "Bicycle Built For Two." It was Evans who had brought Anna Held over from France for the first time in 1896.

Variety itself lost Joshua Lowe—*Jolo*—who died at 72 in London. An American longtime resident in the British capital, he had sat out the London blitz only to be hit by a taxi. Periodically *Jolo* would write letters to the home-office (usually after some severe aerial attack) that he "had to complain to the landlord again last night—too damn much noise upstairs." It was *Jolo* who originated the line, "Good for the big small time," and who also wrote the shortest vaudeville review ever to appear in Variety, as related in a previous chapter.

1950-51 obits included Fanny Brice (59), Vesta Victoria (77), song-writer Harry Armstrong (71), Ivor Novello (57), André Gide (81), Arnold Schönberg (76), Lou Clayton (Jackson & Durante) (63), Decca's Jack Kapp (47), Chi Hotelier Ernie Byfield (59), Damon Runyon (62), Eddy Duchin (41), Warner Baxter (59), John Alden Carpenter (75), John Erskine (72), Mayo Methot (47), Olive Tell (55), Jane Cowl (64), Carla (Mrs. Arturo) Toscanini (73), Variety's Ed Barry (*Edba*) (60), Ashton Stevens (78), Egbert A. ("In the Shade of the Old Apple Tree") Van Alstyne (73), Kelcey Allen (75).

PART SEVEN

VIDEO ERA
1946 - 195-

54

Veni, Vidi, Video, Vaudeo

★

"The Era of Wonderful Nonsense II is over," declared Variety at the close of 1946. "The past year was and henceforth will go down as The Awakening." Gone or going were the jackpots hit by furriers, jewelers, specialty shops and resorts, the wheels of which were spun with black market dollars. Gone or going were the defense workers in shirtsleeves in front row orchestra of the top hits; fabulous gambling in Saratoga and Florida; tipping in large denominations. "It's no gag," Variety observed, "that many a waiter up to now was on his second apartment house, and quite a few maitres can retire to Lake Como without worrying whether their Escoffier sheepskin is in jeopardy."

Although customers were still giving $100 tips for front places at Florida dice tables, war-inflated salaries slumped rapidly. A boxoffice limp was hurting all talent without a big reputation. Daily Variety in Hollywood carried a sign of the times with an ad in March offering an apartment for rent, including the owner's "talent and ability," in exchange for a movie contract. Another ad in an Atlantic City paper announced: WANTED—PIANO PLAYER WHO CAN OPEN OYSTERS AND CLAMS.

It was The Awakening, indeed.

Engaging the attention of show business circa 1946 were such phenomena as plays with dinner intermission; Mr. and Mrs. breakfast shows; 8:00 P.M. legit preem curtains to enable the A.M. newspaper critics to make deadlines; the gradual decline of whodunits on screen and radio, to make way for an upswing of psychological thrillers; the lance-tilting of England's J. Arthur Rank to capture American and world markets for London's celluloid produce; and the French invasion into the United States topflight chansoniers in the class bistros. The Gallic chirpers waxed as rich as French cooking. Edith Piaf, Charles Trenet, Jean Sablon, Lucienne Boyer, Suzy Solidor, not to mention Maurice Chevalier's one-man show as a legit touring attraction, further cemented Franco-American amity with a raft of Continental songs, such as "La Vie En Rose," "All My Love" (née "Bolero") and "C'est Si Bon."

New York's tugboat strike in 1946 played havoc with show biz. Mayor O'Dwyer set up a City Disaster Control Board to put the clamps on fuel-users. Restaurants were allowed to stay open; prepared food was permitted to be served, provided no extra fuel was used. O'Dwyer took to the air and headlines to tell New Yorkers not to go to work on the following day unless advised otherwise. He then shaped an edict shutting down every entertainment place in the city, which would have cost New York show business $2,500,-000. Suddenly, half an hour before it was supposed to go into effect, the order was called off. The strike lasted nine days.

Although the war was over, show business continued to stay in the front lines of patriotic, charity and general welfare work. The American Theatre Wing and USO-Camp Shows continued to play veterans hospitals. Walter Winchell's Damon Runyon Cancer Me-

morial Fund; columnist Ed Sullivan and the Heart Fund; Hollywood's Variety office dispensing free vaccination against a smallpox
epidemic for some 500 actors; $500-a-plate dinner tendered Al Jolson,
to raise funds for an Army hospital being built as a memorial to
Major General Maurice Rose, were part of the unslackening postwar
efforts.

commie probe   1947 was the year that Howard Hughes
made headlines with his Washington testimony; and the un-Ameri-
can Activities Committee probed key Hollywood figures, most of
them writers, for Communistic sympathies. Most of them got prison
sentences. Others, such as Fredric March and his wife, Florence
Eldridge, because of a normal wartime effort for Soviet-American relations, when we were allied against Hitler, found themselves pro-
fessionally embarrassed and forced to sue—and eventually won a
retraction—because the pamphlet, *Counterattack,* put them in a false
light. Edward G. Robinson, whose wartime work was beyond normal
expectancy, including a $100,000 donation to GI welfare, likewise
journeyed to Washington at midcentury to volunteer before a Congressional group as to his past record. Negro singer Josh White
dittoed as did Larry Parks, John Garfield, José Ferrer, and many
others—voluntarily or by subpoena.
    As the anti-Communistic fever snowballed, there were needlessly
embarrassing incidents for any number of radio, TV, Hollywood
and other performers and writers, via the publication of their names
and pseudo-affiliations in the past with Communist-front organizations. Jean Muir's cancellation off "The Aldrich Family" TV series
by General Foods was a minor sensation in 1950. Gypsy Rose Lee
was forced to sue in order to clear her name. Ireene Wicker, vet radio
songstress with a son in the service, found herself "unoptioned" by
what she thought a strange "coincidence," on the heels of the *Red
Channels* "exposé." It was indicated that, in many instances, the
exposé sheet culled from erroneous data in *The Daily Worker* and/or
harked back to anti-Franco or wartime cultural alliances with
Russian artistic groups, at a time when those things were not only
unsuspicious but had a patriotic concept. That some, of course, were
insidious Communist-front groups is something which many
quickly discovered and exited, but the onus lingered, often to their
professional and economic embarrassment or hurt.

In 1947, too, a Boston jurist found the film version of *Forever Amber* so "pure" that he complained it "put me to sleep." Boston cropped up again three years later when it scowled on the Cole Porter musical, *Out Of This World,* with its Amphytrion libretto, and tabooed some of the lyrics and dialogue. A Broadway wag re-dubbed the show "Buttocks and Bows."

In 1947, also, came the cold war, with its front in Berlin. Watching the drama of the air lift, show biz decided to get into the act. Bob Hope, Jinx Falkenburg, Irving Berlin and others left for Germany to entertain the air lift boys for Christmas. On the home front it kept alive the "Purple Heart Circuit," as Eddie Cantor dubbed it, by supporting Veterans Hospital Camp Shows, the successor to USO-Camp Shows.

On the financial side, amusement stocks continued to skid. Shares had been dropping steadily from an average of $22.01 at the end of 1946 to $16.27 at the end of 1947. All phases of show business were beginning to cry the blues, with skating and bowling among the big war-boomers diving hard. The passing of the 5¢ fare in New York changed Coney Island from a "nickel Riviera" to a "10¢ St. Moritz." Steeplechase Park tried to minimize the upped fare by offering free video.

tv goes forward   By 1948 it was clear that the coming era in entertainment belonged to the new baby industry—television. TV gave rise to the most popular pattern of tele entertainment, at least in its initial phases—vaudeville on video, hence "vaudeo."

The first TV World Series was telecast in 1947. Broadway box-office suffered a 50 per cent slump, with matinees kayoed, but bars with television upped 500 per cent. This was the time that gags about "bartender wanted; must be able to fix television set" started. Eventually the World Series, in 1950, were to be sold for $800,000 to Gillette, its long time sponsor. (A subsequent 6-year contract calls for $6,000,-000 for the rights). Considering the fact that the Yanks murdered the Phillies four straight it made $200,000 per telecast pretty expensive sponsorship. Eventually, also, theatres were to attempt coping with major sports events by telecasting them into the cinemas, via large-screen, as part of the b.o. lure. It helped the grosses and the picture houses quickly contracted for "closed circuit," big-screen theatre TV events on an exclusive basis. The only video features that can get them into the theatre, obviously, have to be events not broadcast gratis into the home.

In Portland, Maine, the *Sunday Telegram,* which had published the names of purchasers of horseless carriages back in 1908, now began to do the same for posterity by reporting the locals who were going in for the newfangled video contraption. J. Walter Thompson was the first ad agency to hit $1,000,000 in sponsored tele billings.

Tele began to change the social fabric of the nation. Set owners complained of being deluged by neighbors who elbowed in, made themselves at home, and consumed a fortune in refreshments. Conversation at parties became a dying art, with guests sitting silently and staring at the tele screen in darkness. Women began to complain that when sporting events were being telecast, they were totally ignored—"video widows," Variety explained. Parents became frantic over the problem of how to tear Junior from the tele set, in time to get him to do his homework or go to bed.

Established branches of show business began to get really worried about the new medium. Radio examined with dismay a pulse survey which showed that the TV audience for baseball games outnumbered radio listeners by 33 to 1. Sports, the picture business, book publishers and others started to blame video for any and all ailments. Then they decided it might be better to co-operate with instead of fighting the new medium. To paraphrase Jimmy Durante, pretty soon "everybody wanted to git inta de act." Few were quite sure how.

The National Republican and Democratic conventions, both held in the summer of 1948 in Philadelphia, were accepted by tele as its first major challenge to do a better job than radio or newsreels could. Both radio and tele together spent $1,840,929 for the two convention coverages, with TV emerging as the wonder of the year, even stealing the spotlight from the stormy Democrats themselves. As a followup, 10,000,000 Americans saw President Truman take the inaugural oath of office through video, a total of more people than had seen the 31 presidents combined from Washington to Roosevelt.

There soon became no question that TV would be an influential factor in electing the next President of the United States in 1952. In 1950 TV achieved, for Governor Thomas E. Dewey, what nothing else could—it presented him in a more human light and did much to rid him of that onerous crack about looking "like the bridegroom on the wedding cake."

folsom on tv and politicos   TV helped re-elect Senator Robert A. Taft in face of much labor opposition, as the iconoscope reflected him for a sincere man and wiped out much of the invidious stuff written about him. As Frank M. Folsom, president of the Radio Corp. of America, observed: "He couldn't have been elected dog-catcher in face of the written attacks, but TV mirrored him more sympathetically, brought out much in a man's personality that couldn't be uttered, and Taft won. That figured in the case of Vincent Impelliteri, the successful New York City mayoralty candidate, showing him as a simple, sincere, folksy man. And, by the same token, it crucified others."

The growth of tele was fast and furious. The fashion industry announced it would take heavy time in video. The American Federation of Musicians lost no time in setting a scale for commercial video, which came to 75 per cent of the toll for radio network shows. United Artists became the first major distributing company for television films, via regular film exchanges. But a better b.o. idea was the usage by the Hollywood producers of TV spot commercials to merchandize their choicer new film releases, as against the 10-and-more-years-old pix being telecast gratis.

All of Hollywood sat up and took careful notice when "Ultrafax" was unveiled at a sneak preview in Washington, and hailed as "the seventh wonder of the communication world." It proved the possibility of transmitting full-length movies simultaneously from a film studio to thousands of theatre screens. If this was to be the shape of things to come, the 1948 system of film distribution was doomed to obsolescence. Nobody knew for sure what was coming, but everybody was certain that the movies could not afford to ignore video as they once had radio. The Paramount in Times Square struck an experimental note by televising fights from the Brooklyn Y.M.C.A. on their regulation 18′ x 24′ screen.

Eventually the Broadway Paramount and the Fox, Brooklyn, started to telecast major bouts on their large screens, paying nominal experimental fees and finding it paid off socko at the b.o. Spyros Skouras, meantime, nurtured his pet idea of two-a-day televised programs, of super-boxoffice potency. Linking 20 Fox-West Coast Theatres up and down California to receive special big shows on a twice-daily schedule, in addition to first-run feature films, the showman figured he could achieve grosses of $500,000 to $750,000 weekly on a $1 top scale.

With that sort of b.o. revenue he figured he could play Merman, Crosby, Cantor; anybody; he could book *South Pacific* or the Metropolitan Opera. He knew that his theatres could never saturate the market, and that these theatre-televised shows—they'd never reach into homes or bars, being on a special wavelength—would also serve as boxoffice hypo to any big Broadway musical, the Met, or any top-flight variety programs.

It was too much to expect that Tin Pan Alley would let video pass without a calypso yowl or two, so Paul Specht promptly published a tune by Paul Rebere called "I Tell-A-Vision," while Harry Taylor wrote the ultimate in 1948 love songs, "Let's Build A Coaxial Cable of Love." He forgot to add, "Baby." Not to be left at the technicolor-TV post, Charles and Henry Tobias, with Nat Simon, in 1950 whipped up "A Colorful Little Couple" which was lyrically primed for all the spectrum love words.

TV also got its feet wet in libel and slander that year, when Elizabeth T. Bentley, videoed over NBC's "Meet the Press," charged suspended Department of Commerce official William R. Remington with being a Communist.

While vaudeo looked up, Loew's State on Broadway dropped vaudeville, but a flock of top names streamed to London to play the famous Palladium, most resounding being the smash impact made by Danny Kaye. Jack Benny, Dinah Shore, Betty Hutton, the Andrews Sisters, Sophie Tucker, the Ink Spots and Tony Martin also were among the big Yank hits in austere Britain, but at the other end of the British Commonwealth of Nations, vaude was laying an egg in Australia, with Variety reporting "slim coin and vague dates for United States acts." Eventually, however, Aussie's grosses also started to look up.

The year also saw giveaway shows hitting their peak on the radio. "Stop the Music" went personaling into the Capitol, and "Winner Take All" into the Strand, New York. But the vaude version of the radio jackpots flopped.

Joe Smith and Charles Dale, the oldest vaude team in show business, who were still doing their "Dr. Kronkheit" sketch, and working, celebrated their 50th anniversary together—slightly short of the records of Fox & Ward (58 years) and McIntyre & Heath (52).

Vaude was reduced to pointing with pride at Ken Murray's variety show, *Blackouts,* in Hollywood, which had survived for over seven straight years, passing the 3,224 performance record of *Life With Father,* but flopped in seven weeks when Murray brought it to New York. And to—shades of Willie Hammerstein!—Patricia "Satira" Schmidt, pardoned for the murder of her lover John L. Mee, who rolled up $6,500 on a percentage basis at Harlem's Spanish Mecca, Teatro Las Americas.

55

Upheaval in Radio

★

Emerging from the war as the nation's No. 1 news coverage source, radio strove to hang on to its halos. One of its biggest scoops of 1946 was its eye-witness broadcasts on the dramatic demise of Hermann Goering and the execution of 10 Nazi leaders. It also demonstrated its use as a public service in Minneapolis, when an outbreak of polio caused schools to close. Classes were held as usual, via radio.

In 1946, when the world was buzzing about the significance of the atom bomb, CBS, NBC, ABC and MBS pooled resources to cover the United States atom bomb test at Bikini. Variety ran a very terse and vivid review of the broadcast, to wit:

ATOM BOMB TEST
with Bill Downs, Clete Roberts, Don Bell, W. W. Chaplin, Robert Stewart, Jerome Beatty, others
50 Mins.; 5:30-6:20 P.M. Sunday (June 30)
One Shot

537

Sustaining
CBS-NBC-ABC-MBS.

ZZZ ZZZ FFFTZ ZZZZM
ZZZ PFFFT ZZZZ ZZZZ
ZY PFTTT PFFFF ZZZZ.

Rose

As for entertainment, in 1946 the same radio names that spelled ether stardom 10 years earlier were still in vogue—Bob Hope, Fibber McGee & Molly, Red Skelton, Lux Radio Theatre, Edgar Bergen, Walter Winchell, Mr. District Attorney, Fred Allen, Jack Benny, Jack Haley, Bing Crosby, Eddie Cantor, Kay Kyser, Abbott & Costello and Amos 'n' Andy.

Variety estimated that the end of World War II found radio comics holding the bag for about $150,000 in unused and unusable war gags. Timely gags of the year centered around the railroad strike, coal shortage, under-the-table auto deals, the housing shortage, Kilroy, *The Lost Weekend,* fountain pens that wrote under water, the Brooklyn Dodgers, Petrillo, Truman's piano playing (later switched to Margaret's sopranoing) and Gromyko's U.N. walkout.

Radio humor also took a provincial turn, with increasing emphasis on Southern California, from where most broadcasts originated, and on intra-show biz "insult" gags. These local quips brought loud yoks from studio audiences on the Coast, but frequently left national audiences puzzled, lukewarm or bored. The La Brea tar pits, Mad Man Muntz, gopher holes, smudge pots, California weather, Sinatra's anemia, Fred Allen's nasal twang and the bags under his eyes, Benny's stinginess, Cantor's Ida and 5 daughters, Crosby's boys, clothes and horses, and the noses of Bob Hope and Jimmy Durante became trite and irritating gags of dubious mirth.

Crosby's tape-recorded shows for Philco, the first big-time deal on any network that allowed a star to do his stint away from the live mike, created a precedent. Other stars demanded that they, too, be allowed to wax their shows. Sponsors balked, feeling that they were entitled to live appearances in exchange for the heavy coin paid. They also feared a drop in ratings but eventually many capitulated. Filmed TV, however, was not countenanced until 1951—and certain comedy programs may always remain "live."

Among radio highlights in 1947 was the furore created by Ralph Edwards' highly successful "Who Is Miss Hush?" stunt on "Truth and Consequences"; Margaret Truman's radio debut in Detroit; the first soap opera with an all-Negro cast, sponsor and agency, "Here Comes Tomorrow," in Chicago; and the formation in that city of the first National Association of Disk Jockeys.

The ever-growing threat of television promised to capture the nighttime hours, leaving radio only soap-opera time when housewives were too busy to look as well as listen. Yet radio was still big business in 1948. Over 37,600,000 families were tabulated as listeners, enough to induce sponsors to part with an annual radio revenue of $663,000,000, of which $60,000,000 was net profit—an all-time radio high. ASCAP's cut of the radio melon amounted to $5,000,000. All this despite the Hooper survey that revealed that there was a *status quo* in the number of sets in use and in listening habits between 1940 and 1948, while other branches of show business had shown lush upturns.

radio jackpots   The biggest slugfest of the year was "Stop the Music" which blew the whistle for a giveaway orgy that turned radio into a perpetual "bank nite." Merchandise given away was estimated at $165,000 a week, the jackpot hitting $7,000,000 in only 44 weeks. The merchandise, services, transportation and vacations, were all contributed to the giveaway shows in exchange for free puffs. Frequently sponsors of the Santa Claus shows were hard put to tell who was sponsoring what.

Trouble began when listeners, hypnotized by the possibility of winning a fortune, dialed out old-time radio favorites. They slipped down the Hooper scales as the giveaways climbed up.

Fred Allen, hardest hit program because of the direct competition opposite "Stop the Music," led radio stars in ganging up in a campaign to laugh the giveaway shows off the air—and failed. Their gags were more than goodnatured humor; they had a sarcastic, always frustrated, bite. Allen's "insurance" policy, purporting to compensate any lucky listener called while tuned in to his show, had a reflex effect—in that it focused even more attention on the jackpot program.

Then a no-holds-barred raid by CBS on NBC's top stars highlighted radio in 1948. The raid had TV overtones in that Jack Benny, Amos 'n' Andy and the like were "bought" by CBS board chairman

William S. Paley with an eye to their TV potentials, in the event the AM medium became extinct or passé.

This was a departure for CBS which prided itself on building its own stars. It had a socko showman-salesman in Arthur Godfrey (his personal $400,000 annual gross, from $10,500,000 billings, attested fully to his merchandizing prowess) and was supposedly beyond star-raiding. This was the era of "capital gains" radio deals too. CBS ogled Walter Winchell, whose per-point payoff on his Hooperating made him a highly valuable commodity, but the American Broadcasting Co. kept him on its own network by getting Kaiser-Frazer to payroll a $1,352,000 contract for 90 broadcasts at the rate of $12,500 per 12½-minutes of WW gab on Sunday night.

Hollywood was still riding the crest of the wave in 1946, when $350,000,000 was spent making films. Earnings surpassed those of 1945, and popcorn alone accounted for a $10,000,000 revenue in film houses.

The 1946 film that copped most of the Academy awards was Samuel Goldwyn's *The Best Years of Our Lives*.

bing, bergman, 'bells,' 1946 boffs   The year's top-grossing stars were Crosby and Ingrid Bergman; the top-grossing film, *Bells Of St. Mary's,* which took $8,000,000, followed by *Leave Her to Heaven, Anna and the King of Siam, The Yearling, The Jolson Story* and Howard Hughes' *The Outlaw.*

As regards the boffo Bergman, not too long afterward, such being the mercurial boxoffice sensitivity, her flop *Joan of Arc* (the picture version of her hit Broadway play by Maxwell Anderson, *Joan of Lorraine*) was followed by another flop, *Stromboli.* Despite the Italian-made film's worldwide "advance campaign" (her unconventional romance with Roberto Rossellini, the Italian director who later became her husband), the public wouldn't buy it. Ingrid and Roberto were eclipsed only by the Rita Hayworth-Aly Khan escapade in the public prints.

When Daily Variety polled the Hollywood trade, at midcentury for all-time bests, Miss Bergman was second only to Greta Garbo as the top femme star. In the breakdown of sound pix (as against the silents), she ranked Bette Davis and Olivia de Havilland 1-2-3.

Incidentally, that poll voted *Gone With the Wind* the all-time best, Charles Chaplin and Garbo the top stars; the late Irving Thalberg best producer; and David Wark Griffith, best director. The latter's *Birth of a Nation* rated No. 2 in the half-century poll, with *Best Years Of Our Lives* third.

Ronald Colman and Sir Laurence Olivier tied for No. 2 in the best male star category, with Spencer Tracy runnerup. Behind Garbo and Bergman, came Bette Davis and de Havilland tied for third. Runnerup producer laurels went to Darryl F. Zanuck and Sam Goldwyn. Runnerup directors were Cecil B. DeMille and William Wyler.

A further breakdown in the midcentury appraisal of the best sound pix and the best silents rated Tracy, Olivier and Colman top men; Goldwyn, Thalberg and Zanuck top producers. (Obviously, Thalberg's edge in the silent era gave him the all-time award.)

In the best silent era category, *Birth of a Nation, Big Parade* and *The Kid* were the toprated pix; Chaplin, Valentino and Emil Jannings, male stars; Garbo, Gloria Swanson and Lillian Gish, femme stars.

The year saw the beginning of the cycle of psychological films. After the excitement of the war years, it was tough to hold film audiences with old formulas. The appeal was basically more adult and sophisticated. Another significant change in the Hollywood formula took place in Westerns, with the spurs-and-chaps boys dropping shooting irons and reaching for gee-tars.

The Westerns that flooded the screens from 1948-1950 included semi-historical expositions of epochal proportions. These actioners invariably prove good b.o., and even DeMille's *Samson and Delilah* was described in the trade as "a Biblical Western."

°adult° pix   The cycle for "adult" pix lasted a couple of years. Dore Schary made a short-budgeter at RKO, *Crossfire,* which fared well but Darryl Zanuck's *Gentleman's Agreement* clicked even bigger. Both dealt with anti-Semitism. Zanuck next tackled the Negro question with *Pinky* and clicked, as he did with *Snake Pit,* a picture about mental institutions. Stanley Kramer's *Home of the Brave,* also a Negro theme, registered but a later attempt for "adult" appeal, *The Men* (paraplegics), came a cropper at the b.o.

The cycle having run its course, exhibs suddenly started clamoring for "good, old-fashioned, solid film entertainment about boy-meets-girl, glamour, no 'problems.'"

In 1946 Hollywood began to take increasing notice of what was happening on English film lots. J. Arthur Rank won control of 20 out of 30 sound stages in England, and controlled 1,100 of 4,761 film theatres. All this, and a $220,000,000 combine, from films which started with a short subject against the demon rum! Rank roved his eyes over the American and foreign markets—and eventually was to experience a financial debacle, at least as far as his British production ambitions were concerned.

At first, the United States was highly indifferent to the British product. Even in 1947, when British cameras were beginning to turn out good stuff, Variety headlined: STIX STILL NIX BRITISH PIX. But the sticks were also nixing American pix that year. In Hastings, Nebraska, one exhibitor's marquee read: DOUBLE FEATURE—ONE GOOD SHOW AND ONE STINKER.

By 1948 cool winds were blowing in Hollywood. Hot stars with cold yarns gave the colony only lukewarm profits, which raised the question, "Are stars worth their prices today?" Profits slid 45 per cent, with the seven majors netting only $55,000,000. A wave of economy hit pictures, with heavy layoffs of studio personnel and East coast home office staffs. Producers were jittery, wondering whether this was the first impact of TV, the high cost of living, poor stories or an unhappy combination of all these factors.

There was little clue in the protests of theatre owners who listed sex, crime and costume pictures as the three biggest poison doses at the boxoffice. It was an old cry, and one which rarely stood up under analysis. It represented chiefly the exhibitors' "front" to appease the professional protesters. Hollywood took it with salt, just as it did audience votes for "single feature" programs. The customers invariably voted for one-film bills but went to double features.

divorcement The situation in Hollywood during 1948 rapidly fouled up. The scared majors were afraid to produce for a declining market, while the independents found it hard to drag money out of the banks. The United States Supreme Court handed down its long awaited antitrust decisions forcing the major companies to unload most of its theatres, giving the Big Five a total of five years to get rid of the exhibition end. Paramount and RKO soon settled with the Government via a consent decree. Both divided into two separate companies as Warner Bros. was to do in 1951.

Howard Hughes' buy of RKO startled Hollywood. Few knew him intimately, or what could be expected of him. If he wanted anybody he would call them. If it was urgent, through a series of three 8-hour-a-day, round-the-clock secretaries one might get a message to him and he'd call back. Hollywood wits at first wisecracked, "Hughes will never buy RKO because he can't get it off the ground." But he did, and through the quick consent decree with the Government on theatre divorcement looked fair to cash in by ultimately selling enough RKO theatres to make his studio production and distribution organization purchase a comparative bargain.

The film industry's net profits for 1948 had dwindled from the 1946 peak of $90,000,000 to $55,000,000—still very fancy, however. Paramount's *Road to Rio* (Hope-Crosby-Lamour) was the biggest grosser, garnering $4,500,000. Warner Bros.' $22,000,000 net put that company second to Paramount.

The lowered nets stimulated anew the economy drives that placed emphasis on sharp production cuts, kayo of those fancy $250,000 up to $750,000 story and play properties. Great Britain's 55 per cent quota, and sundry money restrictions quickly influenced other foreign nationals to likewise embargo the American film industry. This forced Hollywood investments in foreign ventures, such as local pix production, hotels, theatres and other foreign-to-showbiz buy-ins, as a device to partially thaw out the piled-up frozen funds in Europe.

If films were on the downbeat, the nation's Drive-In theatres were thriving. Food and drink concessions yielded as much as 50 per cent of the profit. The public yen for outdoor films increased. Pix shown were cheap and profits were high. Some captious showmen called 'em "passion pits with pix." As the vogue of the ozoners increased, a Fly-In theatre opened in Asbury Park—room for 25 planes and 500 cars. A Canoe-Inn cinema was announced for Waltham, Massachusetts. The ozoners—eventually exhibitors preferred to call them auto-theatres—were the lone forward-moving light in the benighted exhibition business. They were a boon to the young marrieds (no baby-sitting problems) and the oldsters (invalids who couldn't navigate in a normal theatre were able to recline in the motors driven by their kin). Drive-in impresarios catered to basic needs by providing bottle-warmers for the infants; quick-lunch and soft drink dispensaries; playgrounds for the kids, some including even miniature zoos; laundromats so that, by the time they saw the picture, the family laundry would be done, and the like. This so-called by-product income accounted for a greater profit margin than the basic show business, and the distributors complained, not for naught, that they were entitled to a percentage on the popcorn and allied profits, since it was the Hollywood product that was the lure to draw the populace to the theatre, be it in or out of doors.

56

Disk Jocks and LP Versus 45s

★

The rise of the disk jockey is a postwar phenomenon of unusual proportions. Originally an economic device, chiefly associated with "one-lungers," as the low-watt hinterland radio stations were called, the turntable impresarios first became important on both coasts via Al Jarvis (Hollywood) and Martin Block (New York), with their "make-believe ballroom" technique of turning disks and making a sales pitch. By exercising a judicious ratio of platter and chatter it made them big-income merchandizers. It was the old medicine show on a larger basis, but with an intimacy that the major networks lacked when the super-shows attempted to sell nostrums, food brands, home equipment, motors, petrol and the like.

Eventually the deejay found himself the No. 1 key man in Tin Pan Alley. As one or another plugged a pet platter; or as such instances cropped up where an old Ted Weems disk ("Heartaches") became the bestseller through the single-handed plugging by a North Carolina disk jockey, music publishers and songwriters looked upon the jocks with new respect.

Incidentally, this al fresco method of creating hits and the uncertainty where the new hits will spring from, became part of the new

ASCAP dividend payoff system under the second Governmental consent decree. Newcomer songwriters benefited better than heretofore, where the multiplicity of plugs was the factor, but it hurt the veteran songsmith who suddenly found his backlog catalog not as valuable for royalty dividends as in former years. This was viewed as an inequity by both factions. Even the newcomers now recognize that, if in future years they had no "active" songs being prolifically performed, they too would suffer on the annual ASCAP royalty melons. A more equitable balance is being worked out within ASCAP and in collaboration with the Government.

The decree, however, makes it easier for ASCAP writers to work with BMI firms, and vice versa. Already there are several music publishers who have both ASCAP and BMI catalogs.

As the public became selective in its plays and pix, so it was on the disks. It cared little if it were a major label like Victor, Decca or Columbia or some obscure brand. The interpretation counted, and that's where the deejay came in. He played them all and plugged those he liked. Sometimes the plugs had a payola connotation but since the public always decides in the final analysis, any artificial respiration can give impetus but never insure acceptance. Thus, a relatively obscure artist like Bill Snyder came to the fore with his unique version of "Bewitched"; Frankie Laine with "Cry of the Wild Goose"; Patti Paige with "All My Love" (nee the French "Bolero"); Red Foley with "Chattanooga Shoe Shine Boy"; Eileen Barton's "Bake a Cake"; Teresa Brewer with "Music, Music, Music"; the colored Billy Eckstine and Billy Daniels, via disks, nitery and vaudfilmeries; the Ames Bros. with "Rag Mop"; and hillbilly singers Tennessee Ernie, Jimmy Wakely and Ernest Tubb with their sundry items.

The deejays soon were wagging the dog. Tin Pan Alley welcomed the development of television which, by its production values, looms as the more logical stimulant to music. The cycle was certainly completed in 1950. The yesteryear, silent movie illustrated song-slides became glorified productions as endowed by Lucky Strike on its Hit Parade video series.

The pop music business boom reached its peak in 1946, collecting $10,000,000 in phonograph royalties and countless millions from sheet music, but subsequently skidded, with the economic downbeat. However, basic copyright values of songs continue to mount in value, in light of new-found incomes from synchronization (film) rights, TV's future values for production rights, and the like. Metro-Goldwyn-Mayer recognized that by buying out its 28 per cent minority partner, Jack Robbins, for $500,000, thus (with 20th-Fox) controlling 100 per cent of a giant copyright pool in the Robbins, Feist and Miller Music holdings, along with their subsids.

Songsmiths found their careers more frequently celluloidized in lavish filmusicals such as Bert Kalmar & Harry Ruby (Metro's *Three Little Words*), Jerome Kern (Metro's *Look For the Silver Lining*), Richard Rodgers & Lorenz Hart (*Words and Music,* again Metro) and Vincent Youmans (Warners' *Tea For Two*). The same was true of Fred Fisher (20th Century-Fox's *Oh, You Beautiful Doll*) and Joe E. Howard (20th's *I Wonder Who's Kissing Her Now*).

battle of the speeds   An evolution of the internecine battle between the two giant networks—CBS' raid on NBC's talent, with the capital gains as the gimmick—was the battle of the speeds. A nation which had been content to get its platter music on 78 revolutions per minute was suddenly in the midst of LP versus 45s. That meant Long Playing (Columbia Records' 33⅓ rpm pattern) as against RCA Victor's 45 rpms. The RCA record is a 7-inch, plastic job (of vinylite texture), with a large spindle hole. The records are tinted, to facilitate ready identification for pops, red seals (classics), hillbilly and blues. RCA propagated that theirs wasn't merely a new record but "an entirely new system of recording"; that experimentation had convinced them that only a certain portion of the band on the 45s reproduced the "truest" music—thereafter it became distorted to the sensitive ear.

Eventually, after the record business experienced a critical year, the transition was made in 1949-1950 into two broad categories—LP (33⅓ rpm) for the classics and the musicomedy scores, and 45s for the pops. Since there were still an estimated 12,000,000 to 16,000,000 oldfashioned 78 rpm players in the market, the 78s continued manufacture, but the rich metropolitan markets, which more consistently supported the record business, soon converted into "three-speed" machines, either alone or in combination with the boom of television which, by 1951, saw nearly 15,000,000 TV receivers in American homes.

The universality of music, as a language which everybody understands, placed music values more and more to the forefront of show
business. American jazz (Duke Ellington and Louis "Satchmo"
Armstrong) once again invaded Europe, and conversely Edith Piaf
and Maurice Chevalier found few linguistic barriers with successful
engagement in the United States. Jazz invaded New York's Carnegie Hall and Town Hall anew at $3 top.

On the longhair side, the Metropolitan Opera House imported
Rudolf Bing to succeed Edward Johnson as managing director and,
with the assistance of "the Broadway touch," via legit stage directors
such as Margaret Webster and Garson Kanin, the Met's 1950-1951
season reopened with Miss Webster's production of Giuseppi Verdi's
Don Carlo to an all-time record gate of $50,000, easily the top one-
night gross in history of all show business on a straight per-ticket
basis, with the exception of some mammoth charity.

Ironically, the sensation of the Met 1950-1951 season was not a
longhair attraction at all, rather a modern version in English of
the ever-popular Johann Strauss operetta, *Die Fledermaus,* with a
new book by Garson Kanin (author of *Born Yesterday*) and new
lyrics by Howard Dietz. Staged by Mr. Kanin and sung by a top-
drawer cast of Met artists including Ljuba Welitch, Patrice Munsel,
Risë Stevens, Set Svanholm, Richard Tucker and John Brownlee,
Fledermaus proved the wisdom of the Broadway legit touch at the
Opera House. A boxoffice socko from its preem performance, the
Strauss favorite vied with smash Broadway musicals for top pop
stage appeal during the season and was the most frequently repeated opus in the Met repertory.

talent raiding   With the battle of the speeds, talent values
boomed. Decca snagged Lauritz Melchior, Frankie Carle and
Tommy Dorsey; RCA took Ezio Pinza away from Columbia and
Columbia retaliated by snaring Leonard Bernstein, Dorothy Kir-
sten, Pablo Casals, Sir Thomas Beecham, Bill Lawrence and Sammy
Kaye. RCA, in turn, annexed Dinah Shore, Risë Stevens, Helen
Traubel and Gregor Piatigorsky.

The vogue for "original cast" albums by the disk companies became complicated by Decca's holdout on Ethel Merman, its exclusive
contractee, despite the fact RCA had 100 per cent bankrolled the

Irving Berlin musical *Call Me Madam,* in which Miss Merman starred.

There was a vogue for duets which soon ran its course, only to be revived again when Mary Martin-Arthur Godfrey and Ethel Merman-Ray Bolger clicked with their novelty "Go To Sleep" and "Dearie" diskings. There was another type of "duet" vogue when Bing Crosby and his son Gary clicked with "Sam's Song" (Decca), followed by Mary Martin and her son Larry dittoing two duets for Columbia. But for a spell, it was a succession of duets by Doris Day-(the late) Buddy Clark, Jo Stafford-GordonMacRae, Margaret Whiting-Jimmy Wakely and Bing Crosby-Andrews Sisters, although he was variously paired with Patti Andrews singly, as well as Ella Fitzgerald, Louis Armstrong, Ernest Tubbs and others. Kay Starr-Tennessee Ernie were another odd coupling of a rhythm singer with a hillbilly specialist, but the folk song vogue was such that anybody and everybody did 'billy tunes as well as the livelier tempos. Fran Warren-Tony Martin were RCA's romantic defi to the Day-Clark and Stafford-MacRae vogue. Incidentally, the platters catapulted both Doris Day and MacRae to Warner Bros. film contracts.

Novelty duets reached "gimmick" proportions as diskeries became imbued with the idea that the more freakish the tunes and/or talent couplings were, the better sales would be. Sometimes it worked. Mario Lanza's surprise boffola, *The Great Caruso,* with its longhair hit parade music, catapulted a wave of middle-and-highbrow music.

RCA Victor's rebuttal was to couple Ezio Pinza with The Sons of the Pioneers in a prairie number titled "The Little Ol' State of Texas." However, his rich basso proved unconvincing when chirping about the wide open spaces. More effective was the pairing of Helen Traubel with Jimmy Durante in the pranksome "A Real Piano Player" and "The Song's Gotta Come from the Heart."

Riding the pop hit paraders were Patti Page, Nat (King) Cole, Frankie Laine, The Weavers with their folk stuff, Rosemary Clooney and Kay Armen. Both of the latter got attention with "Come On-a My House," a little Armenian folk item whipped up by William Saroyan in collaboration with Ross Bagdasarian, who also disked it for Coral.

The 1948 musicomedy season was so sparse that the "society" bandleaders complained there wasn't a good new show tune, and that the most popular requests were the Al Jolson-Decca album tunes, inspired by *The Jolson Story*. Accent was given to the fact that such Tin Pan Alley greats as George Gershwin, Jerome Kern, Vincent Youmans, Walter Donaldson and Con Conrad were gone, and that the bulk fell on the perennial Irving Berlin, Cole Porter and Richard Rodgers. But soon Rodgers & Hammerstein's *South Pacific*, Porter's *Kiss Me, Kate*, Frank Loesser's *Guys and Dolls* and Berlin's *Call Me Madam* scores more than took up the musical comedy slack.

But the music business had to concede that its pop song hits no longer came from the greats. Some hillbilly or newcomer, and many of them via BMI, rather than the lordly ASCAPers, could turn out hits like "You're Breaking My Heart," "Room Full of Roses," "Jealous Heart," "Nature Boy," "Rudolph the Red-Nosed Reindeer," "Careless Hands," "A Little Bird Told Me That You Loved Me," "That Lucky Old Sun," "Don't Cry, Joe," "Riders in the Sky," "Powder Your Face with Sunshine" and the like.

The deejay impact made it open season for all types of songs and songwriters. Just because you were a vet ASCAP songsmith or publisher was no guarantee against some upstart hillbilly song and/or tunesmith from the hinterland bobbing up with such oddities as "Mule Train," "Chattanoogie Shoeshine Boy," "Slippin' Around," "Tennessee Waltz," "If I Knew You Were Comin' I'd Have Baked A Cake," "Cry of the Wild Goose," "Wedding Samba," "Dear Hearts and Gentle People" and "Rag Mop."

broadwayites go hillbilly   The Brill Bldg. and Lindy's set of professional music men who deprecated the oddity of these "awful" songs becoming hits were given the brushoff by Irving Berlin, in a Variety interview, that "any song the public accepts is a good song; and perhaps it is the too sophisticated professional writers who are at fault for turning out their own brand of 'bad songs,' otherwise the public would have reacted more favorably to them." The continued acceptance by the masses of the simple, folksy tunes—the hillbilly genre—didn't leave the ever resourceful veteran songwriter and publisher too smug for too long a period of time, because they did an about-face and started fashioning songs with a Western, folk or hillbilly flavor. What's more, they found them more acceptable than the too hep stuff they had been writing of late.

All this—for there is an affinity between the nation's songs and the state of the nation—was part of the yearning by mass Americana, circa 1948-1951, for a return to the yesteryear *gemütlichkeit*. If the threat of Communism the world over was distressing all hemispheres, at least in their native habitat the Americans seemed to yen for the simple and romantic, as witness these samples of the recent crop of pop hits. From a dispersed people America borrowed and accepted "Tzena, Tzena"; from Huddie Ledbetter ("Leadbelly"), with an assist by musicologist John Lomax, they borrowed "Goodnight Irene." From Italian and Germanic paraphrases came "There's No Tomorrow," "Forever and Ever" and "You're Breaking My Heart." Just as the French impact left its mark on the Hit Parade, the British, too, contributed their quota of international hits with "Galway Bay," "Cruising Down the River," "Hop Scotch Polka" and "Now Is the Hour," although, from London's Denmark Street—the British counterpart of Tin Pan Alley—came protests of the too dominant "Americanization" of English popular music tastes. Periodically, the British Broadcasting Corp. is besieged to "ration" songs so as to give home-grown pop product better representation.

That didn't mean that the songsmiths had forsaken the classics. After the Tchaikowsky, Chopin and Grieg binge of the mid-1940s —Perry Como in 1945 put Chopin on the Hit Parade for many weeks, viz., "Till the End of Time"—the boys were digging into the Italian and mittel-Europa folksongs. Johann Strauss had long since been exhausted, reprised, revived and discarded once again. The refugee, whose first impression of America was that "the people here are all so classical-minded; they whistle the masters and sing and dance to fine old melodies" about summed it up.

Styles in music were chameleon. "Enjoy Yourself (It's Later Than You Think)" became a sort of nitery spending theme song, with the bands propagating the free-spending philosophy. There were attempts at saucy songs which occasionally got network frown or taboo, as for instance the Arthur Godfrey-Mary Martin version of "Go To Sleep." The nation's nostalgic yen for a hark-back to the "good old days," which made the Prohibition era's Jazz Age almost a picnic compared to the Stalin-fomented world unrest, inspired a comeback for the Charleston. This was aided on both coasts by regular Monday night "Charleston contests" at the Mocambo, Hollywood nitery, and by the 1920s theme of the musicalized version of Anita Loos' *Gentlemen Prefer Blondes*. The polka also had its vogue, and with it the zither cycle, inspired by the click of "The Third Man Theme," from the Korda picture of that title. The Dixieland style of dansapation followed the nostalgic urge, and Benny Goodman is in the throes of a swing revival at this writing. Bebop flopped.

passing of many greats The post-World War II era is notable for the passing of a Who's Who of names, who by their fame or achievement, contributed so much to the American scene or to the scene of world entertainment, letters, music and the other contemporary lively arts.

Somehow there is more than a usual quota from the field of music. The names are reprised, chronologically, not so much as a mass recording of obits but for their accumulative name-power and the voids they must leave, excepting where their works have durability or have been recorded for reprise in posterity, be it a George Bernard Shaw or an Al Jolson.

Literary giants like Theodore Dreiser, 74, E. Phillips Oppenheim, 79, Booth Tarkington, 76, Gertrude Stein, 77, and H. G. Wells, 79, were among the 1946 obits. Capt. James Medill Patterson, publisher of the New York *Daily News,* one of the most successful tabloids in the world, died at 67. Others included actors George Arliss, 77, Lionel Atwill, 61, comedians W. C. Fields, 66 and Joe Keaton (Keaton Family), 79, Al Reeves, who discovered Charles Chaplin, died at 77. Others who passed on were film tycoon Jules Brulatour (Eastman Kodak), 76; legit producers George C. Tyler, 78, and William Harris, Jr. 62; Major Edward Bowes, the radio "amateur hour" impresario, 72, and George Foster, 82, founder of England's biggest talent agency. Rose Melville died at 68 (she played Sis Hopkins to 5,000,000 people in 5,000 performances) and Florence Turner, early-day silent film star, died at 61.

al jolson When "the king," as even the other show biz greats called Al Jolson, died in the fall of 1950, this marked the end of a golden era. The surviving wearers of the purple, such as Eddie Cantor, Jack Benny, Fred Allen, Ed Wynn, George Jessel, George Burns and Jimmy Durante recognized it as something historic.

When Jolson went out "like the headliner he always was," by willing his entire $4,000,000 estate to be equally divided among Protestant, Catholic and Jewish charities, he was the subject for acclaim in press and pulpit, as with the public in his rich career of nearly 50 years in all branches of show business. He pioneered *The Jazz Singer* into making the talkers the lifesaver of the silent pix era, and he pioneered stellar entertainment for GIs in World War II, and again by being the first star to go to the Korean war area in 1950. At the memorial service for Jolson in New York the crowds were terrific. Eddie Cantor, who delivered the eulogy in New York, as did Jessel at the actual services in Hollywood, observed, "Jolson turned them away again."

The Government officially recognized Jolson's greatness by awarding him the Legion of Merit. Admittedly Jolson was as much a war casualty as the soldier in battle.

Himself a songwriter, for years he had instructed the American Society of Composers, Authors and Publishers to cede 50 per cent of his income direct to the Northwoods Sanitarium, at Saranac, New York.

sid silverman   The 1950 year's mortalities included Sid Silverman, publisher of Variety, and son of founder Sime Silverman, who willed his dominant ownership in the paper to his 18-year-old son, Syd, now a Princeton undergraduate. Harold Erichs, business head of the paper, and Abel Green, its editor, are the lone individuals owning equal minority shares in Variety, Inc. While an absentee publisher for over a decade, Sid Silverman was very much attuned to the sundry nuances and variations brought about in show business, and with the upcoming of television he was one of its keenest observers and interpreters right until his death at 51.

Other giants of the stage who passed on in 1950 included producers William A. Brady, Arthur Hopkins and Brock Pemberton; stars such as Jane Cowl, Walter Huston, Julia Marlowe, Sir Harry Lauder, Pauline Lord and Maurice Costello; Sid Field, England's No. 1 comic, and Cyril Smith, another w.k. English comedian.

Showman Sid Grauman, notables like Buddy de Sylva, Kurt Weill and Nijinsky, agents Max Hart and Ralph Blum, Lou Clayton (Jackson & Durante), Jack Dean (longtime married to Fannie Ward), Whispering Jack Smith, Alan Hale, Aunt Jemima (Tess Gardella), Tom Patricola, Bull Montana, Hobart Cavanaugh, Lew Lehr, vet New York *World* drama critic Charles Darnton at 80, Col. Lemuel Q. Stoopnagle (of radio), Joe Yule (Mickey Rooney's actor-father), Arthur Ungar, editor of Daily Variety, songwriter

Joe Burke, playwright Edward Childs Carpenter (*Whistling in the Dark*), producer A. B. Marcus (in his prewar "Marcus Shows," which toured the Orient, Danny Kaye first got his real professional start), author Sam Hellman, William M. McBride (the theatre ticket agency man), Eugene O'Neill, Jr. (a suicide at 40) music publisher Jay Witmark, author Edgar Rice Burroughs (of Tarzan fame), silent-screen director Rex Ingram (*Four Horsemen of the Apocalypse*), author Robert S. Hichens (*Garden of Allah*) at 85, Lady Mendl (Elsie de Wolfe), and actor Pedro de Cordoba swelled the mid-century obits.

Composer Herbert Stothart died in 1949 at 64, as did Herman DeVries, 90, dean of Chicago music critics; Congressman Sol Bloom, at 79, who started as a music publisher and whose daughter, Vera Bloom, is a songsmith. Singer Buddy Clark met an untimely death at 38, in a chartered plane crash while returning to Hollywood from a San Francisco football game.

Other 1949 obits comprised Joe Cawthorne, Charles Hanson Towne, producer Crosby Gaige, A. Atwater Kent (pioneer radio tycoon), Sir Seymour Hicks (British stage star), Wallace Beery, Maurice Maeterlinck (author of *The Blue Bird*), Patric J. Cain (Cain's Warehouse), Robert L. Ripley, A. P. Giannini (the California banker so prominent in film financing), David Balaban (& Katz), Mrs. Chauncey Olcott (a playwright in her own right), Frank McIntyre, Al Shean (Gallagher &), George Moran (& Mack), Charles Feltman (Coney Island), Richard Dix, Frank Morgan, Ed Ford (4 Fords), Max M. Dill (Kolb &), Rex Beach, William J. Kelly and Ralph Spence (pioneer silent film gagman).

In 1948, J. Keirn Brennan (74) followed his longtime songwriting collaborator Ernest R. Ball into the beyond, as did Clarence Gaskill ("Minnie the Moocher") 56; Oley Speaks ("Road to Mandalay" and "Sylvia"), at 74; Vernon Dalhart ("Prisoner's Song") at 65; Franz Lehar (the *Merry Widow* composer) at 78; music publisher F. A. (Kerry) Mills at 79; and versatile composer-producer-playwright Earl Carroll, who was killed in a plane crash, at 56, along with his "heart," Beryl Wallace, who was the No. 1 beaut at Carroll's theatre-restaurant in Hollywood. His will requested joint burial, and special municipal permission had to be obtained in Los Angeles for the artistic nude the showman specified over their joint tomb.

The year also saw the passing of David Wark Griffith, the film pioneer; Burns Mantle, the dean of New York drama critics; King Baggot, another early film idol; Carole Landis, a suicide at 29; Elissa Landi; Mary Nolan (Imogene Wilson); Fred Niblo, vet pix director who megaphoned the silent epic *Ben Hur;* Vera Gordon; Viola Allen, Frohman star of yesteryear; Dame May Whitty; Bessie Clayton, the toe dancer, playwright Max Marcin; and Rupert D'Oyly Carte, founder of the great Gilbert & Sullivan opera co.

Harry K. Thaw, the Tommy Manville of his era, died in 1947 at 76, as did J. Herbert Mack, pioneer burlesque impresario, at 91; J. C. Nugent; Lewis E. Lawes, the warden at Sing Sing; Lucille Webster (Mrs. Jimmy Gleason); humorist John P. Medbury; columnist-producer Mark Hellinger; Will Fyffe; pioneer Western star Harry Carey; poet-playwright Richard LeGallienne (father of Eva); Lucius Boomer, the Waldorf-Astoria bossman; J. Warren Kerrigan, silent movie matinee idol; songwriter Bert Kalmar, at 63; Eva Tanguay, vaude's great song interpreter, at 68; Grace Moore, another songbird of a different caliber, at 45; Walter Donaldson, 54, another Tin Pan Alley great; Lieut. Gitz Rice, the Canadian war hero and songwriter ("Dear Old Pal of Mine"); and A. Seymour Brown ("Oh You Beautiful Doll").

The year 1945 saw the passing of such songwriting giants as Jerome Kern, Gus Edwards, Edward B. Marks, James V. Monaco and Al Dubin. A year later Harry Von Tilzer (73); Moritz Rosenthal (83), the Polish pianist-composer; and former Mayor James J. Walker ("Will You Love Me In December As You Did in May?") at 65 joined them in the musical beyond.

Other 1945 obits included the great minstrel man, Al Fields; Billy Watson (né Isaac Levine) of the famed Watson's Beef Trust; playwright Richard Walton Tully (*Bird of Paradise*); Johnnie Jess, 83, another burleycue pioneer; actor George Sidney; musical comedy's Gus Shy; Winfield Sheehan (William Fox's chief aide); producer Oliver Morosco; Charles Coburn (not the actor—né Colin Whitton McCallem English, he wrote "The Man Who Broke the Bank At Monte Carlo"); Albert Geyer, 85 ("World's greatest acrobat," of Geyer & Delhauser); bandleader Glenn Miller (the United States Army officially "presumes" he is dead, victim of a wartime air crash); playwright William Carey Duncan (*Royal Vagabond*); William J. Ferry ("The Frog Man," a vaude and circus great); Kitty Sharp (90), last surviving cast member of the original *The Black Crook*

Company); Julius Keller (81)—he was the first to introduce the cafe floor show to Maxim's, New York, and the first to supply gigolos for lonely ladies at Maxim's tea dansants); newspapermen O. M. (Monte) Samuel (60), Variety's oldest mugg, he started with the paper's founding in 1905; Hype Igoe; Joseph V. Connolly (King Features head); and essayist-critic Benjamin deCasseres.

57

The 'Monster'

★

Show biz already was calling television the "monster," and the continuing $64,000,000 question is, will TV eventually swallow up practically all of show business? The 1951-52 season is undoubtedly the year of decision. Already both Hollywood and TV have decided to go steady. The pix biz figured as long as it can't fight progress it might as well join it, and virtually every major film studio agreed to rent studio space for TV film production. However, film moguls still held out on releasing any relatively recent films to video despite the issuance of lesser if slightly newer British pix. On the other hand, if indie producers want to use studio space for specific vidpix production, the majors are willing to rent their facilities.

But this attempt to protect the 18,000 exhibitors, the long-time customers of the producers, was constantly losing ground. Bill Boyd's Hopalong Cassidy was doing so well with oldie pix that Roy Rogers and Gene Autry got similar ideas for theirs.

United Paramount Theatres dramatized the situation most vividly by a merger proposal with The American Broadcasting Company, and retaining a number of key network executives. Par Theatres' prime objective was to insure TV outlets in 5 key markets, the limitation under existing FCC restrictions.

The show biz axiom about there "being nothing more certain than change in this business" witnessed several changes, shifts, moves, and mergers—all pointing to TV. Henry Ginsberg, former production topper at Paramount, joined NBC as "production coordinator," an ambiguous post at first but keyed to ultimate vidpix production. Billy Rose became a $100,000-a-year TV consultant to NBC. David O. Selznick's Dan O'Shea became an important cog in the CBS top echelon. Louis B. Mayer resigned from Metro-Goldwyn-Mayer, the company he helped found some 27 years ago, in a policy scrap with "the General," as Loew's, Inc.'s prexy, Nicholas M. Schenck, is called. Latter favored production economies and new blood, symbolized chiefly in Dore Schary, the relatively new production boss at the studio. M-G-M is now minus both the Goldwyn (long since gone indie) and Mayer names.

An abortive $25,000,000 deal—at $15 a share for the Warner freres' 24 per cent control—continues to have TV repercussions. Warner's Burbank plant is streamlining its holdings by offering to sell accumulated, heretofore unproduced, scripts, to TV. The Brothers renamed their Broadway Strand showcase the Warner Theatre, in celebration of the "25th Anniversary of Sound," and became the first Main Stem de-luxer to install RCA big-screen television production equipment. The N. Y. Paramount already had its big-screen TV equipment. Even the holdout Loew's Theatre chain is following suit along with other circuits.

subscription television   The click of the Joe Louis-Lee Savold fight, and the "Irish Bob" Murphy-Jake LaMotta fisticuffs exclusive TV showings at theatres sparked renewed interest in "subscription television."

These innovations brought the industry back to Commander Eugene F. MacDonald, Jr., president of Zenith Radio Corp. and proponent of Zenith's subsidiary, Phonevision. Phonevision enables viewers to screen motion pictures at home, the $1 fee per new picture being charged to the individual's telephone bill.

The results were good for the 90-day Phonevision experiment which took place with a special FCC license. This was an about-face for the FCC who had previously frowned on "subscription radio." But new modes and moods brought new rules. Paramount bought control of the Telemeter subscription idea; the Skiatron Corp. had its own Subscribervision system. Based on a coin-in-the-slot principle, the machines unscramble distorted patterns on a special channel. Telemeter claims a unique gauge which automatically records which feature earned which fee, so that it can accurately compute what percentage split goes to what entertainment medium.

The color hassle continued bubbling. CBS got into the field first with a commercial chain telecast, which restricted its own audience because of the complicated CBS system. Later, to offset this difficulty, CBS began manufacturing special colorvision sets. RCA followed with its "compatible" tube system which enabled any black-and-white TV set to receive color. CBS color is a blur when received on an ordinary black-and-white TV set. Somehow manufacturers are sticking with RCA's system, despite the governmental agency's partiality to the CBS system.

The closer affinity of video with the stage, rather than with Hollywood, is figured to hypo the "live" theatre. The plenitude of ballet on TV may or may not be an influencing factor in the fabulous grosses which ballet companies like Sadler's Wells, Roland Petit and his Paris ballet troupe, and others have enjoyed. The English Sadler's Wells ballet netted $134,769 sans tax, in eight shows which exceeds the record set by the national touring company of *South Pacific,* for instance, whose high-water mark was $112,368 in Dallas, and even the still higher gross that *Oklahoma!* did in an Oklahoma City week with $119,811. The Sadler's troupe had over $1,000,000 advance before its second United States tour in 1950—an all-time record in the history of the dance.

Greats, some of whom started in vaudeville and achieved world renown in radio segued into TV and clicked, include Jimmy Durante, Dean Martin & Jerry Lewis (who didn't fare well on radio), Eddie Cantor, Arthur Godfrey, Bob Hope, Jack Benny, George Burns & Gracie Allen, Ed Wynn, Ken Murray, Danny Thomas, Bobby Clark, and Abbott & Costello.

Unlike the more slowly pioneering radio, which was content with such early-day favorites as the Happiness Boys (Billy Jones & Ernie Hare), the A & P Gypsies, Vaughn de Leath, Whispering Jack Smith, Little Jack Little, band pickups such as Vincent Lopez, B. A. Rolfe, Paul Specht and Ben Bernie, TV was big time in no time.

Video interests realized that only big league entertainment would sell receiving sets costing $300 to $500, and more, and sell valuable time to sponsors on the TV networks, so it set out to buy up as much important marquee talent as possible.

Both the William Morris agency and the Music Corp. of America, as well as other talent agencies were equally quick to realize that the pioneering, low-cost era of video would be fleeting. Important money soon became the vogue. Bob Hope's $40,000-a-week (his first Frigidaire-sponsored package was a $130,000 item) set the pace. For the more consistent once-a-monthers such as Eddie Cantor and Jimmy Durante, the "packages" brought $50,000, and with overtime (which the sponsor and network absorbed in part) for rehearsals the shows ran closer to 60G. While the stars could net $20,000 to $25,000 for a month's wages the nature of video is such that more intensive scripting, preparation and rehearsal is necessary. The actor who comes to the radio studio an hour before curtain-time and reads his "ad libs," cues in his songs (with an expert piano accompanist, who anticipates every nuance), or even reads a dramatic script, is a thing of the past. That was AM—not so with TV.

tv's own stars   Meantime TV has been making its own new stars—Sid Caesar, Imogene Coca and Dave Garroway; "plunging neckline" personalities like Faye Emerson, Maggi McNellis, Dagmar, and Eva Gabor; grownup quiz kids, of the Oscar Levant genre, such as Eloise McElhone; and Ken Murray, Clifton Fadiman, Milton Berle, Arthur Godfrey and Ed Sullivan became kingpins as vaudeo entrepreneurs; Ted Mack took the "amateur hour" technique successfully from AM to TV; marionette stars like Kukla, Fran & Ollie and Bob Smith's "Howdy Doody" came to the fore.

By buying back control of his old "Hopalong Cassidy" pix for TV, Bill Boyd put himself into income brackets such as he never before knew. The subsidiary income from "Hoppy" Western regalia and its by-products is astronomical. An example of Boyd's boffo b.o. occurred at the Liberty Theatre, Chicago, which presented "3 Hopalong Cassidys Never Before Seen On TV!"

Godfrey brought back the ukulele to such an extent that music publishers had to reincorporate special uke arrangements on their new sheet music—a practice abandoned after the F. Scott Fitzgerald "Jazz Age" era when raccoon coats and ukuleles were standard flipper-and-flapper equipment.

In line with sophisticated video entertainment—the s.a. gals, adult dramatic scripts, nitery comics' flip gags and the like—there was concern on two fronts. TV wanted to insure itself against any FCC frown by self-regulation; and pix, seeking an alibi for their partial b.o. eclipse, wondered if the "Production Code" (known as the "Joe Breen office" in the trade) should not be relaxed to conform to more "adult" standards. The video cameras have, unquestionably, on occasion, been too revealing, although sometimes accidentally so. There is the instance of the rather prim newspaper gal who appeared on TV in a white decolleté, which through a quirk of the camera, gave her an overall Gypsy Rose Lee appearance. Certain comedians, particularly those from the cafes making guest-shots on the vaudeos, have slipped over an occasional indigo nifty. The dramatic scripts, betimes, also might have gotten "the Joe Breen office" frown if done in Hollywood.

color tv   With the atomic development of post-World War II video, color TV loomed large and menacing in 1950. The two giant networks, CBS and the Radio Corp. of America and its National Broadcasting Co. subsidiary, crossed electronic swords. The Federal Communications Commission's OK on CBS' color TV method over RCA-NBC's touched off an intra-trade and a public battle which made a road company out of their two previous feuds, talent raids and record speed battles.

It is generally agreed that with the coaxial cable now reaching from coast-to-coast the color controversy will catch up with TV's scientific developments, returning the medium to show biz's fundamental—what's the attraction?

TV's importance created another Broadway phenomenon. The easterners who joined the Hollywood pix and radio gold rush came back home. Some sold their Bevhills homes and gave up memberships in the Hillcrest and Lakeside country clubs; most re-established apartments in New York. The Lambs, Friars and NVA club rosters zoomed again as old members returned and lapsed memberships were reactivated but not for long. Already Hollywood is reclaiming some of its lost glory now that the coaxial cable is here.

Fact is that Hollywood, with or without the TV-inspired downbeat of top names—so many of whom hurried back to Broadway, as did scripters and directors—is one of the top datelines in the world. Over 300 correspondents accredited to the "Eric Johnston office" alone attests to that.

Meantime the question of new talent is a continuing one, especially as TV has been devouring so much of it. But somehow new values seem to assert themselves. The mountain summer resorts in the Catskills (New York) and Poconos (Pennsylvania), broadly grouped as the borscht circuit, come up with talent season after season. That, along with niteries and what is left of vaudeville, which heretofore, along with burlesque, was the biggest proving ground for talent, constitutes about the most fertile fountainhead for new faces.

Noted in recent years by Variety's New Act reviews is that over 80 per cent deal with song-and-dance and acrobatic turns—very few comedy acts and talking turns. In vaude's heyday the ratio was about 90 per cent talking acts, and 10 per cent dumb acts or straight singing turns. Yesterday's dumb acts were openers or closers, or an occasional "deuce spot" (No. 2 on the bill). In video, today, they get important spottings. Too often, of course, they're utilized as foils for a Milton Berle comedy antic, for example. But it does pinpoint the paucity of the truly great comics—that's why the few remaining Cantors, Berles, Allens, Bennys, Hopes, Durantes and Wynns must be so carefully rationed around the iconoscopes, on a once-a-month, or even less frequent schedule.

In actuality, video is a blend of or an inspirational force for almost every branch of show biz. Vaude went into the niteries, radio and now video. Legit and ballet, puppets, Little Theatres, circuses and carnivals, musical comedy and revue—all these are now part and parcel of TV. The cycle thus has completed itself, save for minstrelsy which has long become extinct and lingers only in makeshift amateur entertainments by lodges and fraternal organizations.

TV now has permanent circus features as bait for the juveniles, and as an antidote to the Hopalong Cassidy vogue that first seemed to dominate the 5-7 P.M. slots on TV. As regards major outdoor attractions, the Ringling-Barnum & Bailey Circus found TV a boon rather than a b.o. bane, as evidenced by the $6,000,000 record grosses in 1949 and 1950, of which $1,500,000 was from Madison Square Garden alone.

Video's inroads on sports are being offset by underwriting major fights, ball games and the like. TV has helped basketball and hockey, revived wrestling into a clown type of showmanship-sports event, and created popularity for a new sport, the roller derby. Percentage of the TV coin to baseball players, pro gridders, fighters and the like is figured to take up the slack, besides proving a continuing ballyhoo medium for these sports.

Radio's status, meantime, has gone through a gamut of super-shows, such as a 1½ hour, Tallulah Bankhead all-star galaxy that NBC inducted in late 1950 to "knock off Benny at 7," to the petering-out of quiz and jackpot shows. However, the Stop the Music type of show, at its height, did achieve a k.o. on such stalwarts as Fred Allen. For all his fulminating against "radio which makes a frig-idaire the headliner and jackpot the prime entertainment," Allen was forced into retirement, although not for long.

The giveaways assumed staggering and ridiculous proportions until the money and prize-award shows graduated into engaging such expert conferenciers as Groucho Marx, Ralph Edwards, Jan Murray and Joey Adams who merely used the prizes for comedy entertainment values.

The gambling instinct basic with people, combined with the something-for-nothing appeal, gripped the American public. Spon-sors latched on to the millions of phones in American homes as a device for a legal form of a quasi-lottery, and in no time Winchell, the radio columnists, and others were assisting in "the key to the mystery melody" and other inside info, like tipstering sheets.

Amidst the TV hoopla, radio refused to concede defeat and the continuance of AM billings attest to that. Radio is still rich, lush, and thriving. Hinterland independent stations accused the chains of be-coming so big-city sold on TV that they were sabotaging radio, which still paid the freight for all of TV's new excitement. NBC conceded that only 3 of its 5 stations in 1951 were making money, and that the others were only at break-even points.

As for "the monster" taking over all of show biz, Brigadier Gen-eral David Sarnoff, board chairman of RCA, didn't think so. He told Variety, "Television would be a big hit if it only reflected the march of life. In other words, were TV to show only milling crowds in Rockefeller Center, The Loop, or on Market Street, people would want to look at them. It brings the excitement of our world right into the home. Witness the Kefauver committee's investigations, General MacArthur's address to Congress, and major sports events and big entertainment programs."

legit's boom   That fabulous invalid, legit, proved really socko at midcentury. As with all postwar selectivity, you couldn't get into the hits and you couldn't give away the in-betweeners.

The road sagged, but two Rodgers & Hammerstein honeys were continuing to mop up. *South Pacific* bid fair to top the fabulous *Oklahoma!* which, in seven years, rolled up a $4,185,500 profit on the road. In its first year on Broadway, *South Pacific* set a new mark with its $2,635,000 gross, topping Ziegfeld's *Show Boat*.

R & H refuse to have their shows filmed. On Broadway and on tour *South Pacific* and *Oklahoma!* have done more profit than a smash picture which, if costing $1,500,000-$2,000,000 and if realizing a gross twice that amount, is deemed highly profitable. A legit musical's investment today averages $200,000-$225,000 although, of course, the continuing weekly overhead cannot compare with the single-cost investment that constitutes a film's over-all "nut."

Just as *Abie's Irish Rose* was the smash of the 1920s, and *Tobacco Road* with its many road companies was the 1930s topper, so were *Life With Father* and *Oklahoma!* the highlights of the 1940s.

Abie ran on Broadway from 1922-1927 and grossed $2,500,000, garnering its real gravy from myriad road companies, including England, Australia and South Africa besides several national touring troupes in the United States, which piled up another $17,500,000. However, *South Pacific* on its first year grossed $2,635,000. In the comparisons it must not be forgotten that the $2 scale in the 1920s for a light comedy that spelled a $10,000 weekly gross meant a lot of profit.

Tobacco Road grossed $4,300,000, of which $1,820,000 came from its second-longest-run on Broadway record (1933-1941). *Oklahoma!* grossed $12,115,869 all told, and *Life With Father* clocked $9,908,000. *Oklahoma!* as a champ Broadway long-runner is fourth only to *Father*, *Tobacco Road* and *Abie*, the all-American long-runners on Broadway with 3,224, 3,182 and 2,327 performances respectively. Both *Road* and *Abie* also enjoy the dubious distinction of having been roundly panned by the critics but survived the scriveners' barbs, a commentary that is significant in light of recent years when, managers aver, "unless you get a good set of notices you're dead." *Oklahoma!* with 2,248 performances, *Hellzapoppin*, 1,404, and *Annie Get Your Gun* with 1,147 performances are the only three musicals in the top 12.

On the subject of long runs, those wonderful old melodramas of the 19th century, Denman Thompson's *The Old Homestead,* Harriet Beecher Stowe's *Uncle Tom's Cabin* and Lottie Blair Parker's *Way Down East,* really make *Father* and the others look like short-runners. Thompson played in his *Homestead* for 20 years after its first production in 1896. *Tom* troupes roamed the country and the riverboats for decades after its dramatization in 1852. *East* has been a stock company standby for decades after its 1898 premiere.

rodgers & hammerstein   George and Ira Gershwin cornered the musical comedy market in the 1920s with words and music for George White's *Scandals,* Alex Aarons & Vinton Freedley shows (Gertrude Lawrence in *Oh, Kay!*), the Astaires, *et. al.,* but the 1940s and 1950s belong dominantly to Rodgers & Hammerstein & Co. Whereas George Gershwin wrote jazz rhapsodies, jazz operas, and musical comedy scores at a highly accelerated pace during his 38 years, Oscar Hammerstein, 2d, and Richard Rodgers are having richer, fuller careers.

They and their associated stagers, directors, coauthors and co-producers account for a rich heritage in the American theatre, *Oklahoma!* was a signal turning point in the Rodgers & Hammerstein career. It was their first joint effort and it proved a real sock, on the heels of the death of Lorenz Hart at 47 in 1943. Dick Rodgers & Larry Hart had been spoken of as "the American Gilbert & Sullivan." Hart's lyrics were clever and sophisticated, but with the more gentle and poetic Hammerstein, Rodgers was to fashion his even richer scores and to figure as coproducer in some of the best straight comedies.

While the Theatre Guild produced their *Oklahoma!,* the songsmiths in collaboration with Leland Hayward and Joshua Logan, produced *South Pacific.* Alone they presented *The King and I* (Gertrude Lawrence-Yul Brynner). As a production team they also accounted for *I Remember Mama, John Loves Mary* (the latter with Logan), *The Happy Time,* and another fabulously successful musical, *Annie Get Your Gun,* which starred Ethel Merman, with an Irving Berlin score; this was Berlin's takeover of a Herbert & Dorothy Fields book following the death of Jerome Kern at 60 in 1945. Kern was originally to have tunesmithed *Annie.*

The Rodgers & Hammerstein alliances all prospered, as witness the Berlin-Merman musical, *Call Me Madam,* under Leland Hayward's aegis. Hayward, a Hollywood 10 per center turned legit producer, successfully impresarioed *A Bell for Adano, State of the Union, Mister Roberts* (coauthored with and staged by Joshua Logan), *Anne of the Thousand Days* (in association with the Playwrights' Company and authored by Maxwell Anderson). Logan, in turn, was author (from the original *The Cherry Orchard* of Chekov), director and coproducer (with Leland Hayward) of Helen Hayes' *The Wisteria Trees;* coauthor and director of *Mister Roberts* and *South Pacific;* and stager of *I Married an Angel, On Borrowed Time, Two for the Show, Knickerbocker Holiday, Higher and Higher, By Jupiter, Charlie's Aunt, Annie Get Your Gun, Happy Birthday,* and *John Loves Mary.*

south pacific & oklahoma!   The fabulous Rodgers & Hammerstein saga reflected by that sordid economic basis which show biz best understands—the b.o.—is best pointed up by the hit, *South Pacific.* Now in its third year, *Pacific* earns over $20,000 weekly from two companies, over $1,000,000 annual profit. It has already distributed a total of $2,200,000 in profits to the lucky investors.

Oklahoma!'s melon has been $4,275,500, including $60,000 from the 1950-51 season's road tour, as well as British and other foreign managements' rights, record sales, etc. Stock rights have not been leased and there are no picture deals. Ditto *South Pacific.* Rodgers & Hammerstein just can't see undermining their living theatre property by selling celluloid rights.

While it's a Rodgers & Hammerstein era all right, Hayward's *Mister Roberts* didn't do badly, with $1,150,000 in distributed profits so far, and $85,000 in the kitty for cash reserve. And the lucky angels are awaiting another cutting of the melon.

Like Irving Berlin who was accused for 10 years following his marriage of having "lost the common touch" and "the feel of the people," Hammerstein, after a succession of flops, finally wowed 'em with *Oklahoma!* In 1944 he took a memorable ad in Variety telling show biz, I'VE DONE IT BEFORE AND I CAN DO IT AGAIN! And instead of listing *Oklahoma!* or any of his previous successes, Hammerstein's self-kidding ad reprised some of his undistinguished but highly memorable flops, such as *Very Warm for May* (7 weeks), *Ball at the Savoy* (5 weeks), *Sunny River* (6 weeks), *Three Sisters* (6 weeks), and *Free For All* (3 weeks).

It was poetic justice, therefore, that his two outstanding flops—*Ball at the Savoy* and *Three Sisters,* both at London's Drury Lane Theatre in 1933-34—were later wiped off the slate by his being established as the Drury Lane's "longest-run author" in the history of that 288-year-old London theatrical landmark. First came *Oklahoma!* in 1947, which ran over three years (1,343 performances), and *Carousel* in 1950-51 which will have run 1½ years by the time Mary Martin re-creates her *South Pacific* role in the West End in the fall of 1951. (For Miss Martin, too, *South Pacific* is a kind of challenge. In 1946 she flopped in Noel Coward's *Pacific 1860* at the Drury Lane and the comedienne swore she would come back to London and redeem herself.)

Carousel's career at the Drury Lane made it the fourth longest run in the theatre's history, topped only by *Oklahoma!* and two 1920 operettas, *Rose Marie* and *The Desert Song,* on which Hammerstein also collaborated.

$50,000,000 legit biz   As Variety's legit statistician, Hobe Morrison, computed, the legit gross for 1950-51 was $48,216,600, of which $27,886,000 was done on Broadway and $20,330,600 on the road. The 1949-50 season's gross was $49,015,800, of which Broadway contributed $28,614,500; and the year before, legit in the U. S. and Canada grossed $52,498,600, comprising tickets worth $28,840,700 on Broadway and $23,657,900 on the road.

Lemuel Ayers' and Saint Subber's *Kiss Me, Kate* cut up $996,000 in profits and has about $90,000 in other liquid assets. The relatively newer *Gentlemen Prefer Blondes* has cut up $440,000 on a $200,000 investment, with more to come.

Coproducer Joshua Logan, himself an ex-GI, waxed plenty sore at General Thomas T. Handy who banned *Mister Roberts*—which had "soothed" President Truman—from his European command. General Handy's wife thought *Roberts* "too rough" for our German Occupation Army GIs!

Cole Porter's 1951 season entry, *Out of This World,* proved the reverse of *Kate.* It lost $179,000 on a $250,000 production investment. Where the Bard was boff on Broadway in an earlier era, Olivia de Havilland's *Romeo & Juliet* represented a $330,000 setback. *The*

Green Pastures revival cost $200,000; *Billy Budd* gave up with a $105,000 loss; *Make a Wish* was a $250,000 casualty. *Wish* was a handsome production but lacked a good score. Comedian Phil Silvers cracked "Soooo all right, the people will go out humming the costumes!"

The 1951 legit season was notable for the producing team of Feuer & Martin (Ray Bolger's *Where's Charley?* and the Damon-Runyon-inspired *Guys & Dolls*), and, coincidentally, the growing stature of Frank Loesser, composer of both scores.

an actor's year Recent developments indicate that, more and more, "it's an actor's year on Broadway." With Ethel Merman and *Madam,* Carol Channing and *Gentlemen,* Shirley Booth and *A Tree Grows in Brooklyn,* John Gielgud and Pamela Brown in *The Lady's Not for Burning,* Frederic March and Florence Eldridge in Lillian Hellman's *The Autumn Garden,* Celeste Holm in *Affairs of State,* Rex Harrison and Lilli Palmer in *Bell, Book and Candle,* Paul Kelly and Uta Hagen in Odets' *The Country Girl,* Richard Whorf and Nancy Kelly in *A Season in the Sun,* Louis Jouvet's company, Claude Rains with *Darkness at Noon* by Sidney Kingsley, Gloria Swanson and José Ferrer in the MacArthur-Hecht *20th-Century* revival, Gertrude Lawrence and Yul Brynner in *The King and I,* Maureen Stapleton in *The Rose Tattoo,* Charlotte Greenwood in the ill-fated *Out of This World,* Louis Calhern's *King Lear,* Barbara Bel Geddes in *The Moon Is Blue,* Bert Lahr and Dolores Gray in *Two on the Aisle, et al.*

critics' box score 1951 was the year Variety finally acceded to the Legit Critic's long-pending beefs against the Critics' Box Score, and dropped it. Variety pointed out anew that a daily paper's critic's prime function should be to advise his readers whether or not to spend from $3.60 up to $7.20 for a ticket and that pure critical appraisal should not blind the reviewer to the box office objective. Anyway, as Variety pointed out, its 26-year-old box score achieved its purpose: (a) It got reviewers off the fence, because most of them were giving definite opinions; and (b) if there was any backsliding and recourse to fence-sitting it could always be reinstated. In an informal reappraisal of critical opinion, which Variety continues to keep for intraoffice information, it was

noted that there were fewer "definite maybes" given than ever before; that the critics were sincere in their efforts to state definite
opinions. Their papers went further by broadsiding this dubious
acclaim by institutional ads on delivery trucks, office ads in the
newspapers themselves, and the like.

at. midcentury   As show biz rolls into the second half of
the 20th Century, it harks back and wonders. First it was vaude.
Pix knocked that off. Sound knocked off the silents. Radio almost
dittoed, but, somehow pix and other general entertainment entities
were able to capitalize on radio ballyhoo and build-up for b.o. benefit. Now comes video, something unique unto itself. Sight value,
added to sound, brought into the home, and what it does to baby-
sitting problems, are all staggering plusses for TV.

Hold on to your hats, boys, this is where we came in!

Glossary

Admish—admission price.

AM—amplitude modulation radio reception; antithesis of FM

Angel—show-backer.

Anzac—an Australian.

ASCAP—The American Society of Composers, Authors and Publishers.

Aud—auditorium.

Balto—Baltimore.

Belly laff—big comedy reaction.

Big time—big league.

Biz—business.

Blue stuff—dirty comedy or risqué stage business.

BMIer—member of Broadcast Music, Inc., radio's ASCAP counterpart.

Boff—a hit

Baloney—spurious.

Booners—talent scouts, derived from Daniel Boone.

Borscht circuit—broad connotation for Catskill (N.Y.) Mountain resorts booking talent.

B.o.—box office.

B.r.—bank roll.

Brit flick—British film.

Brodied—flopped; derived from Steve Brodie.

Brush-off—to ignore or brush aside.

Budgetitis—trouble with the financial budget.

Burley or burleycue—burlesque.

Caviar set—snobby circle.

Chi—Chicago.

Chiller—melodrama.

Chiz—chiseler; a gyp.

Chowmeinery—Chinese restaurant.

Chump—Broadway sucker.

Cincy—Cincinnati.

Cleffer—songwriter.

Click—a rousing success.

Cliffhanger, or cliffer—melodramatic serial; derived from habit of ending chapters with hero on brink of disaster.

Cocktailery—cocktail lounge.

Coffee-and-cake time—bush league.

Coffee Pot Canyon—Times Square, because of the large number of all-nite drugstores and cafeterias there.

Coin happy—hungry for money, to make money.

Competish—competition.

Crix—critics.

Cuffo—on the cuff; for free.

Damp blanket—bad reviews.

Dancery—dancehall.

Dansapation—syncopated music.

DC—Washington, District of Columbia.

Deejay—disk jockey.

Diskery—phonograph record manufacturer.

Divvy—quarterly dividend.

"Downtown end"—Wall Street, as used in relation to financing a big amusement deal.

Drive—artificial campaign to plug a song into popularity.

Dualer—house playing two films.

Eatery—restaurant.

Emcee—master of ceremonies.

Exhibs—Motion picture exhibitors.

Fanner—fan dancer.

Femcee—mistress of ceremonies.

Femme—female.

Femme looker—pulchritudinous woman.

Filmusical—musical picture, sometimes called tuner.

Finale bend—final bows.

Flesh—live actors.

Flivved—flopped.

Flopped—performance didn't get over.

FM—frequency modulation radio reception; antithesis of AM.

Foldee—a show that folded.

Freeloader—a chiseler; from one who loads up on free drinks and food.

Frisco—San Francisco.

Frolic—performance.

G—$1000.

Gabber—radio commentator.

Gower Gulch—See *Poverty Row*.

Grind—stripteaser's pelvic gyrations.

Grind house—continuous performance theater.

Grunt-and-groaners—those phony TV wrestlers.

Guestar—TV or radio guest artist.

Gyp 'n' take—larcenous show, carnival, etc.

Hand-to-hand music—applause.

Heave-'n'-grunter—wrestler.

Hebe comic—Jewish comedian.

Hip-flinger—cootch dancer.

Hoofery—dancehall.

Hosp—hospital.

Hoss opry—Western film.

Hypo—to stimulate b.o. receipts.

In the test tube—play tryout.

Indie—an independent exhibitor.

Inside stuff—the real lowdown.

Introed—introduced.

Irish justice—burlesque term for skit where judge hits defendant with rubber bladder.

It's the nuts—Sime's brushoff to anything spurious.

Joebreened—script that has been cleaned up; from Joseph I. Breen's, film industry censor.

Joint—nite club, hotel or restaurant, no matter how exclusive.

Juve—juvenile actor.

Kill time joint—cocktail lounge.

Knocked 'em bowlegged—rousing success.

L.A.—Los Angeles.

Laid an omelet—variation of "laid an egg"; a flop.

Layoff—unemployed actor.

Leblang—from Joe Leblang, king of cutrate ticket brokers. When a show goes over "with a Leblang" it profits through cutrate ticket support.

Legit—legitimate theater.

Legmania—acrobatic or intricate dancer.

Life of the party—generally borscht circuit m.c. whose job is to "laff it up" for the resort patrons.

Looker—beautiful woman; in TV dept. could also mean people looking-in on video.

Loop—Chicago's well-known theatrical sector.

L'ville—Louisville.

Mag—magazine.

Mazda Lane—Broadway.

M.c.—See *emcee*.

Megger—Film director; hangover from days when directors used megaphones.

Meller—melodrama.

Mesa meller—Western film.

Mesquiter—Western film.

Met op—Metropolitan Opera Association.

Milk man—actor who "milks" audience for extra laughs.

Mitt-reader—palmist.

Mugg or *Variety mugg*—a Variety staffer.

Muny op—municipal opera.

Mustang meller—Western film.

New faces—new talent.

Nice people—vaude agents' appraisal of actors who gifted them with more than 10% commissions.

Nitery—nite club.

Nix—no, veto, thumbs-down.

No cov joint—joint that doesn't charge cover or minimum.

N.s.g.—not so good.

N.s.h.—not so hot.

NY-to-LA—Broadway to Hollywood.

Oater—Western film.

Obit—obituary.

Ofay—Harlemese for white man.

Oke—OK.

Oke fodder—commercial show; good b.o.

Olio—scenery, in front of which an act, generally a "sidewalk comedy" team performs; also specialties performed between acts in burlesque.

O.o.—once-over.

Op—operation.

Opposish—opposition.

Orange Juice Gulch—Times Square, because of the large number of fruit juice stands there.

Org—organization.

Ork—orchestra, dance band.

Ozoner—drive-in theater.

P.a.—press agent; also personal appearance and public address system.

Pacted—signing of contract or pact.

Pan-Aired West—took Pan-American to Hollywood.

Palooka—an oaf.

Panicked the house—big hit.

Payoff—end result.

Peasants—"unhep" audiences.

Peeler—stripteaser.

Philly—Philadelphia.

Pitmen—musicians in the orchestra pit.

Pitt—Pittsburgh.

Pix—motion pictures or motion picture business.

Platter—phonograph disk.

Plugger—songplugger or music exploitation man.

Plushery—class joint (hotel, nitery, eatery).

Poverty Row—Gower and Sunset in Hollywood, headquarters for quickie producers. See *Gower Gulch*.

Pratfall—comedy fall.

Preem—theatre première.

Prez—president.

Prima—prima donna.

Pro ams—professional amateurs, those pseudo-tyros who constantly appeared on so-called amateur radio and vaudeville programs.

Prostie—prostitute. Variety's sensitized way of describing female characters comparable to those in early Mae West plays.

Pub-ad—publicity and advertising dep't.

Pushover—easy touch or easy make.

Quickie—cheaply made film.

Rave—top critical notice.

Reorg—reorganization.

Risley act—acrobatics that feature foot balancing.

Round actors—See *flesh.*

Round heels—a pushover.

S.a.—sex appeal.

Sagebrusher—Western film.

Schnozzle—nose (viz., Jimmy Durante).

Scram—exit.

Shoestringer—inexpensive or cheap theatrical operation.

Show biz—show business.

Shubert Alley—private street off Broadway, between 44th and 45th, where legits congregate.

Silo circuit—strawhat circuit, summer stock companies.

Situash—situation.

Small time—bush league.

Songplugger—exploiter of songs.

Spec—a spectacle; occasionally, ticket speculator.

Staffer—reporter.

Starrer—starring vehicle.

Stoky—Leopold Stokowski.

Stooge—grotesque comedy aide to a comedian; also a foil.

Strawhat—summer stock company.

Stripper—striptease dancer.

Stubholders—audiences.

Super-Chiefed east—went to New York on the Super-Chief.

Tab show—tabloid version of a musical.

Tad comic—Irish comedian.

Talkers—sound films; rarely called "talkies" in Variety.

Tea-reader—fortune teller.

10%er—theatrical agent.

Termer—a term contract.

Terpery—dance hall.

Terps—dancing.

Terp team—ballroom dance team.

They-went-thatawayer—Western film.

Third sex—a homosexual.

Tin Pan Alley—Music publishers' row, derived from the open-windowed brownstone houses west of Broadway on New York's 28th St. in the early 1900s when show business activities were focused between Union and Longacre (later Times) Square. Theatrical reporter Monroe H. Rosenfeld is credited with having coined the term in an interview with songwriter-publisher Harry Von Tilzer, and from that interview stemmed the legend that Von Tilzer coined it. TPA is still used because of its color although the music business has moved largely to the Brill Building uptown at 1619 Broadway; also Radio City.

Tinter—Technicolor film.

Took a bath—went into bankruptcy.

Took the veil—retired from public life.

Torcher—torch singer.

Torso-tosser—cootch dancer.

Toscy—Arturo Toscanini.

Trench unionist—musician in the orchestra pit.

Tuner—musical picture, or filmusical.

Turk day—Thanksgiving.

TV—television.

TVA—Television Authority.

TWA'd to the Coast—flew to Hollywood via TWA.

Vaudery—vaudeville theater.

vaudfilm—house showing films and vaudeville.

Ventro—ventriloquist.

Video—television.

Vidpic—films especially made for television.

Whodunit—mystery show.

Wickered—wastebasketed.

w.k.—well known.

Wowed the customers—big hit.

Yocks—big laughs.

Index

Index

Index   588

Index